Labor Economics:
The Emerging Synthesis

Robert M. Fearn
North Carolina State University

WINTHROP PUBLISHERS, INC.
CAMBRIDGE, MASSACHUSETTS

Library of Congress Cataloging in Publication Data

Fearn, Robert M
  Labor economics.

  Includes index.
  1. Labor economics. 2. Labor and laboring classes
—United States. I. Title.
HD4901.F3   331   80–39637
ISBN 0–87626–473–9

Production Editor: Clive Martin

Cover design: Richard Spencer

10 9 8 7 6 5 4 3 2 1

To Pris, my wife, lover, companion and friend of many years, in grateful appreciation of her patience with and understanding of my other love affair—that with labor economics.

Contents

Acknowledgments

I am indebted to my departed colleague, James G. Maddox, for encouraging me to examine the nature of the synthesis which has developed and is continuing to develop in modern labor economics. My thanks also go to James Easley, who assisted with the early drafts of Chapters 1 and 2, and to Magdi M. El Kammash and Jim Jonish, who reviewed the manuscript and made many useful suggestions. The various faculty and graduate student participants since 1966 in the Labor Economics and Human Resource Development Workshop and in the Labor and Applied Economics Workshop at North Carolina State University and the University of North Carolina (Chapel Hill), respectively, have provided me with valuable analytical insights. I am particularly appreciative of the interaction with my triangle university colleagues: Loren Ihnen, Thomas Johnson, Robert Clark, Walt Wessels, Steve Allen, Dan Sumner, Solomon Polachek, Thomas Kniesner, Juanita M. Kreps, T. Dudley Wallace, and H. Gregg Lewis, and with my former Ph.D. students: Ann D. Witte, Theodore Lianos, Alvin Cruze, Aldon Turner, John Warner, Jim Rook and Wuttithep Indhapanya. Their collective impact upon my understanding has been substantial, although they are obviously innocent of any of my errors. Many undergraduate students also deserve my thanks for they have brought home to me in dozens of unique and enjoyable ways the benefits of using economic theory in the examination of labor market phenomena.

A very special debt is owed to Deborah Hilliard, who typed most of the manuscript—some parts many times, as I changed my views about the presentation of these materials. Janet Leggett also assisted in typing the final manuscript.

Material in Chapter 3 from *Married Women in the Labor Force: An Economic Analysis* by Glen Cain (Chicago: University of Chicago Press, 1966) is reprinted by permission of the University of Chicago Press. "Anna Imroth" and the excerpt from "Dynamiter" in Chapter 10 are from *Chicago Poems* by Carl Sandburg, copyright 1916 by Holt, Rinehart and Winston, Inc., copyright 1944 by Carl Sandburg; "The Mayor of Gary," also in Chapter 10, is from *Smoke and Steel* by Carl Sandburg, copyright 1920 by Harcourt Brace Jovanovich, Inc., copyright 1948 by Carl Sandburg. These poems are reprinted by permission of Harcourt Brace Jovanovich, Inc. Figure 12-1 is reprinted by permission of Robert J. Barro, Herschel I. Grossman, and the *American Economic Review*.

Introduction

The ideas of economists and political philosophers, both when they are right and when they are wrong, are more powerful than is commonly understood. Indeed, the world is ruled by little else.
    J. M. Keynes, *The General Theory of Employment, Interest and Money*[1]

Every academic discipline or subdiscipline represents an evolving confluence of theory and evidence. The subdiscipline of labor economics is no exception. From its origin among the common theoretical traditions of economics, labor economics has gradually evolved into a separable body of knowledge. That evolution was not without trauma and controversy, and the emerging synthesis in this area of knowledge is a relatively recent event.

This brief introduction exposes the reader to the ancient and recent academic controversies and to the resulting creative tensions in the field. As a brief overview, it is necessarily incomplete. Nevertheless, it should serve to acquaint the reader with some key terms and concepts and to provide for him a historical background. This introduction also discusses the organization of the text and how the textual material is related to the emerging synthesis.

The Decline and Reemergence of Economic Theory in the Study of Labor Markets

Modern labor economics has its origin in three distinct modes of thought: the classical-neoclassical approach, the institutionalist approach, and the demographic approach. Despite differences in emphasis and analytical techniques, the intent of the various investigators has been identical—to understand better the activities by which labor time is applied to the productive progress and the resulting distribution of real and money income.

The traditional approach of classical-neoclassical economists to labor markets was analogous to the classical-neoclassical approach to product markets. Each individual was assumed to be seeking to maximize his net utility (or, more narrowly, his net income). A classic quote from Adam Smith's *Wealth of Nations* (1776) shows the usefulness of that analytical assumption:

> *The whole of the advantages and disadvantages of different employments of labour* [*and stock*] *must, in the same neighbourhood* [read: labor market], *either be perfectly equal or continually tending to equality. If in the same neighbourhood there was any employment evidently either more or less advantageous than the rest, so many people would crowd into it in the one case or so many would desert it in the other, that its advantages would soon return to the level of other employments. This at least would be the case in a society where things were left to follow their natural course, where there was perfect liberty, and where every man was perfectly free both to choose what occupation he thought proper, and to change it as often as he thought proper. Every man's interest would prompt him to seek the advantageous and to shun the disadvantageous employment.*[2]

This citation not only develops the concepts of labor supply and market equilibrium, but also emphasizes the idea of compensating wage differentials for the nonpecuniary aspects of employment *the whole of the advantages and disadvantages.* . . . In general, of course, the classical economists saw an unfettered economic system *where every man was . . . free . . . to choose what occupation he thought proper . . .* as a powerful engine for the generation of wealth and higher levels of living.

The alleged failure of the capitalist economic system to promote upward mobility among the proletariat and a reaction to the social "inequities" which developed during the burgeoning industrial revolution gave rise to strong attacks on Smithian (or classical) logic from both Marxist and more traditional quarters. By 1874, John Cairnes specifically recognized the class limits of choice (an insight also emphasized by the Marxists in a different analytical structure) and the possibility that, under certain constraints, occupational wage differentials could readily be greater than necessary to compensate for the unpleasantness of the occupations or the cost of training which might be required. After recognizing the "competitiveness" of a common laborer with other common laborers and the emergence of compensating differentials among low skilled activities, Cairnes noted:

> . . . *But beyond this, he* [the common laborer] *is practically shut out from competition. The barrier is his social position and circumstances, which renders*

his education defective, while his means are too narrow to allow of his repairing
the defect or of deferring the return upon his industry 'till he has qualified himself
for a skilled occupation.[3]

In particular, Cairnes introduced the notion of a binding capital constraint *his means are too narrow to allow . . . .*

By the time of Alfred Marshall,[4] the amount of labor time demanded
in response to wage differences was shown to be derived from underlying
production relationships and product market conditions. With the elaboration of marginal productivity theory by Marshall, John Hicks, Paul
Douglas, and others in the late 1920s and early 1930s, the classical-neoclassical approach was well developed. The various concepts of compensating differentials, noncompeting groups, factor demand, and the like
were linked directly to the general theory of choice and market determination of prices and quantities. The concepts were part of the intellectual
equipment of all neoclassical economists, although few of them specialized in labor questions. Most neoclassical writers recognized that labor
(services) cannot be separated from the worker himself, and therefore,
that labor markets present some questions or problems which are absent
from or of less import in commodity markets. These distinctions, however,
were not emphasized. Thus, labor market analysis was viewed as an
integral and not-too-different part of general economic analysis, and usually followed the commodity analogue.

In contrast, the institutionalists emphasized the uniqueness of labor
markets from commodity markets. Rather than tracing labor market
behavior to individual choice in a utility-maximizing framework, the
institutionalists sought to understand labor market behavior by investigating the habits, customs, and legal frameworks surrounding and per-
meating the workplace, and by investigating the supposedly unique (or
at least distinctive) psychology of the working classes or "the laborers."[5]
Labor leaders, some politicians, and many other citizens throughout the
industrial West supported that general view. The Clayton Anti-Trust
Act of 1914 in the United States, for example, sought to distinguish
labor markets from commodity markets by declaring that "the labor
of a human being is not a commodity or article of commerce."[6]

These emphases resulted from the concern of John R. Commons,
Selig Perlman, and others with the rise of corporations, trusts, labor
unions, and other groups. They saw behavior being molded by these
new, powerful forces and regarded the rise of such institutions as vitiating
the individual choice "mechanism" that is central to the neoclassical
approach.[7] In general, the approach of the institutionalists was historical
or legal with either Marxist or social-psychological overtones. The institutionalists, many of whom were at the University of Wisconsin, emphasized empirical research, concentrating upon the specific "rules of the
workplace" in contrast to the "ivory tower" approach of the neoclassical

school. Like their intellectual cousins of the German historical school, the institutionalists compiled substantial amounts of empirical data about the nature of the workplace and the "workingman." Moreover, the institutionalist approach was by its nature neutral (or at least nonantagonistic) toward the growth of labor unions and union positions concerning the problems of the workplace. If any bias was discernible, it was a positive one, for the institutionalists looked with intellectual (if not personal) favor upon institutional developments that could increase their levels of understanding. Certainly, the variegated union movement provided ample opportunity to apply their historical, legal, and social-psychological approaches to gain more insight. This nonantagonistic (or even positive) view contrasted sharply with the neoclassical approach that saw unionism implicitly, at least, as a monopolistic influence which could only reduce market efficiency.

The neoclassicists and institutionalists also differed in their approach to unemployment. The pre-Keynesian neoclassicists assumed the presence of full employment or a persistent tendency of the economy to move toward full employment. Institutionalists did not. Rather, they saw periodic unemployment and the resulting desire for security to be important determinants of the behavior of workingmen. The early institutionalists did not attempt to explain periodic spells of unemployment, although later work at the National Bureau of Economic Research and elsewhere probed the causes of business cycles.

During the 1930s, the neoclassical approach to labor and indeed all of traditional economics fell into disrepute in both academic and nonacademic circles. The proximate cause of this "fall from grace" was the apparent inability of traditional (neoclassical) economic theory to explain the persistence of widespread unemployment. Moreover, neoclassical labor economics seemed to offer few insights into the rapid development of unionism in the United States—particularly the industrial unionism fostered by the Congress of Industrial Organizations (CIO). From a neoclassical viewpoint, unions were seen largely as monopolies (or potential monopolies) whose growth could impose substantial losses on society. Both "failings" of the neoclassical economists were disturbing in the socially conscious and prounion milieu of the depressed 1930s. It is not surprising that institutionalist approaches increased in popularity and that criticisms of received neoclassical doctrines increased in intensity. See Fig. 1 for the relative strengths of the neoclassical, institutional, and Marxist approaches at that time.

As noted above, neither the neoclassical nor the institutionalist approach addressed itself directly to the problem of unemployment. Marxists regarded the unemployment phenomenon as endemic to capitalism as "capitalism proceeded with historic inevitability to destroy itself." Thus, policy makers in the industrialized West turned to government agencies for the measurement and analysis of unemployment. In the

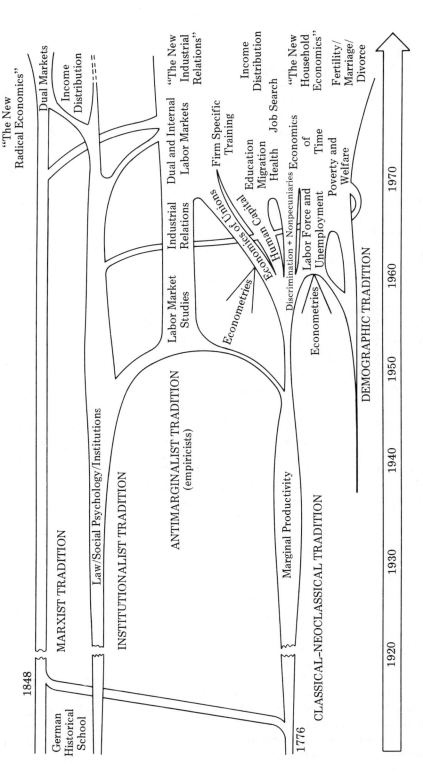

Figure 1   Labor Economics—The Emerging Synthesis

United States, the Works Progress Administration and then the Bureau of the Census were called upon to provide regular, consistent data on the labor force, employment, and unemployment status of the working age population together with other related data. The Department of Labor also began to collect employment and earnings statistics on a more regular basis. While the procedures for collecting and aggregating these data were statistically respectable, they were not guided by either the general theory of choice or by the legal-historical approaches of the institutionalists. As sampling variances permitted, however, these data were collected and analyzed within categories familiar to demographers such as age, sex, race, color, marital status, and so on. Hence, a demographic approach evolved.

As the field emerged from the World War II period, the three approaches—neoclassical, institutionalist, and demographic—were quite distinct and each had strong overtones of cultism. As suggested above, interest in a "better" explanation of unionism and a feeling of disquiet concerning the "unrealism" of the neoclassical approach predated World War II. The full flowering of criticism and revisionist sentiments, however, did not come until after the war. Led by Richard Lester of Princeton University, a group which can be called the antimarginalists mounted a strong attack on traditional neoclassical theory.[8]

The antimarginalists and the institutionalists had several common characteristics: for example, an emphasis on the "security mindedness" of workers and a feeling that responses to wage or compensation changes were usually small or negligible. In contrast to the institutionalists, however, the antimarginalists were rooted in the general theory of choice. They sought to improve the "realism" and predictive power of traditional theory. Consequently, they directed their attention toward worker responses to various stimuli—wage or compensation changes, changes in job security systems, unionism, etc. They examined union wage and employment effects and, in some instances, saw unionism or minimum wages as operating to counterbalance the (presumed) monopsony power of employers. In general, they sought a comprehensive revision of labor market theory.[9]

Although the proposed revision never quite jelled, the criticisms increased in popularity. By the mid-1950s, most undergraduate and graduate labor texts and courses were *not* market-oriented and "labor economics" was increasingly divorced from the general theory of choice. Particular, if not exclusive, emphasis was given to unionism, labor law, and collective bargaining—often from a historical or institutional viewpoint. Those sections of textbooks concerned with the theory of labor markets pointed to the inadequacies and "unrealism" of marginal analysis in general and marginal productivity in particular. Often marginal productivity theory was seen implicitly as an attempt to justify nonunion labor markets, representing a sociopolitical or normative rationalization of nonunion shops rather than an analytical approach. Where neoclassical approaches were employed, great emphasis was given to the theory of bilateral monopoly and the texts called for a new, more realistic theory of labor markets. Moreover, many universities established "industrial relations centers" or "institutes" which were interdisciplinary or multidisciplinary in nature, giving primary attention to institutional, legal, or policy matters pertaining to collective bargaining. "Labor courses" were often taught outside departments of economics, further divorcing the analysis of labor markets and collective bargaining from economic theory. Even the terms "labor economics" and "the economics of labor" became increasingly synonymous with "industrial relations" despite the fact that union membership represented only about 25 percent of the civilian labor force.

Like the institutionalists, the antimarginalists emphasized empirical research. By the mid-1960s, the antimarginalist movement had generated a spate of labor market studies.[10] Not all of these studies were conducted by detractors of traditional theory, but the questions considered were largely those raised by the antimarginalists.

Concurrently and in part as a result of the antimarginalist criticism, there was a resurgence of interest in the application of neoclassical analysis to labor market problems. That resurgence began in earnest in the mid- to late-1950s, but its foundation had been laid earlier by Paul Douglas and the other "Chicago School" economists in the United States and by John Hicks in England.[11] Douglas's *Theory of Wages,* his *Real Wages in the United States, 1890–1926,* and his investigations of the labor supply curve (with his students) mark him as the grandfather (or godfather) of the neoclassical resurgence in the United States. A stream of economists—including H. Gregg Lewis and then Albert Rees at Chicago, and Melvin Reder at Stanford in particular—spearheaded the resurgence.[12]

As so often happens, intellectual revivals are influenced by forces outside as well as inside the halls of ivy. This one was no exception. Three circumstances can be cited:

1. the existence of measured unemployment levels in the United States from 1957–58 through 1963–64 which were substantially above the expected normal (or "frictional") level of 3–4 percent,
2. the Schultzian or "human capital" revolution,[13] and
3. substantial improvements in statistical and econometric competencies among economists, together with the concurrent computerization of economic research.

As unemployment failed to return to the expected frictional level after the 1958–59 recession, public and academic interest rose substantially. Some of this interest centered around a broad controversy about the existence and possible growth of structural unemployment—related to "automation," education, or regional adjustments.[14] A second level of inquiry, also based upon census data, probed the accuracy of the labor force and unemployment estimates. Part of this latter concern was addressed to the "discouraged" or "added worker" problem,[15] while another part considered the accuracy and usefulness of the statistics themselves.[16]

The wide-ranging public and academic discussions culminated in numerous "shotgun" legislative efforts to treat what came to be known as "manpower problems." In the process, the demographically based labor force estimates of the Bureau of the Census began to be interpreted in the light of economic analysis.[17] Labor force participation studies and other economic interpretations were "grafted" onto the demographic base, with economic hypotheses concerning labor force choice being tested with the relatively newly developed statistical and econometric competencies. The public and academic interest also led to a new annual manpower report of the President and highlighted the moribund state into which *broad* labor economics had fallen by the late 1950s and early 1960s. As one consequence, numerous incentives (including research grants) were established through the Manpower Development and Training Act to induce new personnel and direct new energies into labor economics, broadly conceived.[18]

Meanwhile, the thinking of Theodore Schultz at the University of Chicago and his disciples concerning the development of human productive capacities began to clarify the linkages between neoclassical labor market theory, the economics of education and training, and the institutions through which competencies are acquired. Schultz emphasized the usefulness of viewing education, training, or schooling as investments in the "human agent": the creation of human capital from which would or could flow increased productivity and higher income streams. Even though the Schultzian approach smacked of treating "laborers" (or humans) as if they were "commodities" or, more correctly, as if they were analogous to machines, the Schultzian revolution also had a base in institutionalism. Because the school systems through which skills are often acquired are largely "outside" the market and because of the role of foregone income in the cost of education, it was apparent that existing institutions might limit or otherwise alter the level of human capital investment. Thus, analysts were led to consider the possibility of increasing growth rates and/or rates of public and social returns to education by altering institutions or relaxing capital constraints.[19] The work implied, therefore, that the acquisition of skills may be related not only to labor market forces and structures, but also to the myriad legal and institutional characteristics stressed by the earlier Wisconsin-based institutionalists. Alternatively viewed, Schultz and then Gary Becker picked up and reemphasized the Cairnesian conception of "noncompeting groups," laying a theoretical foundation for the "stock" aspects of labor which was consistent with and supportive of neoclassical theory while leaving room for considerations of existing institutional structures and constraints.[20]

Finally, the growth of econometric and statistical competence among economists permitted the neoclassicists and the antimarginalists to test their notions concerning the important determinants of labor market behavior. These tests ranged across the board—from measurements of the effect of trade unions on relative wages and employment to a wide spectrum of labor market analyses and to the raft of labor force participation studies noted above. The heavy empirical emphasis was, in part, the result of the antimarginalist and institutionalist challenges to traditional neoclassical theory. Because those challenges suggested that traditional, "unrealistic" theory could not be expected to predict and explain the complex phenomena of "real world" labor markets, attention was focused directly on the testing of hypotheses derived from theory.

Thus, modern labor economics has emerged from the creative confluence of the several separate approaches, traditions, and concerns. With the aid of a revitalized neoclassical theory and the development in human capital theory, labor economists "got it all together" or more precisely "got much of it together" in the 1960s and 1970s. The theory of choice once again became the touchstone of analysis, but the emphasis was and is on empirical studies and hypothesis testing via modern econometric techniques. Moreover, most analysts now recognize the role of institutions and legal settings in conditioning and altering behavior and/or seek to measure those effects.

From the emerging synthesis have come many new areas of analysis, indicated in Fig. 1. Several are directly traceable to a single economist, Gary Becker of Columbia University and the University of Chicago. Becker was responsible for advances in human capital theory, major works in the economics of discrimination and the economics of time, and a portion of the "new household economics." Other economists of the 1960s and 1970s are introduced below as their particular contributions to the synthesis are relevant to the textual discussion.

The Approach of This Text

In light of the history of the subdiscipline, one could logically develop a labor economics text around the subject matter areas or the historical controversies discussed above. Such an approach would be particularly useful for graduate students who have a solid background in economic theory and an understanding of the relevant institutions, and who are already heavily committed to understanding the nuances and details of such controversies. Given the differences in backgrounds and objectives of graduate students and nonprofessional readers, however, the controversy- or research-related approach seems less appropriate for the nonprofessional (including the undergraduate student). Nevertheless, some topical approach should prove useful to the average nonprofessional both for sustaining and intensifying interest and for indicating how the tools of the trade—the various theories, concepts, and approaches—help one to analyze and understand existing "practical" problems or situations.

This text employs such an approach. A series of topics are considered including:

1. labor markets and labor force attachment,
2. welfare programs and work incentives,
3. the economics of women's liberation,
4. the economics of human capital,
5. the economics of minimum wages,
6. the economics of job search,
7. the economics of internal labor markets (and segmented labor markets),
8. the demand for human capital,
9. discrimination in employment, earnings, and human capital,
10. the economics of unions,
11. the economics of migration,
12. unemployment and underemployment,
13. the distribution of income.

The topics are arranged so that the reader is exposed sequentially to the relevant theory and institutions. For example, topics 1 and 2 above develop from the theory of the allocation of time to labor market activities (flow supply). Topic 3 develops from flow supply, labor force participation, and the economics of time. Topic 4 considers questions of skill development (stock supply or human capital). Topic 5 involves the demand for labor time and its characteristics together with the workings of the (external) labor market. Topic 6 looks at the role of information and search costs in labor markets. Topic 7 develops the theory of the internal labor market and so on. By the end of topics 7 and 8, the reader should have a good feel for the emerging synthesis of neoclassical, institutional, demographic, and antimarginalist approaches and concerns.

Although the approach is topical, the emphasis throughout the text is on the generalizability of the theoretical approach and the usefulness of that approach in understanding the practical workings of the labor market. In each chapter, only a portion of the topic is examined. The reader should recognize from the outset that the concepts and approaches developed in the several chapters can be applied to a much larger set of problems or questions than those specifically addressed in the text.

The topics and subtopics considered here, however currently relevant, will wane in time. The generalizable theory is more lasting.

An alternative approach to the writing of this labor economics text would be to eschew "relevance" and present only the "bare bones" of the theory without any appreciable reference to contemporary problems or topics. Most readers probably would find such an approach "deadly dry," and they would justifiably conclude that economics deserves its appellation as "the dismal science." The topical approach, therefore, seems preferable if only to prevent the further denigration of the discipline of economics or the subdiscipline of labor economics. Without further ado, we proceed to the discussion of labor markets and labor force attachment.

Notes to Introduction

1. John Maynard Keynes, *The General Theory of Employment, Interest and Money* (New York: Harcourt, Brace & Co., 1936), p. 383.

2. Adam Smith, *An Inquiry into the Nature and Causes of the Wealth of Nations* [1776] (New York: The Modern Library, 1937), bk. I, chap. 10, p. 99.

3. John E. Cairnes, *Some Leading Principles of Political Economy Newly Expounded* [1874] (New York: Augustus M. Kelley, 1967), pp. 65–66.

4. Alfred Marshall, *Principles of Economics,* 8th ed. (London: Macmillan & Co., 1922), especially bk. IV, chaps. 1–3, and bk. V, chap. 4.

5. Many of Thorstein Veblen's writings also reflect a concern with the influence of institutional and social-psychological forces. See, in particular, Thorstein Veblen, *The Engineers and the Price System* (New York: Viking Press, 1921).

6. See any "labor history" for a discussion of the attempt via the Clayton Anti-Trust Act to exempt labor unions from provisions of the Sherman Anti-Trust Act and from criminal conspiracy charges under the common law.

7. See John R. Commons, *Legal Foundations of Capitalism* (New York: Macmillan Co., 1924), pp. 5–6. Also see Robert F. Hoxie, *Trade Unionism in the United States* (New York: D. Appleton & Co., 1920), pp. 3–6.

8. The antimarginalist group has also been called "the empiricists." See R. A. Lester, "Shortcomings of Marginal Analysis for Wage Employment Problems," and F. Machlup, "Marginal Analysis and Empirical Research," *American Economic Review* 36, no. 1 (March 1946): 63–82, and 36, no. 3 (June 1946): 519–54, respectively. Also see Simon Rottenberg, "On Choice in Labor Markets," *Industrial and Labor Relations Review* 9, no. 2 (January 1956): 183–99.

9. Lloyd Reynolds, *The Structure of Labor Markets* (New York: Harper and Brothers, 1951). Also see Clark Kerr's classic article, "The Balkanization of Labor Markets," in *Mobility and Economic Opportunity,* ed. E. Wright Bakke et al. (New York: John Wiley & Sons, 1954).

10. See M. Lurie and E. Rayack, "Racial Differences in Migration and Job Search: A Case Study," *Southern Economic Review* 23, no. 1 (1966): 81–95,

for a tabulation of these studies and of findings on employee job search up to 1966.

11. See Paul Douglas, *The Theory of Wages* (New York: Macmillan & Co., 1934). On the other side of the Atlantic, a book by the same name was copyrighted two years earlier: J. R. Hicks, *The Theory of Wages* (London: Macmillan & Co., 1932). Hicks noted in the preface to his 1948 edition:

> *Such a reconsideration of wage theory seems long overdue. For the most recent comprehensive statements of a positive theory of wages in English—of anything more than an elementary character—are now thirty to forty years old. We have to go back for them to Marshall's* Principles *and Clark's* Distribution of Wealth. *Since that time important work on the subject has indeed been done, but it is nearly all special studies; even Professor Pigou's treatment of labour, in the* Economics of Welfare, *ought probably so to be reckoned for our purposes.*

Also see Paul Douglas, *Real Wages in the United States, 1890–1926* (New York: Houghton Mifflin Co., 1930), and E. H. Schoenberg and P. H. Douglas, "Studies in the Supply Curve of Labor," *Journal of Political Economy* 45, no. 1 (February 1937): 45–79.

12. See, in particular, H. G. Lewis, "Hours of Work and Hours of Leisure," and M. V. Reder, "The Cost of a Shorter Work Week," *Proceedings of the Ninth Annual Winter Meeting of the IRRA* (Madison, Wis.: Industrial Relations Research Association, 1956), pp. 196–221; H. G. Lewis, *Unionism and Relative Wages in the U.S.* (Chicago: University of Chicago Press, 1963); and Albert Rees, *The Economics of Trade Unions* (Chicago: University of Chicago Press, 1962). Also see John T. Dunlop, "The Task for Contemporary Wage Theory," in *The Theory of Wage Determination,* ed. John Dunlop for the International Economics Association (London: Macmillan & Co., 1957), pp. 3–27, for a somewhat more eclectic approach.

13. For an example of the breadth of "Schultzian" thought and approaches, see National Bureau of Economic Research, *Human Resources: Fiftieth Anniversary Colloquium VI,* NBER General Series, no. 96 (New York: Columbia University Press, 1972).

14. For representative examples, see Charles C. Killingsworth, "Full Employment and the New Economics," *Scottish Journal of Political Economy* 16, no. 1 (February 1969): 1–19; Joint Economic Committee, Subcommittee on Economic Statistics, U.S. Congress, *Higher Unemployment Rates, 1957–1960. Structural Transformation or Inadequate Demand,* 87th Congress, 1st Session (Washington, D.C.: U.S. Government Printing Office, 1961), often known as the Knowles-Kalachek report; Barbara R. Bergmann and David E. Kaun, *Structural Unemployment in the United States* (Washington, D.C.: U.S. Department of Commerce, May 31, 1966).

15. See, for example, C. D. Long, *The Labor Force Under Changing Income and Employment* (Princeton, N.J.: Princeton University Press, 1958); T. F. Dernberg and K. T. Strand, "Hidden Unemployment 1953–62," *American Economic Review* 56, no. 1 (March 1966): 71–95; and Jacob Mincer, "Labor Force Participation and Unemployment: A Review of Recent Evidence," in *Prosperity and Unemployment,* ed. R. A. and M. S. Gordon (New York: John Wiley & Sons, 1966), chap. 3, pp. 73–112.

16. President's Committee to Appraise Employment and Unemployment Statistics ("the Gordon Committee"), *Measuring Employment and Unemployment* (Washington, D.C.: U.S. Government Printing Office, 1962).

17. Glen G. Cain, *Married Women in the Labor Force: An Economic Analysis* (Chicago: University of Chicago Press, 1966); William G. Bowen and T. A. Finegan, *The Economics of Labor Force Participation* (Princeton, N.J.: Princeton University Press, 1969); Marvin Kosters, *Income and Substitution Effects in a Family Labor Supply Model,* reprint monograph P-3339 (Santa Monica, Calif.: The Rand Corporation, December 1966).

18. See Manpower Administration, *The Manpower Research Institutional Grant Program: The First Three Years, 1966–1969* (Washington, D.C.: U.S. Department of Labor, 1969), and any issue of *The Manpower Report of the President,* 1964–1973.

19. Because of the volume of the "human capital" literature, no comprehensive list or detailed discussion of analytical developments is attempted here. See Mark Blaug, *Economics of Education: A Selected Annotated Bibliography* (London: Pergamon Press, 1966), and Mark Blaug, ed., *Economics of Education 1 and 2* (Middlesex, England: Penguin Books, 1968 and 1969).

20. Also see Walter Y. Oi, "Labor as a Quasi-fixed Factor," *Journal of Political Economy* 70, no. 6 (December 1962): 538–55, and Gary Becker, *Human Capital: A Theoretical and Empirical Analysis, With Special Reference to Education* (New York: Columbia University Press, 1964).

1 | *Labor Markets and Labor Force Attachment*

Humphrey: . . . *I'd like to ask one question about the new communes [in China].* Khrushchev: *They are old-fashioned, they are reactionary. We tried that right after the Revolution. It just doesn't work. . . . You know, Senator, what those communes are based on? They are based on the principle 'From each according to his abilities, to each according to his needs.' You know that won't work. You can't get production without incentive.*

Hubert H. Humphrey,
The Education of a Public Man[1]

I thank Thee for all Thy blessings, but especially for letting me live in the happiest possible society, and practice what I hope is the truest religion. If I am wrong, and if some other religion or social system would be better and more acceptable to Thee, I pray Thee in Thy goodness to let me know it. . . .

Thomas More, *Utopia*[2]

Almost all elementary and intermediate textbooks in economics begin with a statement that humankind is faced by scarce resources relative to seemingly insatiable wants and desires. Therefore, the texts assert, *the* economic problem is one of scarcity and the allocation of limited resources among competing ends. The texts then move very quickly to a discussion of markets as the mechanism for allocating the available resources among ends and among individuals in the society. Market mechanisms, including the firm and the household, product markets, factor markets, and money payments for services rendered or goods exchanged, are usually introduced without any meaningful consideration of alternate forms of social or economic organization.

This text is concerned with production and distribution through labor markets, but there are alternative ways in which production and distribution can be organized. The commune is an alternative form, one that has attracted some of the greatest minds through the ages. Slavery is another form.[3] Before assuming market allocations of labor time and goods and services, therefore, one needs to question why most labor time is allocated via a market process (individually rented in exchange for claims on goods and services) rather than being supplied communally or by some other "system." Obtaining an answer to this question is a first step in understanding labor market processes and problems. Alternatively stated, if one does not know the circumstances under which communes and other arrangements are viable forms of organization for the production and distribution of real goods and services, one's knowledge and appreciation of labor markets is quite limited.

In order to consider why labor market processes exist and to examine what we mean by labor force attachment (or participation), this chapter concentrates on one key question: Under what conditions are communes viable forms of economic organization?

First, of course, one must define *a* commune or *the* commune so that it is analytically distinct from any other organizational form for production and distribution. The following working definition should suffice for our purposes: A commune is a group of persons whose production and consumption activities are based on two principles: (1) that consumption or claims on consumption are separated from and not necessarily proportional to productive effort or payment for that effort, and (2) that property rights in physical capital, for the most part, are held jointly by the group—by agreement if not by law. Thus, the "pure" commune involves more than social, collective, or public ownership of physical capital—land, machinery and so on, properly called socialism. It also includes the requirement that consumption be separated from productive effort. A "pure" voluntary commune would operate according to the principle From Each According to His Ability—To Each According to His Needs (as one conceives of his "needs").

Before one joins Nikita S. Khrushchev in scoffing at the unrealism of such an institution, it is useful to recognize that the nuclear and, to a considerable extent, the extended family operate on this basis and have so operated for millennia. Indeed, when viewed as an economic unit for production and distribution, the family is related closely to a commune. Perhaps that is why modern street and agricultural communes often call themselves "families." Generally, however, when one refers to a commune, one is describing a collective of individuals who are not necessarily biologically related to each other in any direct sense, and who exceed the average number of persons in a nuclear family or most extended families. Nevertheless, this investigation into the viability of communes also helps us to make useful distinctions between the household or family sector of an economy and the market sector.

In the United States, communes experienced considerable popularity during two historical periods. The first occurred in the early 1800s, encompassing the activities of the New England perfectionists and the settlements at New Harmony, Indiana, Oneida, New York, and Brook Farm, Massachusetts, among others. In one way or another, these communes attempted to preserve the close feelings of community and personal relationships which were threatened by the emerging industrialization and urbanization of the time. During this period (call it Walden I), the communes differed in their internal social organization and in their religious emphases, but the basic economic organizational principles applied at all.[4] A second wave of communal interest (Walden II?) occurred in the late 1950s and the 1960s with the emergence of both street and agricultural communes, often among young adults. The founders of these communes, like their historical forebears, sought (in modern terminology) "to find a meaningful social relationship apart from the dehumanizing humdrum of contemporary America," "to get back to the soil and real values," and so forth.

A similar but much more grandiose attempt to apply the principles of "commune-ism" was made by the early leaders of the Union of Soviet Socialist Republics. During the period of "War Communism" soon after the Communist Revolution, Soviet leaders sought to eliminate what they called "commodity production," substituting "production for use" within a communal production and distribution system. As Khrushchev indicated, that attempt failed, as did most of the early American communes. In each instance of failure, a wage system tying productive effort to consumption was substituted for the communal system.[5] Obviously, the distribution of income was affected by each changeover from a communal to a market system of distribution.

In view of these experiences, the social scientist and the thoughtful observer are prompted to ask, Why has the communal system generally failed to provide a satisfactory answer to the problems of production and distribution *when it has been applied to groups larger than the family or extended family?* One should not expect to find the answer to that question in the social or public ownership of physical capital or land. Although socialist systems face many organizational problems, they have existed for many years in many places. The answer would appear to be related either to the separation of production from consumption, or to the personalities and peculiarities of the commune members and their leaders, or both. Economists as a species have little to contribute to the understanding of personality and social adjustment problems in communes,[6] but economic theory does provide some insight into the viability or expected viability of communes via an analysis of the separation of production from consumption. Moreover, as suggested above, analysis of the communal form of production and distribution provides an interesting springboard for considering labor markets and their operations.

Indifference Curve Analysis and Communal Distribution

Consider a hypothetical communard who values both leisure time and real goods and services. Assume further that prior to entering the commune, he or she had no claims on real goods and services other than those claims produced by the direct use of his or her labor time in some productive process (i.e., no "nonwage" income). Assume also at the outset that the communard's time can be transformed into goods at some constant rate per unit time, given the availability of other cooperating inputs—land, capital, etc.

One can describe the tastes of our hypothetical communard for leisure time and for real goods and services by constructing an indifference or utility map. Consider the choices between a given bundle of goods and leisure (say, point A on Fig. 1–1) and various other bundles (B, C, D, or E). If our hypothetical individual values (places positive utility on) or receives satisfaction from both leisure and goods, he will prefer any position in quadrant I (say, B) to A. That is, he will prefer more of the "commodities" (including leisure) he values to fewer of them. He will also prefer B' to A, for at B' he has the same claims on real goods and services but more leisure than at A. Similarly, he will prefer A to C'. If our communard's tastes are not contradictory (i.e., if they follow logically throughout the taste area being considered), there will be some position in quadrant IV (say, D) at which the communard will be indifferent to the mix of goods and leisure at A and an alternative mix at D. By similar argument, there is an equal indifference point (say, E) in quadrant II. Moreover, because one can set any point as the origin of this Cartesian coordinate system, one can replicate this exercise with B, C, or any other point in the leisure-goods space.

Connecting the points of indifference for all combinations of goods and leisure produces Fig. 1–2—a map of our individual communard tastes for leisure time and goods. Any position (say) on U_1 involves more utility (satisfaction) than any point on U_0. Similarly, $U_6 > U_5 > U_4 > U_3 > U_2 > U_1 > U_0 > U_{-1} > U_{-2}$, etc. The serious-minded reader will find it useful to determine (1) why indifference curves cannot cross or touch, and (2) why indifference curves must be convex to the origin (T_p). The reader should also note that some part of the available time per unit time is necessarily reserved for "productive consumption," a minimum amount of nondiscretionary time (OT_p) used for sleeping and eating (recreation?) in order to maintain the productive potential of the human asset. If inadequate time is allowed for these activities, our hypothetical communard is "eating his capital" in a very real sense. Such a situation cannot be a long-term equilibrium condition, although obviously it may exist for a short period. College students who have experienced one or

Figure 1–1 *Leisure Goods Choice and Rankings*

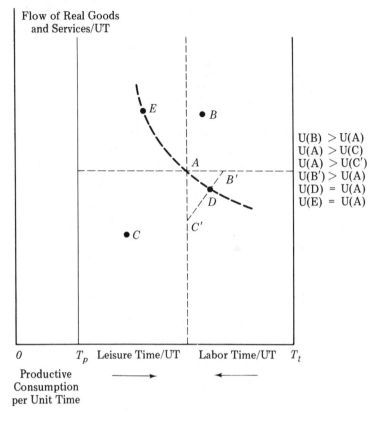

U(B) > U(A)
U(A) > U(C)
U(A) > U(C')
U(B') > U(A)
U(D) = U(A)
U(E) = U(A)

Time/Unit Time (UT) in Hours, Weeks or Whatever

more long "football," "beach," or "party" weekends already understand this part of the analysis.

The indifference map in Fig. 1–2 shows all tradeoffs that our hypothetical individual is willing to make between goods and leisure while considering himself equally "well off" or "better off."[7] That is, he will be willing to move to higher utility levels (say, from U_0 to U_1) and along any indifference curve. The choices made by a man free to choose between leisure and goods will therefore reflect his particular tastes—if we know the other constraints under which he operates. Note that one can subdivide the goods and leisure axes in any number *(n)* of dimensions and thereby examine tradeoffs for more than one "kind" of good and/or one "kind" of leisure. Because the essentials of the analysis are the same

Figure 1–2 *Indifference Curves for a Hypothetical Communard*

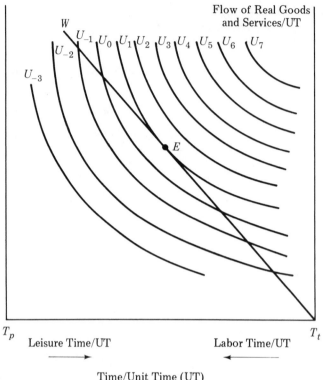

in two (2) as in n $(n \geq 2)$ dimensions, and because more than two dimensions are difficult to present on two-dimensional paper (at least for this author), the discussion will be limited largely to homogeneous goods and homogeneous leisure.

The production or wage line, WT_t in Fig. 1–2, represents the rate at which time (in cooperation with other inputs) can be converted into goods or income. A movement leftward (and upward) along this line entails a greater allocation of time to "goods production" and less to "leisure production." The slope of WT_t represents an implicit wage *(w)* determined by an individual's productive ability. That wage is assumed here to be constant for all rates of time input. Alternatively stated, the linear WT_t assumes constant marginal productivity—no change in the ability to produce per unit time as more time inputs are added. Alternatively, we could have assumed diminishing marginal productivity, represented by a curve "bowed out" from the origin, T_p.[8] Constant marginal productivity is assumed for simplicity of exposition.

Faced with a restriction on the amount of time available per unit time and with some rate at which time can be converted into goods, the communard can maximize his level of satisfaction if he moves to the point of tangency between WT_t and the highest indifference curve he can reach, i.e., U_1 at point E. At E, the rate at which *he is willing to exchange time for goods* is just equal to the rate at which *he can exchange time for goods*. At no point along WT_t (a line of maximum attainable combinations of leisure and goods) will "U"—the index of satisfaction or utility—be as high.[9]

A Small Commune, or Tea for Two

Assume now a geographically isolated commune (family) of two individuals with the following characteristics:

1. each commune member is free to decide how much he will produce or consume,
2. the tastes for leisure and goods differ between the two commune members,
3. the productive ability *(w)* of the two commune members is equal,
4. the relative amount of productive consumption of the two commune members is equal, and
5. neither member "draws down" on his human capital by consuming time from the amount necessary for productive consumption.

In Fig. 1–3, therefore, one can plot two indifference maps (solid and broken lines) and one productivity (or wage) line.[10] It follows from the argument above that in this voluntary commune, the total free choice output per unit time is $Y_r + Y_b$. It also follows that the maximum communal level of consumption is $Y_r + Y_b$, but does not follow that either member's consumption will be limited to his own production level. Indeed, if the latter were the case, the commune would exist only in name.

What then induces either member to consume less than his maximum attainable consumption level—the level at which he would choose to produce and therefore *could* consume if he were unattached? The answer lies in the presence of another axis or dimension of our utility analysis—a dimension representing the consumption level of the other member(s) of the commune. Assuming rational behavior on the part of both members, each will consume less than he voluntarily produces only if the additional utility (or satisfaction) derived *by him* from contributing to the other person exceeds the utility obtainable from his own consumption. In general, then, the consumption of one member or the utility of one member must enter the other's utility function. In contrast to the

Figure 1–3 *A Two-person Commune: Different Tastes for Goods and Leisure, and Equal Productivities*

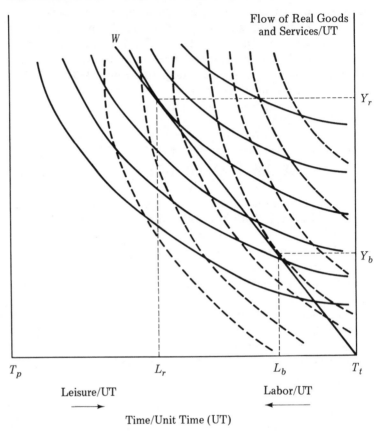

utility function of an individual whose concern is only for himself—a rare and perhaps endangered subspecies of humankind, the communard's utility function includes others (see insert below). Specifically, in order for $C_r < Y_r$ on a voluntary basis, the marginal utility to r of the other's consumption or of the other's utility, $\Delta U_r / \Delta C_b$ or $\Delta U_r / [\Delta U_b(C_b)]$, must be greater than an equivalent amount of personal consumption, $\Delta U_r / \Delta C_r$, where $C_r = C_b$. Less formally stated, one member must get more utility from some given amount of consumption by the other than is obtainable from an equal amount of consumption by the first member himself. I choose to call this utility characteristic LOVE.[11]

In the absence of love, the "contributor" of time and real goods and services has several options, assuming that $C_r < Y_r$ within the commune. He can remove himself from the commune, continue to produce

Extreme Individualist	Communard
$U_I = U_I(C_I, L_I)$	$U_r = U_r(C_r, L_r, C_b)$,
	$U_r = U_r(C_r, L_r, C_b, L_b)$, or
	$U_r = U_r(C_r, L_r, U_b)$
where C denotes consumption per unit time, L is leisure per unit time, and U is an index of utility	

at Y_r, and consume "the fruits of his labor." That is, he can produce elsewhere and withdraw from communal distribution of his earnings. Alternatively, if he is constrained from leaving the commune in the short or the long run, he may reduce his level of productive output to his level of desired consumption ("soldier on the job") or raise his personal consumption within the commune so that it conforms to his productivity. Given the output-budget constraint of the commune $(Y_{max} = Y_r + Y_b)$, however, these approaches may cause allocative difficulties. Total consumption cannot be greater than total voluntary output. Finally, if constrained from leaving the commune, he may seek to institute a program of activity (at some cost in real resources) to change the tastes of the other parties so that they conform more closely to his. A close reading of George Orwell's classic, *Animal Farm*, will yield examples of each of these techniques or responses.[12] If interaction with others raises productivity above that possible on the basis of individual effort, the analysis becomes somewhat more complicated. Under those conditions, incentives exist for individuals to cooperate in productive activities and to reap the individual and collective benefits of their complementaries in production. Communal distribution as distinct from communal production, however, still requires love.[13]

It is not surprising, therefore, to find concern with frugality, "peace and love," and ethical and moral traditions *vis-à-vis* fraternal obligations within operating communes. Moreover, in view of the close relationship which may exist between love and sex, it is not surprising that communes may involve and have often involved plural marriages, "free love," and the like. One need only add the caveat that sexual relations may or may not involve love.

Assume now a new case in which the two persons in the commune exhibit identical tastes for goods and leisure but have sharply different productivities. Figure 1–4 shows that this situation leads one to the same conclusion as before—that the welfare (consumption or utility) of each member of the commune must enter the utility map of the other member if communal distribution of the product is to be a satisfactory form of distribution and if the commune is to maximize its voluntary output of goods, services, and leisure. Wherever sufficient mutual concern and

Figure 1–4 *A Two-person Commune: Identical Tastes for Goods and Leisure, and Unequal Productivities*

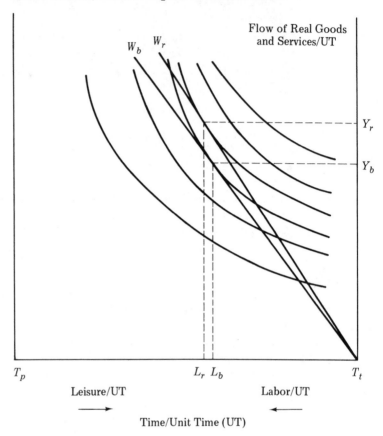

accommodation does not exist, we would expect the particularly productive individuals not to lower their levels of ultimate consumption below privately attainable levels or, alternatively, to lower their productive effort to equal some consumption standard. Thus, when insufficient love exists, economic connections or transfers among individuals will tend to be either forced exchanges (via a command structure) or market exchanges rather than a sharing of available output on the basis of individual but mutually acceptable "needs."[14]

The argument above suggests that even a totalitarian state may find it difficult or impossible to establish a communal distribution system. Without sufficient love, the leaders of any communal movement may be forced to compromise with "practical considerations" and to use market rather than communal distribution systems. The communal ideals, however, may live on. For example, the Soviet Union cancelled its early "War Communism" experiment with communal production and distribution for many of the reasons considered above, but the official ideology continued to support the communal approach. Even in 1961:

. . . *There is evidence that the Soviet leadership is consciously attempting to substitute leisure and* [publicly distributed] *consumption for private consumption. Khrushchev has specifically excluded from the U.S.–Soviet economic 'race' any major competition in production and ownership of private automobiles, and a similar prejudice against 'wasteful' and socially unapproved consumption is apparent throughout Soviet economic publications. . . . Furthermore, Soviet wage theory as enunciated in articles on wage and hours adjustments and in textbooks, insists that the rate of increase in average wages be less than the rate of growth in productivity. If* [output] *plans are met, therefore, the relative share of production being distributed as wages will decline secularly. This pattern has been justified ideologically as the natural concomitant of the movement toward Communism, during which an increasing share of a worker's real income is derived from his 'needs' rather than from his 'work.' In practice the ideology coupled with wage theory suggests that social benefits or governmental transfer payments—such as old age and disability pensions, the provision of kindergartens, boarding schools, rest and vacation areas, and other state grants like 'free' housing—will increase more rapidly than average wages, therefore representing a growing proportion of each individual's real income.*[15]

Note, however, that the Soviet approach still waives the vital questions of (1) the "equitable" distribution of social services, (2) whether the social service rendered is valued as highly by the recipient as by the giver (the net grantor and/or the state), and (3) whether social, political, or market conditions permit dissatisfaction to be communicated to the policy makers and policies to be altered in response to that communication. In the absence of sufficient love or a feeling of equity, all of the responses open to our communard above are open in principle to Soviet workers.[16]

It follows from this analysis that voluntary communes will be more viable:

1. the more similar are the tastes of commune members concerning the leisure-income mix,
2. the more similar are productive abilities among commune members, and
3. the more closely related psychologically are the members of the commune: i.e., the more interdependent are the utility functions of the members.

It is not surprising, therefore, that those voluntary communes which have indicated some temporal viability (1) have been composed of persons linked to a particular faith or philosophy, (2) have emphasized a simple life or a set of particular crafts, and (3) have been relatively small. The size of the commune is important because the larger the group, the more apt is it to experience diversity in taste, background, and productivity—all of which require a greater measure of love as the "tie that binds" (in the words of the old Protestant hymn). Involuntary communes, where ersatz communality is enforced by the coercive power of a governmental or eclesiastical entity or both, may, of course, last longer and be larger in size.[17] Finally, a partial or imperfect commune may exist for some time through the establishment of an internal wage or compensation (work chit) system. That system serves as a proxy for a market exchange which interconnects production and consumption.[18] Note, however, that this arrangement is not the "pure" voluntary commune defined above.

There are other mixed communal-market systems. For example, the Swedish Ministry of the Budget—operating with a decentralized and largely capitalist market economy—planned in 1977/78 for very substantial income transfers (the vast majority of central government expenditures) and for total governmental expenditures representing about 44 percent of the gross national product.[19] Communality in Sweden is obviously substantial. The analysis above would suggest that governmental redistribution of income from one group of citizens to another via taxation and grants (or other programs) should be relatively easier (evoke less resistance) the more homogeneous is the population of the respective nation. Perhaps this explains the greater relative success of the Scandinavians in "social programs" relative to the experience of less homogeneous peoples. Casual empiricism would suggest that the various and extensive transfer programs in Sweden, Norway, and Denmark have had widespread popular support although a degree of coercion may be involved for some persons. Governmental transfer programs will be discussed further in Chapter 2.

Communes and "Copping" or "Opting Out"

The popular movement toward communes in the United States in the 1950s and 1960s seemed often to have been viewed by communards as a way of copping or opting out of "the contemporary American rat race." One observed instances in which persons "gave up" high paying occupations or activities to join communes where, by any reasonable measure, the individual's productivity would be lower and/or his claim on real goods *and* leisure would be lower as a member of the commune. It is of no consequence to the positive economist whether this action was or is justified with or without rancor with respect to the larger society. Alternatively phrased, it is of no consequence to the analyst whether the fledgling communard's attitude is expressed positively (e.g., evidencing a desire to "return to the soil" or "the simpler, fundamental things in life") or expressed negatively (e.g., refusing to conform to the "overly materialistic expectations of a rotten and decadent society"). As Adam Smith argued, it is "the whole of the advantages and disadvantages of the various employments" of labor which condition human behavior with regard to the uses of time (where such choice is "permitted" by the prevailing legal or social environment).[20] To explain such behavior, therefore, we seek to incorporate the nonpecuniary aspects of employment into the analysis, albeit that such nonpecuniaries are difficult to measure.

Suppose that a prospective communard had the option of working "inside the establishment" for wages or "doing his thing" within a commune with a much lower productivity. His choice would then depend upon the strength of his tastes for or against working with "the establishment." Consider that "s," a shame coefficient ranging from positive 1 to negative infinity, is attached to all wage payments from "the establishment." Then, the prevailing establishment wage (w) will be discounted to produce an effective wage: $w^* = w(1 - s)$. Where an individual's "s" ranges from 0 to +1, he has tastes against the nonwage aspects of employment within the establishment and $s(w)$ represents the dollar value per unit time necessary to compensate for these nonpecuniaries. Where the "s" ranges from zero to negative infinity, our hypothetical individual has positive tastes for the nonpecuniary aspects of employment for or "with" the establishment.

Figure 1–5 shows an individual with two wage offers or productivity relationships: w—off the commune—and w_c—on the commune—where $w > w_c$. If $s(w) > w - w_c$, our hypothetical individual would opt for the lower wage position in order to maximize his own level of satisfaction. Note that each "establishment $" is treated as if it were equal to $(1 - s)$$'s where $0 \leq s \leq 1.0$. Thus, Y in "establishment" dollars can be less in utility terms than a smaller number of "commune" dollars. In no way can such behavior be considered "irrational" against the backdrop of the communard's tastes. Figure 1–5 shows that our hypothetical individual would not only opt for a lower wage and lower income, but might work longer hours to achieve that lower income. However, given his tastes with regard to the nonpecuniary conditions of employment, our hypothetical individual is making a rational choice even though "straights" or noncommunards might regard him as "a bit weird."

Thus, if potential earnings off the commune are higher than implicit productivity on the commune (given, say, the presence of more complementary factors in the "outside world") and if the communards *all* have very strong feelings concerning the distastefulness of working in the "outside world," the group might necessarily forego very substantial

Figure 1-5 *The Dilemma of the Anti-Establishment Communard and the Shame Coefficient*

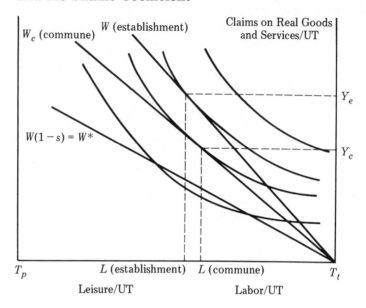

claims on real goods and leisure in exchange for their tastes. Bearing the costs of one's own tastes is the essence of Gary Becker's economics of discrimination, developed more fully below.[21]

Communes, Households, and Labor Force Attachment

As suggested above, all (adult) able-bodied commune members are expected to contribute to the commonweal in accordance with their respective abilities. In the absence of communal production and distribution systems, other economic units—firms, businesses, etc.—emerge. Such units are exclusively or predominantly devoted to production, and the interconnections between firms and individuals are largely market relationships.[22] Under these circumstances, it is useful for labor economists and policy makers (1) to measure the proportion of the population who have an attachment to the market, (2) to observe how that proportion changes over time and place, and (3) to examine the determinants of those changes. Measures of labor force attachment (or participation) would make little sense in a commune where participation is always 100 percent by definition. In a market system, however, the measures provide useful information about how choices are made between market and household participation.

Before describing these useful measures and some related data, one general caveat is necessary: measures of labor force attachment, employment, and so on—i.e., measures of those who work or seek to work for pay—do not capture all of the productive activity in the economy. The household still exists as a productive unit. Indeed, households can best be regarded as economic units producing "commodities" (like nutrition, child services, recreation, etc.) by combining household time and market inputs (goods and services) and distributing those commodities largely in a communal manner.[23] The fact that the goods and services are obtained largely through the market and that persons in the household are not paid does not imply either that households are exclusively consuming units or that adults who are exclusively in the household sector (housewives or househusbands) are nonproductive. Just as in the case of the communard, the labor force choice of each household member is related to productivity (and compensation) in the market (noncommunal) sector relative to productivity in the household.

The data collected by the U.S. government provide good examples of useful labor force, employment, and unemployment measures. These data fall into three basic sets known as:

1. household data,
2. establishment data, and
3. unemployment insurance data.

The names reflect the manner in which the data are collected rather than the coverage of the collection effort. There are, however, important differences in coverage, and an understanding of these data and their differences are important to anyone trying to understand modern labor economics.

Household Data

Household data are collected by the U.S. Bureau of the Census via the Current Population Survey (CPS) and are published regularly in *Employment and Earnings* (previously called *Employment and Earnings and the Monthly Report on the Labor Force*). These data are also available in numerous other government publications and news releases.

Systematic attempts to measure labor force, employment, and unemployment totals are relatively recent. Prior to and for the most part during the Great Depression, the United States had no regular survey on labor force status, employment, or unemployment. The decennial census did collect data, however, by household and/or personal enumeration on the number of "gainful workers." A "gainful worker" was one who (or whose family) responded positively to an occupational query. If a man or woman had an "occupation"—regardless of his/her employment or unemployment status—he or she was counted as a gainful worker. Thus, a complete count of gainful workers in the United States was available every ten years, but no regular measure of employment or unemployment was available as a guide for national economic policy. During the 1930s and under the pressure of "high unemployment," the Works Progress Administration (WPA) began to experiment with different concepts of labor force and unemployment status. In 1937, a national post card registration of the unemployed was undertaken and other techniques were sought to estimate unemployment on a nationwide basis. A (WPA) sample survey of unemployment began in March 1940, and the effort was transferred to the Bureau of the Census in 1942. The sample was revised in 1943. This approach with modifications continues to be used to date.

The estimating technique involves a sample survey of a given number of eligible households (56,000 per month covering 614 primary sampling units in 1979)—a stratified random sample. The data reflect behavior during the second week of each month—specifically, the week including the twelfth. The household respondents, often the housewives, are asked to report the labor force, employment, and unemployment status of all members of the household together with a number of other characteristics. The stratified random sample data are then "blown up" to estimate labor force, employment, and unemployment numbers and characteristics for the nation as a whole. These estimates are benchmarked to the same data collected by total "household enumeration" every ten years in the decennial census and by special surveys.

Table 1–1 shows a portion of the U.S. Current Population Survey interview form used to acquire the raw data, specifically, Budget Bureau form 41-R 1202.14. As can be seen from this form, the survey obtains data on many dimensions of economic life other than just labor force and employment status. These data provide a wealth of knowledge concerning changes in economic relationships and are regularly published in the various Ps series of the Bureau of the Census. Among the data regularly collected by the CPS is information on hours of work and hours of work by usual status, school enrollment, educational attainment, veteran's status, income levels, social security payments, and mobility across states and counties, to name but a few of the series. One could spend considerable time discussing the problems of obtaining accurate data via a household survey, classification procedures, and response errors. These problems are legion and were explored in great depth during the 1960s by the so-called Gordon Committee—the President's Committee to Appraise Employment and Unemployment Statistics. They were also among the subjects studied by the National Commission on Employment

Table 1–1 *Excerpt from the Current Population Survey Form: CPS-1*

---

18. LINE NUMBER

19. What was . . . doing most of LAST WEEK –

Working
Keeping house
Going to school
or something else?

Working *(Skip to 20A)* . . . . . WK
With a job but not at work . . J
Looking for work . . . . LK
Keeping house . . . . H
Going to school . . . . S
Unable to work *(Skip to 24)*. U
Retired . . . . R
Other *(Specify)* . . . . OT

20C. Does . . . USUALLY work 35 hours or more a week at this job?

Yes ○ What is the reason . . . worked less than 35 hours LAST WEEK?

No ○ What is the reason . . . USUALLY works less than 35 hours a week?

(Mark the appropriate reason)

Slack work . . . .
Material shortage . . . .
Plant or machine repair . . . . . .
New job started during week . ○
Job terminated during week . . ○
Could find only part-time work ○
Holiday *(Legal or religious)* . . .
Labor dispute . . . .
Bad weather . . . .
Own illness . . . .
On vacation . . . .
Too busy with housework, school, personal bus., etc.
Did not want full-time work . .
Full-time

---

20. Did . . . do any work at all LAST WEEK, not counting work around the house? *(Note: If farm or business operator in hh., ask about unpaid work)*

Yes ○ No ○ *(Go to 21)*

20A. How many hours did . . . work LAST WEEK at all jobs?

20B. INTERVIEWER CHECK ITEM

49+ *(Skip to item 23)*
1-34 *(Go to 20C)*
35-48 *(Go to 20D)*

20D. Did . . . lose any time or take any time off LAST WEEK for any reason such as illness, holiday or slack work?

Yes ○ How many hours did . . . take off?

(Correct 20A if lost time not already deducted; if 20A reduced below 35, correct 20B and fill 20C; otherwise, skip to 23.)

No ○

20E. Did . . . work any overtime or at more than one job LAST WEEK?

Yes ○ How many extra hours did . . . work?

(Correct 20A and 20B as necessary if extra hours not already included and skip to 23.)

No ○

(Skip to 23)

OFFICE USE ONLY

INDUSTRY	OCCUPATION
○ ○ A ○	○ ○ ○ N ○
I I B ○	I I I P ○
ē ē C ○	ē ē ē Q ○

---

21. *(If J in 19, skip to 21A.)* Did . . . have a job or business from which he was temporarily absent or on layoff LAST WEEK?

Yes ○ No ○ *(Go to 22)*

21A. Why was . . . absent from work LAST WEEK?

Own illness . . . . ○
On vacation . . . . ○
Bad weather . . . . ○
Labor dispute . . ○
New job to begin within 30 days ○ *(Skip to 22B and 22C2)*
Temporary layoff *(Under 30 days)* ○ *(Skip to 22C3)*
Indefinite layoff *(30 days or more or no def. recall date)* ○
Other *(Specify)* . . ○

21B. Is . . . getting wages or salary for any of the time off LAST WEEK?

Yes . . . . ○
No . . . . ○
Self-employed ○

21C. Does . . . usually work 35 hours or more a week at this job?

Yes ○
No ○

(Skip to 23 and enter job held last week)

---

22. *(If LK in 19, skip to 22A.)* Has . . . been looking for work during the past 4 weeks?

Yes ○ No ○ *(Go to 24)*

22A. What has . . . been doing in the last 4 weeks to find work? *(Mark all methods used; do not read list.)*

Checked with –
pub. employ. agency ○
pvt. employ. agency ○
employer directly . . ○
friends or relatives ○
Placed or answered ads . . . . ○
Nothing *(Skip to 24)* . . . . ○
Other *(Specify in notes, e.g., MDTA, union or prof. register, etc.)* . . . . . ○

22B. Why did . . . start looking for work? Was it because . . . lost or quit a job at that time *(pause)* or was there some other reason?

Lost job . . . . ○
Quit job . . . . ○
Left school . . . . ○
Wanted temporary work ○
Other *(Specify in notes)* ○

22C. 1) How many weeks has . . . been looking for work?
2) How many weeks ago did . . . start looking for work?
3) How many weeks ago was . . . laid off?

22D. Has . . . been looking for full-time or part-time work?

Full ○ Part ○

22E. Is there any reason why . . . could not take a job LAST WEEK?

Yes ○ Already has a job . . . . . ○
Temporary illness . . . . ○
Going to school . . . . . . ○
No ○ Other *(Specify in notes)* ○

22F. When did . . . last work at a full-time job or business lasting 2 consecutive weeks or more?

1970 or later *(Write month and year)* . . ○

---

and Unemployment Statistics during the late 1970s.[24] As a result of the deliberations of the initial committee, the "Gordon Report" produced a number of changes in the CPS. These changes are discussed in detail in the November 1966 and February 1967 issues of *Employment and Earnings and the Monthly Report on the Labor Force.*

With this background, one can develop the simple mathematics of the demographic accounting system as follows:

1. Establish a population of labor force age and measure the size of that population on a sample basis and/or by a complete census. Call that number $N_{p(14+)}$ or $N_{p(16+)}$ depending upon the lower population age limit.[25]

2. Following the answers to the household survey, divide the population of labor force age into those *in* the labor force and those *outside* the labor force:

(1–1) $$N_p = N_L + N_N$$

3. Because the labor force includes all persons employed or seeking employment, divide N_L into two parts:

(1–2) $$N_L = N_E + N_U$$

4. Finally, express these data in ratio form:

(1–3) $\dfrac{N_L}{N_p} = L' =$ labor force as a fraction of the population of labor force age (or for any subset of that population); $(L' \times 100) = L =$ the labor force participation rate

(1–4) $\dfrac{N_E}{N_L} = E'$ where $(E' \times 100) = E =$ the employment rate

(1–5) $\dfrac{N_U}{N_L} = '$ where $(U' \times 100) = U =$ the unemployment rate

Obviously, N_E, N_U, and N_L are all summations of dichotomous variables across individuals and/or groups of individuals. Each person either is or is not in one of these categories, and the summations of these 1–0 variables represent proportions among the various groups. Alternatively stated:

$$E' + U' = 1.00 \text{ and}$$
$$L' + N' = 1.00 \text{ where } N' = \frac{N_N}{N_p}.$$

Some persons have used a variant of this approach for research work, defining an employment population ratio—i.e., N_E/N_p. The measure is not presented in that form, however, in any regular publication of the Labor Department or the Bureau of the Census.

Although the mathematical presentation above is ultrasimple, it can be very useful. For example, it indicates the many ways in which measures of unemployment are quite different from measures of nonemployment—being out of the labor force. Note that:

$$N_U \neq N_N, \ U' \neq N', \text{ and } U \neq N.$$

Similarly, being in the labor force does not imply being employed, being out of school, or not being engaged in household activities. Moreover, the simple mathematics above help one to avoid confusion between unemployment, unemployment insurance, and welfare. A clear distinction between unemployment and welfare is required to address a number of contemporary labor market and poverty problems. Note that by definition one must be in the labor force to be unemployed, but that welfare eligibility may or may not depend upon one's labor force status (as in the case of general welfare support or aid to families with dependent children). Note also that not all those counted as unemployed by CPS count may be eligible for unemployment insurance because unemployment insurance programs may impose other conditions (particularly prior employment) in determining eligibility for payments.

Table 1–2 presents the U.S. labor force and employment status of the noninstitutional population from 1947 to 1978. These data were taken from the *Employment and Training Report of the President* (formerly called *The Manpower Report of the President*). Further statistical details, of course, are available in the various census volumes and tapes. Monthly data compiled from the CPS sample appear in the various monthly issues of *Employment and Earnings* (from the U.S. Bureau of Labor Statistics). Examination of both these sources of data is essential for a full understanding of the statistical *tour de force* performed by the Bureau of the Census.

A complete discussion of these data and of the associated definitional and measurement problems is neither appropriate nor possible in a textbook on labor economics. Government manuals are available for those purposes. Two examples of definitional problems will suffice to acquaint the reader with the nature of these questions. Consider the following:

1. the determination of the labor force status of a man or woman on vacation, and
2. the determination of the labor force status of a man or woman on strike.

A man on vacation is regarded (1) as in the labor force, (2) as employed, and (3) as "with a job, but not at work." Such a designation of his labor force status seems eminently reasonable for he has clearly indicated his intentions to be attached to the labor force, and he is not currently

Table 1–2 *Employment Status of the Noninstitutional Population 16 Years and Over, by Sex: Annual Averages, 1947–78*[a] *(Numbers in thousands)*

Sex and Year	Total Noninstitutional Population	Total Labor Force, Including Armed Forces		Civilian Labor Force						Not in Labor Force
		Number	Percent of Noninstitutional Population	Total	Employed			Unemployed		
					Total	Agriculture	Nonagricultural Industries	Number	Percent of Labor Force	
BOTH SEXES										
1947	103,418	60,941	58.9	59,350	57,039	7,891	49,148	2,311	3.9	42,477
1948	104,527	62,080	59.4	60,621	58,344	7,629	50,711	2,276	3.8	42,447
1949	105,611	62,903	59.6	61,286	57,649	7,656	49,990	3,637	5.9	42,708
1950	106,645	63,858	59.9	62,208	58,920	7,160	51,752	3,288	5.3	42,787
1951	107,721	65,117	60.4	62,017	59,962	6,726	53,230	2,055	3.3	42,604
1952	108,823	65,730	60.4	62,138	60,254	6,501	53,748	1,883	3.0	43,093
1953	110,601	66,560	60.2	63,015	61,181	6,261	54,915	1,834	2.9	44,041
1954	111,671	66,993	60.0	63,643	60,110	6,206	53,898	3,532	5.5	44,678
1955	112,732	68,072	60.4	65,023	62,171	6,449	55,718	2,852	4.4	44,660
1956	113,811	69,409	61.0	66,552	63,802	6,283	57,506	2,750	4.1	44,402
1957	115,065	69,729	60.6	66,929	64,071	5,947	58,123	2,859	4.3	45,336
1958	116,363	70,275	60.4	67,639	63,036	5,586	57,450	4,602	6.8	46,088
1959	117,881	70,921	60.2	68,369	64,630	5,565	59,065	3,740	5.5	46,960
1960	119,759	72,142	60.2	69,628	65,778	5,458	60,318	3,852	5.5	47,617
1961	121,343	73,031	60.2	70,459	65,746	5,200	60,546	4,714	6.7	48,312
1962	122,981	73,442	59.7	70,614	66,702	4,944	61,759	3,911	5.5	49,539
1963	125,154	74,571	59.6	71,833	67,762	4,687	63,076	4,070	5.7	50,583
1964	127,224	75,830	59.8	73,091	69,305	4,523	64,782	3,786	5.2	51,394
1965	129,236	77,178	59.7	74,455	71,088	4,361	66,726	3,366	4.5	52,058
1966	131,180	78,893	60.1	75,770	72,895	3,979	68,915	2,875	3.8	52,288
1967	133,319	80,793	60.6	77,347	74,372	3,844	70,527	2,975	3.8	52,527
1968	135,562	82,272	60.7	78,737	75,920	3,817	72,103	2,817	3.6	53,291
1969	137,841	84,239	61.1	80,733	77,902	3,606	74,296	2,831	3.5	53,602
1970	140,182	85,903	61.3	82,715	78,627	3,462	75,165	4,088	4.9	54,280
1971	142,596	86,929	61.0	84,113	79,120	3,387	75,732	4,993	5.9	55,666
1972	145,775	88,991	61.0	86,542	81,702	3,472	78,230	4,840	5.6	56,785
1973	148,263	91,040	61.4	88,714	84,409	3,452	80,957	4,304	4.9	57,222
1974	150,827	93,240	61.8	91,011	85,936	3,492	82,443	5,076	5.6	57,587
1975	153,449	94,793	61.8	92,613	84,783	3,380	81,403	7,830	8.5	58,655
1976	156,048	96,917	62.1	94,773	87,485	3,297	84,188	7,288	7.7	59,130
1977	158,559	99,534	62.8	97,401	90,546	3,244	87,302	6,855	7.0	59,025
1978	161,058	102,537	63.7	100,420	94,373	3,342	91,031	6,047	6.0	58,521
MALE										
1947	50,968	44,258	86.8	42,686	40,994	6,643	34,351	1,692	4.0	6,710
1948	51,439	44,729	87.0	43,286	41,726	6,358	35,366	1,559	3.6	6,710
1949	51,922	45,097	86.9	43,498	40,926	6,342	34,581	2,572	5.9	6,825
1950	52,352	45,446	86.8	43,819	41,580	6,001	35,573	2,239	5.1	6,906
1951	52,788	46,063	87.3	43,001	41,780	5,533	36,243	1,221	2.8	6,725
1952	53,248	46,416	87.2	42,869	41,684	5,389	36,292	1,185	2.8	6,832
1953	54,248	47,131	86.9	43,633	42,431	5,253	37,175	1,202	2.8	7,117
1954	54,706	47,275	86.4	43,965	41,620	5,200	36,414	2,344	5.3	7,431
1955	55,122	47,488	86.2	44,475	42,621	5,265	37,354	1,854	4.2	7,634
1956	55,547	47,914	86.3	45,091	43,380	5,039	38,334	1,711	3.8	7,633
1957	56,082	47,964	85.5	45,197	43,357	4,824	38,532	1,841	4.1	8,118
1958	56,640	48,126	85.0	45,521	42,423	4,596	37,827	3,098	6.8	8,514
1959	57,312	48,405	84.5	45,886	43,466	4,532	38,934	2,420	5.3	8,907
1960	58,144	48,870	84.0	46,388	43,904	4,472	39,431	2,486	5.4	9,274
1961	58,826	49,193	83.6	46,653	43,656	4,298	39,359	2,997	6.4	9,633
1962	59,626	49,395	82.8	46,600	44,177	4,069	40,108	2,423	5.2	10,231

Table 1-2 *(Continued)*

Sex and Year	Total Noninstitutional Population	Total Labor Force, Including Armed Forces		Civilian Labor Force						Not in Labor Force
		Number	Percent of Noninstitutional Population	Total	Employed			Unemployed		
					Total	Agriculture	Nonagricultural Industries	Number	Percent of Labor Force	
1963	60,627	49,835	82.2	47,129	44,657	3,809	40,849	2,472	5.2	10,792
1964	61,556	50,387	81.9	47,679	45,474	3,691	41,782	2,205	4.6	11,169
1965	62,473	50,946	81.5	48,255	46,340	3,547	42,792	1,914	4.0	11,527
1966	63,351	51,560	81.4	48,471	46,919	3,243	43,675	1,551	3.2	11,792
1967	64,316	52,398	81.5	48,987	47,479	3,164	44,315	1,508	3.1	11,919
1968	65,345	53,030	81.2	49,533	48,114	3,157	44,957	1,419	2.9	12,315
1969	66,365	53,688	80.9	50,221	48,818	2,963	45,854	1,403	2.8	12,677
1970	67,409	54,343	80.6	51,195	48,960	2,861	46,099	2,235	4.4	13,066
1971	68,512	54,797	80.0	52,021	49,245	2,790	46,455	2,776	5.3	13,715
1972	69,864	55,671	79.7	53,265	50,630	2,839	47,791	2,635	4.9	14,193
1973	71,020	56,479	79.5	54,203	51,963	2,833	49,130	2,240	4.1	14,541
1974	72,253	57,349	79.4	55,186	52,519	2,901	49,618	2,668	4.8	14,904
1975	73,494	57,706	78.5	55,615	51,230	2,801	48,429	4,385	7.9	15,788
1976	74,739	58,397	78.1	56,359	52,391	2,716	49,675	3,968	7.0	16,341
1977	75,981	59,467	78.3	57,449	53,861	2,639	51,222	3,588	6.2	16,514
1978	77,169	60,535	78.4	58,542	55,491	2,681	52,810	3,051	5.2	16,634

[a] Source: *Employment and Training Report of the President* (Washington, D.C.: U.S. Government Printing Office, June 1979), Table A-1.

or actively seeking employment (except in the sense that all persons may constantly be seeking alternative employment). A man or woman on strike represents a somewhat less clear-cut case.

Note that under American law, any person on strike can be replaced while on strike, but that he may not be fired "because" he is on strike. Since the 1930s at least, strikes have generally been considered by the courts to be legitimate union activities. Employer attempts to interfere with employees' rights to engage in legitimate union activities (including collective bargaining and strikes) have usually been held to be unfair labor practices, subject to injunction and restitution procedures. While the union is on strike, however, a man can hunt for and/or take other employment. "Hitting the bricks" often involves part-time work elsewhere.

Before the 1967 changes in definitions, "strikers" were counted as unemployed (or as employed if they had alternative part-time or fulltime jobs). Under the procedures adopted since 1967, however, men on strike are seen as analogous to men on vacation. A striker's attachment is considered to be to that employment about which his union is negotiating. The current practice of most large employers in not hiring replacements ("strike breakers" or "scabs" in the union terminology) supports such a determination. Thus, by Census Bureau definitions, strikers are considered to be "with a job, but not at work."

Classification of strikers as "with a job, but not at work" *cleaned* the unemployment statistics of an undesirable element that was contrary to the national purposes for collecting labor force and unemployment statistics. From the beginning, these statistics have been intended for and have been used to guide national monetary, fiscal, and expenditure policies. Inclusion of strikers among the unemployed not only raised the level of unemployment, but raised (or would raise) that level more in periods of prosperity than in periods of depression, since strike activity is procyclical. Thus, the redefinition eliminated "noise" in the unemployment series.[26]

Establishment Data

Establishment statistics are drawn from the financial records of a large number of cooperating companies and are particularly accurate in the areas of average hourly earnings, average weekly hours, and average weekly earnings. The data are carefully classified into industry subdivisions by the Standard Industrial Classification Manual code. These data provide great detail on the characteristics of the occupational, earnings, and industrial mix of the employed, but reveal nothing about the unemployed or about labor force participation rates or levels. Moreover, the range of cooperating companies in the establishment data set is not universal or uniform across industrial areas. For example, coverage of the firms in finance, insurance, and real estate or in retail trade is much less complete than in durable and nondurable manufacturing.

Considerable attention could be given to the details of the establishment statistics. Because one can read the details of these programs in various government manuals, this text discusses only the broad differences among the various sets of statistics.

Unemployment Insurance Data

The U.S. unemployment insurance program is administered by a joint federal-state arrangement—the U.S. Employment and Training Administration, successor to the U.S. Bureau of Employment Security, together with the bureaus of employment security of the various states.[27] In the course of providing unemployment compensation for qualified applicants and in seeking to place the unemployed, considerable amounts of labor force, employment, and unemployment data are obtained. Unlike the CPS data, however, the "operational statistics" are local and industry-specific, and depend upon the set of contacts and coverage each local "BES" has with prospective employees. Moreover, some of these data are not definitionally consistent because standards of eligibility for unemployment compensation differ among states. Nevertheless, the data, emerging largely as a byproduct of the unemployment insurance laws, do provide some additional insight into labor force, employment, and unemployment differences particularly across geographic areas.

The CPS data historically have been of questionable reliability for subdivisions smaller than the regional level—for most states and standard metropolitan statistical areas (SMSAs), and for cities, central cities, or neighborhoods. Because neither the CPS nor establishment data provide local geographic coverage and because of concern with structural unemployment during the 1950s in certain regions or states (e.g., New England and West Virginia), various acts passed by the Eisenhower and Kennedy administrations required the national BES to estimate unemployment by *local* labor market areas. Among these was the Area Redevelopment Act of 1961 which provided for government assistance and low-cost loans to areas with "substantial and persistent unemployment." Therefore, beginning with the "operational statistics," the various state bureaus estimate the labor force, employment, and unemployment totals for each geographic area via a "building block method." In brief, this method uses "operational data" as a base to which are added estimates of employment and unemployment for groups that are largely out of contact with the bureaus of employment security. The groups include:

1. new entrants or reentrants into the labor force (unqualified for unemployment compensation),
2. strikers, and
3. the number of unemployed who have exhausted their eligibility for unemployment compensation (usually those unemployed for more than twenty-six weeks).

There are, of course, several possible biases in any such estimating technique, and there have been substantive and important questions asked concerning the validity of the "building block method."[28] As a result, data for the states and for thirty major labor market areas since 1976 have been based on the concepts and methods used in the CPS. Thus, these subaggregates have been made more comparable to the national aggregates.[29] The unemployment insurance data, however, remain the sole source of local area labor force and unemployment information for most localities throughout the nation. Table 1–3 displays excerpts from a *State Labor Summary* for North Carolina, a report based on the "building block method." Figure 1–6, also based largely upon these data, shows unemployment in sixteen Appalachian SMSAs at two business cycle peaks. The national unemployment figures in that chart, however, were obtained from the CPS household survey. With reference to the "structural unemployment" problems noted above, one can see that most of these Appalachian SMSAs experienced local unemployment rates that

Table 1-3 North Carolina State Labor Summary, March 1980

Employment Developments: Total employment in the state was estimated to be 2,565,600 during the mid-week of March, 1980. That was a significant net monthly gain of 30,600 (+1.2 percent). All three of the main employment categories experienced noticeable increases over the month. Agricultural employment continued its seasonal growth with the addition of 5,700 workers (+10.1 percent), the "all other" nonagricultural employment segment enjoyed an increase of 3,200 people (+1.2 percent) and nonagricultural wage and salary employment (excluding dual jobholders) displayed a healthy net monthly increase of 21,700 persons (+1.0 percent).

Manufacturing employment (including dual jobholders) showed a very slight drop of 100 workers from mid-February to mid-March of this year. The durable goods segment remained constant over the month with most of its industries displaying subtle mixed trends. Primary metals added 200 workers (+2.6 percent) over the month, while electrical machinery grew by 500 employers (+1.0 percent). The nondurable goods segment sustained a loss of 100 persons over the month. The tobacco industry continued to exhibit a normal seasonal decline with the reduction of 900 workers (−3.9 percent), many of whom were in stemmeries. On the positive side, the textile industry experienced an increase of 1,200 employers (+0.5 percent) due to a general increase in business.

During the past thirty days, nonmanufacturing employment experienced an impressive increase of 16,800 persons (+1.1 percent). Several of the industry groups displayed measurable over-the-month gains. The construction industry added 6,000 workers (+5.2 percent) over the month, the result of a mild seasonal upswing. Trade employment grew by 3,400 people (+0.7 percent) as both wholesale and retail segments experienced increases. Also, service and miscellaneous employment advanced by 3,700 workers (+1.1 percent) as hotels and recreation areas began increasing their staffs in preparation for the tourist season.

North Carolina's manufacturing employment sustained a minor loss of 1,200 workers (−0.1 percent) from March, 1979, to March, 1980. On the other hand, nonmanufacturing employment showed a yearly gain of 63,600 persons (+4.2 percent) as several industry groups exhibited strong growth: finance, +4,500; transportation, +6,000; government, +8,400; service, +19,900; and trade, +23,900.

Manpower Resources: Total unemployment in the state was estimated to be 151,900 people during the mid-week of March, 1980, an over-the-month increase of 3,900 persons (+2.6 percent). As a result of that unemployment gain, North Carolina's unadjusted rate of unemployment rose from 5.5 percent in February, 1980, to 5.6 percent in March, 1980. In March, 1979, economic conditions were quite a bit better with 118,600 people out of work for a rate of 4.5 percent. The national unadjusted rates of unemployment were 6.6 percent in March, 1980, 6.8 percent in February, and 6.1 percent one year ago. The national seasonally adjusted rates of unemployment were 6.2 percent this March, 6.0 percent in February, and 5.7 percent twelve months ago. Seasonally adjusted unemployment data are not developed for the state.

Available Applicants: As of March 31, 1980, there were 186,474 active job applicants registered for work with the local Job Service offices throughout the state,

Table 1-3 *(Continued)*

---

a slight over-the-month decline of 340 persons (− 0.2 percent). The under twenty-five segment was once again the largest applicant group by age with 61,605 or 33.0 percent of the total. The second largest applicant group fell between the ages of thirty and thirty-nine and numbered 43,893 or 23.5 percent. The sixty-five and over segment accounted for the fewest number of applicants with just 1,407 or 0.8 percent of the total. Most of the active applicants were male with 93,917 or 50.4 percent. Whites (not Hispanic), who numbered 105,130, comprised 56.4 percent of the total. The vast majority of the active applicants (170,377 or 91.4 percent) were not working when they registered with the Employment Security Commission. The following table provides additional information from the state-wide active applicant file as of the end of March, 1980.

North Carolina Civilian Labor Force, March 1980[a]

Item	Number			Change to Current Month from:			
				February 1980		March 1979	
	March 1980[b]	February 1980[c]	March 1979	Net	%	Net	%
Civilian Labor Force	2,717,500	2,683,000	2,632,400	+34,500	+ 1.3	+85,100	+ 3.2
Employment, Total	2,565,600	2,535,000	2,513,800	+30,600	+ 1.2	+51,800	+ 2.1
Agricultural Employment	62,000	56,300	66,600	+ 5,700	+10.1	− 4,600	− 6.9
Nonag. Wage & Sal. Employ.[d]	2,236,400	2,214,700	2,182,500	+21,700	+ 1.0	+53,900	+ 2.5
All other Nonag. Employ.[e]	267,200	264,000	264,700	+ 3,200	+ 1.2	+ 2,500	+ 0.9
Unemployment, Total	151,900	148,000	118,600	+ 3,900	+ 2.6	+33,300	+28.1
State Unadjusted Rate	5.6	5.5	4.5	+ 0.1	XXX	+ 1.1	XXX
National Rate (Unadjusted)	6.6	6.8	6.1	− 0.2	XXX	+ 0.5	XXX
(Seasonally Adjusted)	6.2	6.0	5.7	+ 0.2	XXX	+ 0.5	XXX

[a] All data revised to reflect 1979 benchmark revisions.
[b] Preliminary estimates.
[c] Revised estimates.
[d] Adjusted to exclude dual jobholders and the effects of worker commuting.
[e] Includes self-employed workers, unpaid family workers, and domestic workers in private households.

---

were substantially above the national level in 1960, in some cases by a factor of two or more. By 1969 almost all the unemployment levels were within one percentage point of the national level and seven out of sixteen SMSAs were below the national level. Table 1–4 presents the unemployment rates for several labor market areas.[30] The areas were especially

Figure 1–6 *Unemployment in the Sixteen Appalachian SMSAs at Two Business Cycle Peaks*

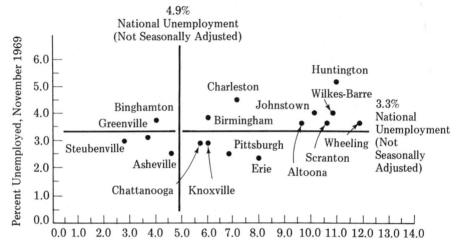

Source: U.S. Department of Labor, *Area Trends in Employment and Unemployment*, various issues, 1960–1971.

Table 1–4 *Unemployment Rates in Selected Labor Market Areas, March and May 1956–60*[a] *(Not deseasonalized)*

Time	Washing- ton, D.C.	Provi- dence, R.I.	Birming- ham, Ala.	Wilkes- Barre, Pa.	Duluth, Minn.	Charlotte, N.C.
1956						
March	2.2	8.8	3.4	12.6	8.0	3.7
May	1.7	9.0	3.3	13.6	3.7	3.8
1957						
March	2.4	10.3	4.1	11.7	7.6	3.7
May	1.7	10.0	3.2	11.8	4.1	3.8
1958						
March	3.4	14.7	7.4	17.0	13.7	4.9
May	2.7	15.1	7.5	16.4	12.4	5.2
1959						
March	2.6	11.7	6.5	17.0	13.2	3.9
May	1.9	9.1	4.8	14.1	8.2	3.4
1960						
March	2.7	7.9	7.1	13.8	11.4	5.2
May	2.1	6.5	6.5	10.9	7.6	2.9

[a] Unpublished data from the U.S. Bureau of Employment Security. Complete tabulation for the period is available in Robert M. Fearn, *Labor Force and School Participation of Teenagers* (Ph.D. diss., University of Chicago, 1968).

selected to indicate differences in the variability of unemployment across labor market areas and across the business cycle.

With this introduction to the demographically based system of labor force accounting, we can proceed to a consideration of welfare systems in market economies and the potential effects of those systems.

Notes to Chapter 1

1. Hubert H. Humphrey, *The Education of a Public Man* (Garden City, N.Y.: Doubleday & Co., 1976), p. 201.

2. Thomas More, *Utopia* (Baltimore: Penguin Books, 1965), p. 128.

3. Slavery is discussed in some detail in Chapter 4.

4. See Charles Nordhoff, *The Communist Societies of the United States* (New York: Harper & Brothers, 1875). Also see the excellent film on one of the early communes, *The Shakers,* distributed by Tom Davenport Films, Delaphane, Va. For an interesting contrast in time, see R. Farfield, *Communes USA: A Personal Tour* (Baltimore: Penguin Books, 1972), and Mack Reynolds, *Commune 2000 A.D.* (New York: Bantam Books, 1974). Note that Reynolds's book "solves" the economic problem by satiating the demand for all market goods. For an examination of communes of the 1960s and 1970s and of the mystical-religious aspects of those associations, see Lawrence Veysey, *The Communal Experience* (Chicago: University of Chicago Press, 1978).

5. See Paul Craig Roberts, *Alienation and the Soviet Economy: Toward a General Theory of Marxist Alienation, Organizational Principles, and the Soviet Economy* (Albuquerque: University of New Mexico Press, 1971). For a discussion of the subsequent Soviet wage system, see Robert M. Fearn, *An Evaluation of the Soviet Wage Reform, 1956–62* CIA/RR ER 63–22 (Washington, D.C.: Central Intelligence Agency, August 1963).

6. See, however, Stewart H. Holbrook, *Dreamers of the American Dream* (Garden City, N.Y.: Doubleday & Co., 1957), Part 1. "The Perfect Society," for a discussion of the role of personal and social adjustment processes within communal structures.

7. One might reasonably question whether the "type" of persons who form communes is properly portrayed by the preference map approach. They are often called "nonacquisitive," "moralistic," "idealistic," "security-minded," etc. In considering this question, note that the axes are not restricted to "market goods" and can represent goods such as solitude and contemplation (which are also "produced" by the use of time). Thus, the argument against applicability may rest more upon presumptions of the labels on the axes than upon the usefulness of the technique itself.

8. Technically, constant marginal productivity means that $\partial Y/\partial L > 0 = W$ and that $\partial^2 Y/\partial L^2 = 0$ where output $= Y = f(L, Z)$ and where Z represents a vector of nonlabor inputs. The "more realistic" assumption of diminishing marginal productivity assumes that $\partial Y/\partial L > 0$ and $\partial^2 Y/\partial L^2 < 0$.

9. Note, however, that U_6, U_5, U_4, etc., are ordinal, not cardinal measures.

10. This assumes no interaction in team production; that is, it assumes that the marginal product of the team of two persons is no greater than the sum of the marginal products of each separately. See Armen A. Alchian and Harold Demsetz, "Production, Information, Costs, and Economic Organization,"

American Economic Review 62, no. 5 (December 1972): 777–95, for a discussion of team productivity and the nature of the economic firm. The model presented here is a variation and simplification of that developed separately by Gary Becker, "The Theory of Social Interactions," *Journal of Political Economy* 82, no. 6 (November/December 1974): 1063–93.

11. Some readers might be concerned that the economic definition of love used here is oversimplified. One might argue, for example, that love is a psychogalvanic response to a series of psychological and physiological stimuli powerful in their effects, diverse in their origins, and resulting in nonpredictable and erratic behavior patterns. One can hardly argue with such an elegant definition, but its usefulness is questionable. In the absence of a better one, the definition of love (or economic love) used here will suffice for our purposes. For a closely related discussion of equality, see James M. Buchanan, "Equality as Fact and Norm," *Ethics* 81, no. 3 (April 1971): 228–40.

In this context, love may be divided into two types depending upon whether the utility or only the consumption level of one member enters the other member's function. The latter implies maternalistic or paternalistic love, for the weights applied to the particular consumption tradeoff are the contributor's weights. The other form, wherein the weights entering the contributor's utility function are effectively the receiver's weights, may be characterized as "mature" or mutually reinforcing love. See the description of the relationships between Adam and Henrietta Swan in R. F. Delderfield, *God is an Englishman* (New York: Simon and Schuster, 1970), Part 3. "Cobb at Large: 1862–1863," for an excellent example of the difference between the two kinds of love.

12. George Orwell, *Animal Farm* (New York: Harcourt, Brace & Co., 1946).

13. More complex models involving "his" and "her" utility and "his" and "her" goods (i.e., goods for a partner which do not enter into the other's utility function) have also been elaborated. See Marjorie Bechtel McElroy and Mary Jean Horney, "Nash-bargained Household Decisions: Toward a Generalization of the Theory of Demand" (unpublished paper, Duke University, 1978).

14. One might argue in an analogous fashion that markets economize on that very scarce resource, love. Clarence Philbrook in "Capitalism and the Role of Love," *Southern Economic Journal* 19, no. 4 (April 1953): 458–66, argues that capitalism is a very effective substitute for love in organizing productive activities. Most of his arguments apply, however, to capitalist market systems *or* socialist market systems.

15. Robert M. Fearn, *An Evaluation of the Program for Reducing the Workweek in the USSR* CIA/RR ER 61–13 (Washington, D.C.: Central Intelligence Agency, March 1961), pp. 20–21.

16. Political or ideological matters may outweigh economic ones in collective decisions involving (1) or (3) above. Individual behavior responses to such politically or ideologically motivated decisions, however, can be analyzed with the indifference curve approach. Such an analysis may imply a conflict or "contradiction" between the distribution system desired by the nation's leadership and that which would result if the tastes of the population could be effectively implemented.

17. Chinese agricultural communes are a case in point. Note, however, that the complexity of modern industry and the greater heterogeneity of the urban Chinese militate against the use of the communal form. Thus, urban

patterns are consistent with the general analysis of communes developed above. Moreover, differential compensation systems may be used even in rural Chinese communes in order to supplement the power of comradely affection. See T. A. Hsia, *The Commune in Retreat as Evidenced in Terminology and Semantics Studies in Chinese Communist Terminology,* Center for Chinese Studies, Institute of International Studies, no. 11 (Berkeley, California: Summer 1964). Note also that the argument between "The Gang of Four" and the "practical" Chinese leaders was concerned, in part, with the efficacy of communal approaches.

18. For an example of a work credit or work chit system, see B. F. Skinner, *Walden Two* (New York: Macmillan Co., 1948). Such work credit (or wage) systems may be varied from week to week to induce sufficient work response. The linkage of consumption to production in this fashion, however, does not represent a pure communal system. Rather, it represents a small Langian system of market socialism. See Oscar Lange and Fred M. Taylor, *On the Economic Theory of Socialism* (Minneapolis: University of Minnesota Press, 1938), or Ota Šik, *Plan and Market Under Socialism* (White Plains, N.Y.: International Arts and Sciences Press, 1967). It will also be useful for avid readers to determine how the *Walden Two* program of behavioral conditioning is related to the economic model developed above.

19. Ministry of the Budget, *The Swedish Budget 1977/78* (Stockholm: Goteborgs Offsettryckeri AB, 1977).

20. Adam Smith, *An Inquiry into the Nature and Causes of the Wealth of Nations* [1776] (New York: The Modern Library, 1937), p. 99.

21. Readers will find it useful to examine the effects of hard drugs and drug addiction on the viability of communes. In their examination, they should think about the effect of drugs (1) on productivity, (2) on levels of "needs" or desired consumption, (3) on love or mutual utility relationships, and (4) on the shape of the leisure-goods tradeoff map itself. Note that the effect of drugs on productivity (or what passes for it) may not always be negative. Consider, for example, the productivity of hard rock groups or jazz drummers who, in the vernacular, "are bombed out of their skulls" relative to their productivity without the aid of stimulants.

22. This is the essence of "commodity production" as distinguished by the Marxists from "production for use."

23. See Gary Becker, "A Theory of the Allocation of Time," *Economic Journal* 75, no. 229 (September 1965): 493–517. In this work, the household is viewed as producing commodities for consumption by combining time inputs and market goods: $Z_i = f(T_i, x_i)$ where the Z_i's are basic commodities such as recreation services, child services, nutrition, etc. The T_i's are time inputs and the x_i's are the goods inputs used for production. The household maximizes $U(Z_1, Z_2, \ldots, Z_m)$ subject to an income constraint, $\Sigma p_i x_i = I = V + T_w \overline{w}$, and a time constraint, $\sum_{i=1}^{m} T_i = T_c = T - T_w$. In the constraints, the p_i's are goods prices, I is real spendable income, V is (real) nonwage income, T_w is labor market time, $\overline{w}$ is the market wage or foregone income for each unit of household production/consumption time, and T is total time per unit time. Given particular time and goods requirements per unit of the respective commodities, $T_i \equiv t_i Z_i$ and $x_i \equiv b_i t_i$, one can collapse the time and goods constraints into one: $\Sigma \Pi_i Z_i = (p_i b_i + t_i \overline{w}) Z_i = V + T \overline{w}$. Thus, the consumer's budget constraint is not just spendable

income, *I*, but total time evaluated at the market wage plus nonwage income—"full income" in Becker's terminology. Π_i, the price per unit of each Z_i, contains two components—a goods price and a time price. Using Becker's approach, one can distinguish between time-intensive production-consumption, such as "eating in," and goods-intensive production-consumption, such as "eating out." Moreover, his approach permits us to view household activities, labor market supply, and product market expenditures as closely interrelated. For example, let nonwage income rise for a family. Both conventional and Beckerian theory lead us to expect an increase in the purchase of all superior (or normal) goods. In conventional theory, no household production effects are described or suggested. The economics of time leads us, however, to expect both an increase in the purchase of market goods and a reduction in labor time supplied to the market. Moreover, Beckerian analysis predicts a simultaneous shift in the time intensity of consumption. The approach has also been applied in many other areas. For applications to family-size decisions and to the quantity and quality of children, see the March/April 1973 supplement to the *Journal of Political Economy*.

24. President's Committee to Appraise Employment and Unemployment Statistics, *Measuring Employment and Unemployment* (Washington, D.C.: U.S. Government Printing Office, 1962); John E. Bregger, "A New Employment Statistics Review Commission," *Monthly Labor Review* 100, no. 3 (March 1977): 14–20; and National Commission on Employment and Unemployment Statistics, *Counting the Labor Force* (Washington, D.C.: U.S. Government Printing Office, 1979).

25. Following the suggestion of the Gordon Committee, the lower age limit for the population of labor force age was raised from 14 to 16 years of age in 1967.

26. See President's Committee, *Measuring Employment and Unemployment,* for other questions of definition, measurement, and interpretation. See also Chapter 12 below.

27. The state agencies are called by various names: the Employment Security Commission, the Department of Employment Security, the Department of Industrial Relations, and the like.

28. For estimating methods, see U.S. Department of Labor, *Handbook on Estimating Population of Labor Market Areas, Estimating Unemployment, Handbook on Defining Labor Market Areas,* and *Estimating Area Employment of Self-Employed, Unpaid Family and Private Household Workers—Nonagricultural Total,* BES nos. R-183, R-185, R-186, and R-187, respectively (Washington, D.C.: Bureau of Employment Security, March 1960–August 1963). See also U.S. Department of Labor, *Area Manpower Guidebook,* BES no. R-174 (Washington, D.C.: Bureau of Employment Security, 1957). For discussions of the accuracy of this approach to the estimation of labor force aggregates, see J. E. Ulman, "How Accurate are Estimates of State and Local Unemployment?" *Industrial and Labor Relations Review* 16, no. 3 (April 1963): 434–52, and President's Committee, *Measuring Employment and Unemployment,* chap. 7.

29. See Table D-4, p. 282, and "Note on Historic Comparability of Labor Force Statistics," pp. 171–72, in *Employment and Training Report of the President* (Washington, D.C.: U.S. Government Printing Office, May 1978).

30. In most cases, labor market areas (or labor areas) and standard metropolitan statistical areas are coterminus.

2 | *Welfare Programs and Work Incentives*

Let welfare be a private concern.   Barry M. Goldwater,
                                        The Conscience of a Conservative[1]

*Let those of us who are well-fed, well-clothed, and well-housed never
forget and never overlook those who live on the outskirts of hope.*
                                        Lyndon B. Johnson[2]

*In a welfare state, the benefits an individual receives are political
rights, not charity, and there should be no occasion for apology
or embarrassment in applying for them. Moreover, the services made
available by a welfare state will parallel in quality and coverage
those open to individuals who are able to draw on private resources.*
                                        Andrew Hacker, *The New York Times*[3]

In recent years, concern with the "welfare mess" in the
United States has been widespread. Advocates of various positions and
policies have been vocal and sometimes vociferous. It has been and is
still often alleged that welfare encourages idleness, reduces work incentives and labor force participation, and even increases illegitimacy. These
allegations are made against a background of real or expressed concern
with the level of living otherwise attainable by welfare recipients. The
economic, social, and political problems of welfare are not simple and,
quite obviously, cannot be addressed here in any relatively complete
fashion. This chapter will therefore concentrate on one question that
is central to many of our "welfare problems": What is the effect of welfare
payments on labor force participation, labor supply, and the work ethic?

Neither labor supply nor the work ethic have been defined, as yet,
in this text. These definitions will emerge from the application of the
indifference model developed in Chapter 1 to the question of welfare
and work incentives. Institutional data will be supplied whenever necessary to the analysis.

Figure 2–1 represents the indifference map of a welfare recipient eligible to receive Y_o claims on real goods and services per unit time (for whatever reason the sociopolitical system may regard as "valid"). Note that in contrast to the productivity line of the communard in Chapter 1, the productivity or wage line for the welfare recipient does not "begin" at the right-hand origin, but at Y_o.

Now, consider the labor time response of our welfare recipient to (presumed) alterations in the productivity (or wage) line, $Y_o Y_o$ to $Y_o Y_1$, $Y_o Y_1$ to $Y_o Y_2$, etc. As before, the slopes of the lines represent various wage rates per unit time. At $Y_o Y_o$, the maximum utility position for the welfare recipient will be at zero (0) labor time per unit time. Thus, the recipient will seek *not* to be in the labor force. In order for the recipient to be able to "locate" at L_o, Y_o must at least meet minimum consumption "needs" as seen by the recipient, and "welfare payments" must be available without a work or labor force participation "requirement." Only when the slope of the productivity line is greater than the slope of the indifference curve at "0" labor time per unit time (L_o) will

Figure 2–1 *Indifference Curves and the Support Level (Y_0) for a Hypothetical Welfare Recipient*

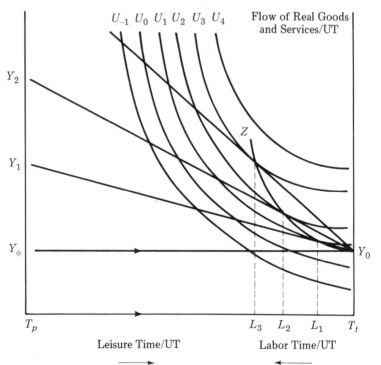

the recipient *voluntarily* offer *any* time to the labor market. Thus, for each individual—given his Y_o and his tastes for market goods and leisure (or nonmarket goods)—there will be some reservation wage (W_o) just high enough to induce him into the labor force. This interpretation of labor force participation is economic as distinct from demographic, and it emphasizes the choices available to and the choice made by each individual as he attempts to maximize his utility, given his tastes for leisure and other uses of time (say, in the household), given Y_o, and given an expected market wage.

Returning to Fig. 2–1, note that the recipient faced with $Y_o Y_1$ (a higher "W" than at $Y_o Y_o$) will maximize his utility by offering L_1 units of labor time to market activities. Similarly, at $Y_o Y_2$, L_2 will be offered, at $Y_o Y_3$, L_3 will be offered, etc. Connecting these offers of time per unit time creates an *offer curve (Y_oZ)*.

Because the slope of the productivity line (in each case) is a wage (or expected wage), we can alternatively plot labor time offered as a function of the wage rate, given the value of Y_o and tastes. Thus, we have derived the labor supply curve

(2–1) $\qquad L_i = f(W_i \,|\, Y_{oi}, \, \ldots \, , \, T_i)$

> where L represents labor time offered, Y_o represents some level of nonwage but guaranteed income, and T represents the taste map of the ith welfare recipient.

In general, then,

(2–2) $\qquad L_i = F(W_i, \, Y_{oi}, \, \ldots \, , \, T_i)$

> where changes in wages or expected wages, support levels, and tastes all influence the labor time offered.

From the arguments above, one can also see that the labor force participation of a welfare recipient will depend upon the same variables; that is,

(2–3) $\qquad LP_i = g(W_i \,|\, Y_{oi}, \, \ldots \, , \, T_i)$

> where $LP_i = 1$ if $W \geq W_o$; $LP = 0$ otherwise,

and in general,

(2–4) $\qquad LP_i = G(W_i, \, L_{oi}, \, \ldots \, , \, T_i).$

Despite the similarities of the L and LP functions, one should remember that L is expressed as time per unit time and that LP is a $1 - 0$ or "dummy" variable. Figure 2–2 shows the supply curve for our hypothetical welfare recipient. As the wage or expected wage rises, the additional labor time offered per additional wage becomes smaller and eventually negative. The slope of the supply curve (and its relative slope or elasticity[4]) depends upon the relative magnitudes of two effects: a substitution effect and an income effect of a wage change. Consider an increase in wage rates or expected wage rates. The higher expected or actual wage implies a higher opportunity cost for leisure and/or for time used in household activities. Hence, there will be a tendency to substitute additional time in the labor market for time in the household. Concurrently, the higher wage implies a higher income at or above the old rate of hours worked. If leisure and household activities are superior goods, one would expect the recipient to buy more of such goods (i.e., offer less labor time) as potential earnings or wages rise. If the substitution effect dominates (as it is more apt to do at lower income levels), higher wage rates will elicit more hours offered to the labor market. If the income effect dominates, work time (in some time dimension) will decline as wages rise. The supply curve will "bend backward."

In Fig. 2–2, W_o represents the reservation wage. That wage is influenced by many considerations, among others the productivity of the individual in the household relative to the market. Becker has argued that the household ought to be considered a "producing" enterprise. But what determines the value of one's household time? In general, one might argue that the value of household time (or the implicit household wage) should depend upon the family or household size, the relative size and type of residence (for example, a third-floor, two-room apartment versus a nine-room farmhouse with vegetable and herb gardens), the ages of children (for one of the functions of the household has been to rear— not just bear—children), and so forth. Moreover, a little thought will convince the reader that W_o also depends upon Y_o, the support or nonwage income level, and T. Note, in particular, that the steeper the slopes of the leisure/goods indifference curves and the higher the implicit value of time in the household, the higher will W_o be at any support level (Y_o). Furthermore, as long as leisure is a superior (or normal) good, W_o will be positively related to Y_o itself. (The diligent reader can prove this to himself by drawing a few graphs and observing the effect of Y_o on W_o.)

In trying to understand the "welfare mess," it is useful to sum the supply curves of the various recipients into an aggregate (or market) supply curve. The resulting sum represents the labor time offered by the entire recipient group at various hypothetical (or possible) wage rates, given the Y_{oi}'s, T_i's, and household productivities of the respective recipients. Two assumptions must be made in order to sum up the individual supply curves:

1. that the skills possessed by the recipients over whom we are summing labor time (offered) per unit time are either identical or similar, or alternatively, that we can convert different productive abilities per unit time into comparable efficiency units and sum those units,[5] and
2. that the labor supply decisions of each individual have no influence on the tastes for labor and leisure of other individuals.[6]

Under these assumptions, the market supply curve is a simple summation of the individual supply curves.

   We now turn to an analysis of a proposed welfare program—the Family Assistance Plan (FAP) initially proposed by the Nixon administration in 1969. Although many plans have been proposed, FAP contains several elements crucial to our analysis. Thus, our "findings" should carry over somewhat to the analysis of any other plan or operating welfare system.

Figure 2–2 *Supply Curve for a Hypothetical Welfare Recipient (or anyone else receiving Y_0)*

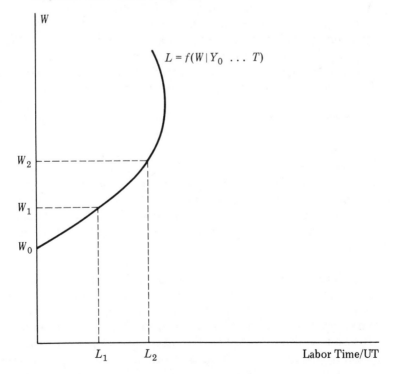

The "Nixon Family Assistance Plan": An Illustration of Behavioral Consequences

Much of the concern with the federal-state welfare system has been directed toward one of the categorical welfare programs—Aid to Families with Dependent Children (AFDC). That program is by any measure the largest and fastest growing in recent years. The others, including Aid to the Blind, Aid to the Aged,[7] Aid to the Disabled,[8] and General Welfare, have been less controversial and have been increasing less rapidly in size and expense. In 1972 the U.S. Congress replaced the state-run programs for the blind, the disabled, and the aged by Supplementary Security Income (SSI), administered from Washington, D.C. and structured in part as a negative income tax. The U.S. food stamp program was also expanded in the early 1970s.[9] Moreover, experimental "pilot programs" requiring a work commitment as a requirement for receipt of the stamps were established in eight locations during 1979. In general, all welfare programs involve an element of communality because the tax system transfers claims on the available goods and services from some taxpayers to the welfare recipients. The transfer, therefore, may not be entirely voluntary. Moreover, governmental transfers involve some explicit or implicit voting process in which the recipient may play a role. Thus, it is not certain that the "tie that binds" in this case is entirely one of compassion or love. Indeed, it is likely that the distribution of willingness to contribute is not uniform among taxpaying groups or individual taxpayers, and that some will feel aggrieved (coerced) by the community decision to supply any particular socially determined support level.

President Richard Nixon unveiled his Family Assistance Plan in a nationwide radio and television address on August 8, 1969.[10] It was aimed, he stated, "at getting everyone able to work off welfare rolls and onto payrolls . . ." and ". . . at ending the unfairness in a system that has become unfair to the welfare recipient, unfair to the working poor, and unfair to the taxpayer."[11]

In that broadcast and in a subsequent bill, S.2986,[12] President Nixon and his legislative associates presented a program with the following major elements:

1. A national family assistance floor for each family based on a standard formula such that levels of support would increase in the states previously providing the lowest levels of support and such that the federal share of the payments would increase in all states. Former support levels under AFDC and AFDC(UP), Aid to Families with Dependent Children with Unemployed Parent(s),[13] would continue in all states previously paying above the national floor—usually called a "hold harmless" provision.

2. Inclusion of male-headed families under the act [where not already permitted by AFDC(UP)].

3. Exclusion of the first $60 per month in earnings and 50 percent of monthly earnings above $60 from consideration in determining the monthly support level (Y_o).

4. A requirement that all adult FAP recipients be in the labor force or in work training (excluding only those physically unable to work and mothers of preschool children).

5. A variable (declining) scale of payments per child for female-headed families.

In his arguments in favor of the plan, President Nixon noted that it would remove the incentive for welfare recipients "not to work" and substitute "an incentive to work"; that it would remove "the incentive for families to break apart" and substitute "an incentive for families to stay together"; and that it would help "this Nation work its way out of poverty."[14]

Each of these allegations is amenable to theoretical examination and empirical verification. First, however, it is necessary to develop the specifics of the family assistance bill itself. Luckily, the essence of the bill can be presented in three formulas: we will call them an income eligibility formula, an asset eligibility formula, and an income payment formula.

First, under the provisions of the bill, eligibility depends upon an actual or expected annual income level. To be eligible for the program, the family unit must have earned an annual income less than the following:

(2–5) $\qquad Y < (\$500)\,(2) + \$300\,(n-2)$ where

$$Y = Y_e + Y_o - [\$720 + W_s + Y_{IRR} + Y_{cc} + Y_{FS} + Y_T + Y_{HP} + 0.5\,Y_o]$$

and where Y_e = earned income,

Y_o = nonwage (other) income,

n = number of members in the family which is itself defined to have 2 or more members,

W_s = earnings of students in the family,

Y_{IRR} = irregular income,

Y_{cc} = expenditures for child care,

Y_{FS} = the dollar equivalent of food stamps contributions (another transfer or welfare system),

Y_T = dollars of expenditure incidental to training plus any training allowance (@ $30 per month), and

Y_{HP} = dollar value of home produce.

Thus, a family of four earning less than $1,600 per year after exclusion of expenditures and compensations deemed to be "incidental to the purposes of the act" would be eligible on income account for FAP support. The family must also meet asset eligibility requirements such that

(2–6) $\qquad A < 1,500$ where $A = A_T - (H + H_G + 0)$ and where

A_T = the total (market) value of family-owned assets,

H = the (market) value of a home,

H_G = the (market) value of household goods and personal effects, and

0 = the (market) value of other goods which in accordance with and subject to limitations "of the Secretary of Health, Education and Welfare" are so essential to the family's means of self-support as to warrant their exclusion.[15] This category was certainly intended to encompass automotive and other means of transportation.

If eligible, the family would receive an FAP payment per year or a proportion thereof in accordance with the following equation:

(2–7) $\qquad Y_{FAP} = \$500\,(2) + \$300\,(n-2) - 0.5\,(Y_e - \$720) - 0.5\,(Y_o)$
where

Y_{FAP} = the FAP rate per annum,

Y_e = earned income per annum above $720; $(Y_e - 720) = 0$ otherwise,

Y_o = nonwage income.

Some additional provisions, which are ignored here, were made for federal compensation to states that were already providing benefits above the national floor specified in Eq. (2–7).[16]

One can analyze the consequences of the proposed FAP with the indifference map approach developed above. Assume, for simplicity, that we have two general categories of recipients according to their previous eligibility status—male-headed and female-headed families. Assume further that the indifference maps relevant to female-headed families will reflect a higher relative valuation of nonmarket activities than will the indifference maps relevant to the activities of males in male-headed families. Remember also that most male-headed families also include an adult female, while most female-headed families do not include an adult male. The steeper indifference curves for the females amount to assuming that females will value more highly their home time (used heavily for the nurturing of children) than will male heads value their home time. These not-too-unrealistic assumptions are incorporated into Figs. 2–3 and 2–4.

In Fig. 2–3, the FAP alters the area of attainable combinations of income and leisure from TOW to $TOCBA$ where OC represents the grant payment for which the family would be eligible per annum (Y_o) and where the horizontal distance between B and C represents \$720 per annum. The slope of OW and CB, of course, represents the relevant market wage per unit time. The slope of AB is 0.5 of the slope of CB (or OW), representing the effect of a marginal tax rate of 0.5 on earnings above \$720 per year. As one can readily observe, the new program will imply some reduction in the amount of labor time offered per unit time (a backward shift in the labor supply curve). The amount of that reduction for each potential welfare recipient depends solely upon the "flatness" of each recipient's indifference curve. Some recipients will possess indif-

Figure 2–3 *The Effect of the FAP on the Labor Supply of a (Previously Exempted) Male Family Head with a Given Wage*

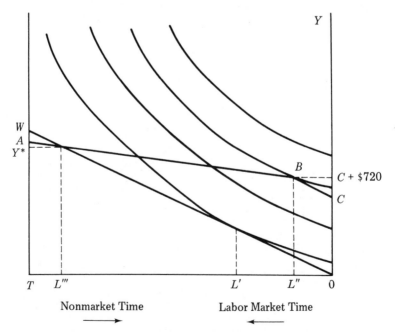

ference curves which "hang them on the corner," so to speak, with their maximum utility being achieved at B with L'' offered to the market. For those with flatter indifference curves, the time offered will vary from L' to L''. The magnitude of the net change (but not its "sign") is then an empirical matter. Note also that the "breakeven" income (Y^* at L''') has no behavioral significance for individuals already receiving assistance.[17]

Finally, if leisure is a superior (normal) good, the reservation wage will increase with an increase in support payments. Thus, one might logically expect some decrease in labor force participation *if market wages are close to reservation wages*. Given the labor force insensitivity to wage changes generally observed among adult males, and given the relatively low support levels envisioned by the Nixon program, no significant reduction in labor force participation would be expected. Thus, we are led to expect that among males:

1. labor force participation will not decline appreciably, if at all, and
2. labor time offered per unit time will decline, although the average magnitude of that reduction is uncertain.

Figure 2–4 *The Effect of the FAP on the Labor Supply of Female Family Heads Previously Eligible for AFDC*

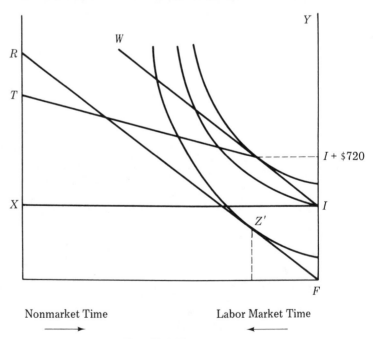

Note, finally, that the changes in labor time may occur in various dimensions, for example, in weeks per year as opposed to hours per week. Empirical studies testing these hypotheses are discussed below.

Turning now to Fig. 2–4 and AFDC mothers, the opportunity set and behaviors are sharply different from those in the male case. Note first that many female-headed families for whom coverage was to be provided under FAP were already receiving AFDC support at or near FAP levels. Moreover, even though marginal tax rates (MTRs) differed among states, those rates under AFDC were often greater than 50%. Historically, MTRs for welfare recipients have been as high or higher than 100 percent. The line *FIX* in Fig. 2–4 shows the 100 percent marginal tax rate situation.

Under AFDC, mothers with relatively low earning power (productivity) and highly valued home activities are given a choice between *Z'* and some position along *FIX* whenever the implicit tax rate on earnings is high or close to 100%. Positions along *WI*, which would be attainable by the welfare mother at 0 marginal tax rates, have been effectively foreclosed by the dollar-for-dollar (or high proportion thereof) reduction of support for each dollar of earnings. Thus, despite verbal attempts to foster work efforts among welfare recipients, the "implicit incentives" of the AFDC program itself induce the welfare mother to locate at *I*. Her next best alternative under the "opportunities" made available to her is to move to *Z'* at a lower utility and income level. It is very likely that both she and society regard that alternative income level as "inadequate." She would move to *Z'*—drop out of the welfare program—only if her "shame coefficient" lowers Y_o enough so that $U(FI(1-s)) < U(Z')$ $= U(I^*)$. Notice that under these conditions the shame (or pride) of the welfare mother results in lower family income and a smaller number of market goods and services for her growing children.[18] I leave to others analysis of the *psychological* consequences of this conflict between shame and the need for sustenance for the children.

Figure 2–4 can also be used to describe the Nixon FAP plan. If the FAP support level were approximately equal to the AFDC level, the lower marginal tax rate for the first $60 a month of earned income would be expected to induce many welfare mothers into the labor force. Some would offer labor time up to the point where the MTR jumps to 50 percent. Indeed, our presumptions concerning the value of work at home would lead us to expect a number of these women to be "hanging on the corner"—engaged in part-time work—under FAP. Some might, of course, move beyond the corner if their indifference curves were relatively flat. Provision of day-care centers, of course, will flatten indifference curves and raise labor force efforts. Finally, in those states where the FAP support level might increase relative to the old AFDC level, we would expect to see a smaller relative increase in labor force participation than in the remaining states.

Consider, now, the least skilled of the AFDC mothers—those with the lowest w's. Even with "0" marginal tax rates, such women may seek to remain at I. Under FAP, however, women without children under six years of age would not be permitted to do so, and they would have the following choices:

1. enter the labor force for the smallest amount of time necessary to satisfy the authorities and maintain eligibility,
2. undergo training, or
3. have additional children.

Figure 2–5 graphs the problem. The first option above is clearly unsatisfying and is a nonequilibrium solution, for a movement from I to S involves a reduction in utility. Under this option, not only would recipients seek to do as little "work" as possible, but at the same time they would feel abused by the work requirement. More likely, they would opt for training to the degree that the training permitted more time at home and more time flexibility than part-time work. The "load" that this option could place on training centers is obvious: (1) the centers would be attempting to raise the market productivity of a number of individuals with the lowest marketable skills, and (2) motivation for learning would probably be weak since the training requirement would

Figure 2–5 *The 'FIX' of a Welfare Mother with Low Market and High Household Productivity under the FAP*

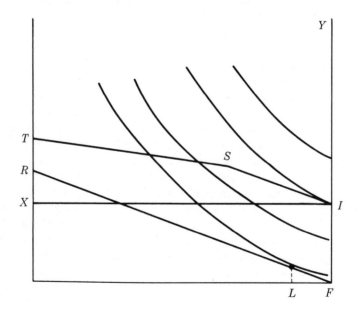

be viewed in the same light as the work requirement. Finally, note that children born to a female-headed family, male absent, are almost always defined as "illegitimate" even if the child or children were sired by a legal but "absent" husband.

This "illegitimacy" or family disformation incentive is implicit in AFDC-type programs. Most have required the absence of a male "bread-winner" (on the records, if not in fact) for the family to be eligible for support (an interesting if not laudable example of sexism). As President Nixon suggested, the inclusion of male-headed families in FAP would have eliminated the incentive for family disformation so readily apparent in the AFDC program.

To summarize our model of FAP, it is clear that the program was not intended to alter tastes for leisure, market goods, or household time or to increase or decrease shame coefficients. Rather, it concentrated on opportunity factors. Thus, for Eq. (2–8),

(2–8) $L = F(Y_o, s, w, t, \ldots, T)$ and $LP = G(Y_o, s, w, t, \ldots T)$
where

L and LP are as used above,

$Y_o =$ the support level,

$s =$ the shame coefficient (or some average shame coefficient among recipients),

$w =$ the appropriate market wage,

$t =$ the marginal tax rate, and

$T =$ the individual's tastes,

we would expect that:

1. $\dfrac{\Delta L}{\Delta w} \gtrless 0$ depending upon income and substitution effects with a presumption that $\Delta L/\Delta w$ will be more positive for females than for males, *ceteris paribus.*

2. $\dfrac{\Delta LF}{\Delta w} > 0$ with a presumption that the effect may be negligible for males and measurably positive for females, *ceteris paribus.*

3. $\dfrac{\Delta L}{\Delta Y_o} < 0$ with a presumption that $\Delta L/\Delta Y_o$ will have a larger (negative) effect for females than for males, *ceteris paribus.*

4. $\dfrac{\Delta LF}{\Delta Y_o} < 0$ with a presumption that $\Delta LF/\Delta Y_o$ will be $\approx$ to zero for males, *ceteris paribus.*

5. $\dfrac{\Delta L}{\Delta t} < 0|\,w$ with a presumption that $\Delta L/\Delta t$ will be greater (in absolute magnitude) for females than for males, *ceteris paribus.*

6. $\dfrac{\Delta LF}{\Delta t} < 0|\,w$ with a presumption that $\Delta LF/\Delta t$ will be measurably negative for females and $\simeq$ to zero for males, *ceteris paribus.*

Empirical Measures of Labor Supply and Participation Responses to Welfare Programs

It is now time to examine some studies of various welfare arrangements as illustrations and tests of the supply responses discussed above. One cannot hope to summarize all of the recent studies here, but three are particularly enlightening—two conducted by Leonard Hausman and one by Mathematica, Inc. The studies asked the question: What are the magnitudes of the effects one might expect on labor force participation and on labor supply from changes (or differences) in support levels and/or marginal tax rates among AFDC mothers and, alternatively, among prime-age males (heads of poverty families)?

Dr. Hausman's early studies were supported by both the President's Commission on Income Maintenance Programs and the Labor Department's Institutional Development Grant to North Carolina State University. The first of these studies attempted to indicate the potential for financial self-support among AFDC recipients in New York City. In that study,[19] Hausman found that relatively few welfare mothers could support themselves and their families at or near their current welfare support level even if they were to devote full-time (40 hour weeks, 2,000 hour years) to employment. Given their educational levels and work experience, the productive potential of the mothers was very low relative to the level society deemed to be a minimum for their respective families (in some cases, *any* family). Hausman concluded that income levels and support levels for children simply could not be maintained if the welfare mothers were forced into the labor force by cessation of benefits. Moreover, at the time, MTRs were relatively high. Thus, Hausman argued that the *"FIX"* situation depicted in Fig. 2–4 above was not unrealistic. In a second study, Hausman employed multiple regression techniques to isolate the effects of particular variables on the work efforts of AFDC mothers in three states—Alabama, Kentucky, and Mississippi. Variations in the level of support and in the implicit tax rate on the earnings of AFDC mothers did appear to have substantial and statistically significant effects upon work effort in the expected directions.[20] Hausman concluded, in part, that:

1. *The labor force behavior of AFDC mothers in Alabama, Kentucky and Mississippi is sensitive to changes in their family incomes, whether this income is received in the form of welfare payments, income-in-kind from food aid programs, or support payments and other types of non-welfare income. Raising their incomes by raising their welfare payments or by instituting a negative income tax program that provides more money than AFDC would induce some labor force withdrawal and/or reduction in work effort. This anticipated response may or may not be desirable, depending on one's values and objectives. Some may look upon raising welfare payments as a way of freeing AFDC mothers from virtual compulsion to work. Others may view raising payments as a means of inducing slothfulness.*

2. *The mothers would, seemingly, participate in the labor force, even at a somewhat higher level of income, if the implicit tax rate was set at an appropriate level. This makes economic (and common) sense for persons at such low income levels with young and/or many children.*

3. *The sensitivity to the economic aspects of the AFDC program was observed in states in which welfare administrators may be relatively demanding of AFDC mothers, insofar as market labor is concerned. One might guess, therefore, that in the other states the observed sensitivity to the same economic variables might be greater than it is in the three states studied here.*

4. *Caution is advisable in attempts to generalize these results and conclusions. AFDC mothers in other states are, firstly, living at much higher levels of income; and, secondly, may have very different attitudes towards work, leisure, and welfare. Their responses to equivalent changes in income and/or implicit tax rates may be different from those observed in these states.*[21]

In general, Hausman found the expected effects on the labor force participation rate and on what he called the labor force intensity rate (labor force participation weighted by hours worked). If one were to apply Hausman's findings to a hypothetical AFDC-FAP changeover with support levels constant and MTRs falling by 50 percent, one might expect a 14 percent increase in the labor force participation of welfare recipients to about 26 percent, as compared with 23 percent of the relevant AFDC population. The change in the labor force intensity rate would be even larger—a 22 percent increase.[22.]

The Mathematica study, sponsored by the Office of Economic Opportunity and called the New Jersey Graduated Work Incentive Experiment, involved a three-year panel study of male-headed families in New Jersey/Pennsylvania. In exchange for providing detailed budgetary and labor force information, participating families received cash payments which varied in amounts according to the earning levels of family members. Control groups with similar sociodemographic characteristics were also surveyed. Participating families were provided with various support levels and subjected to various marginal tax levels. This procedure was intended to provide estimates via multiple regression analysis of the net effect of the support program on the work effort of all members in male-headed families.

The preliminary results of the New Jersey study were widely disseminated during early congressional consideration of the Nixon welfare program.[23] They were based on the Trenton, New Jersey sample and indicated no appreciable effect on the work efforts of the male heads in the affected families. Given the strong attachment of males to the labor force, this result is what one might expect with respect to labor force participation; particularly in an experiment of limited duration. Moreover, if the labor supply curve is relatively inelastic within the relevant earning range, little effect might be seen in that dimension. Some of the preliminary data seemed to show a tendency for male recipients to spend more time searching for new positions after they were unemployed than was the case in the absence of support (a slight backward bend in work time *per year?*).

These preliminary conclusions were buttressed and elaborated in the *Final Report of the New Jersey Graduated Work Incentive Experiment*, which incorporated results from the other sample sites: Paterson-Passaic, Jersey City, and Scranton, Pennsylvania.[24] Figure 2–6 shows the general structure of the experiment with various cash payments and various marginal tax rates beginning at "0" earnings. Hours, earnings, and participation effects were then observed for the various support-tax packages. Note from Fig. 2–6 that both income and tax effects serve to reduce work effort.

In general, labor force participation among white and black male heads did not change under the program, but there was a slight (and statistically significant) reduction in labor force participation among Spanish-speaking male heads. Work hours declined slightly for white and Spanish-speaking male heads, but not for blacks. Among whites and Spanish-speaking male heads, however, the effects were larger for the smaller net support levels than for the more generous levels—contrary to expectations. Thus, substantial questions remain.

For married women, labor force participation rates fell among whites and, to a smaller degree, among blacks. They rose slightly, however, for Spanish-speaking women. Hours of work rose significantly for black married women, but fell overall because of the negative impact among white married women. All in all, these changes were not very large absolutely, but given the low initial labor force participation for these low income women, *relative* changes in labor force participation and in net labor supply were sizable.

Summarizing the results of the study, Albert Rees wrote:

In general, the estimated effects of the experimental treatment on labor supply are in accord with our expectations. The major surprise is the absence of any negative effect on the labor supply of black households. For white and Spanish-speaking families, and for the group as a whole, the effects are negative, usually

Figure 2–6 *A Schematic Representation of the New Jersey Guaranteed Work Incentive Experiment*

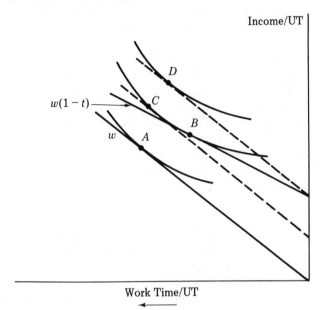

Horizontal distance *AB* = observed work effect

Horizontal distance *AC* = *CD* = the income effect of the program (*C* is observable only where *t* = 0)

Horizontal distance *CB* = the substitution or tax effect of the program

significant, but not very large. They consist of a reduction in hours of white male heads, an increase in the unemployment rate of Spanish-speaking male heads and a large relative reduction in the labor force participation of white wives.[25]

Rees admitted that the patterns of response were "not as clear" as the experimenters had expected. Particularly puzzling was the unexpectedly positive effects in black households.[26] Among the possible explanatory factors to the various puzzles were the following:

1. the problems of (selective?) attrition losses (migration back to Puerto Rico, etc.),
2. the perceptions of the recipients (if the support was regarded solely as a temporary windfall and if the effect of the marginal tax rate was clear), and
3. the introduction of a generous AFDC(UP) plan in New Jersey during the term of the experiment.

Nevertheless, the results of the Hausman and the New Jersey studies, if generalizable, would support the notion that an FAP or similar program would produce small and expected alterations in work efforts. Concerns about the degree of generalizability, perception, and interpretation, however, prompted the Office of Economic Opportunity to support other experiments in the following rural and urban areas: Duplin County, North Carolina; Calhoun and Pocahontas Counties, Iowa; Seattle, Washington–Denver, Colorado; Gary, Indiana.[27] Thus, despite remaining questions, studies of the type discussed here are helping to clarify (or bracket) the magnitudes of the responses that might accompany the establishment of an FAP or other welfare program.[28] Certainly, the expected economic responses, together with the political parameters faced by legislators and other public servants are important determinants of their positions on welfare reform.[29]

Indifference Curves, the "Work Ethic," and the Other Social Sciences

The indifference curve or utility map approach developed in Chapter 1 and applied in both Chapters 1 and 2 provides economists with a theoretical "picture" of individual tastes and preferences without requiring them to look into the origins of the tastes. Such inquiries are left largely, but not exclusively, by economists to the practitioners of sister social sciences, chiefly to the psychologists and sociologists. Within their own paradigms, psychologists and sociologists are attempting to increase our collective understanding of "tastes," and the individual and group patterns from which such tastes are derived or by which tastes are generated. Psychologists, in addition, concentrate on the degree of rationality exhibited by humans (and animals) under various stresses. In the parlance of indifference or utility analysis, psychologists, among their other activities, examine both the shifts in taste maps (in their many dimensions) and the transitivity conditions assumed by economists. Sociologists and anthropologists concentrate on the degree to which differential behavior among groups and cultures produces differential taste maps and on the social and institutional constraints upon individual choice within a particular social milieu. Political scientists investigate group decision making and relationships involving the coercive power resident in the governmental structure—however that structure is defined or established—together with the differential origins of and rationalizations behind the use of coercive power. Thus, indifference or utility analysis creates a useful division of labor, separating areas of potential research for economists from those usually investigated by other social scientists.

As noted in the introduction, institutionalists and antimarginalists have argued that institutional, political, and social (customary) forces play important—perhaps dominant—roles in determining labor market behavior. The "compleat" labor economist, they suggested, ignores or abstracts from these influences at his own risk. Although not always fully satisfying, it is convenient for labor economists to proceed with their analysis under the assumptions of given tastes and institutional conditions, concentrating their attention on the degree to which changes in "opportunity factors" (wages, income levels, unemployment, prices, etc.) influence labor market behavior.

It is nevertheless possible to discuss, albeit somewhat hesitantly, the influence of welfare on "the work ethic," i.e., tastes. In utility map parlance, the work ethic is closely connected with the slope of the utility curves in the income-leisure space. If the "work ethic" means anything, it must represent a willingness to trade leisure and household time for claims on market goods and services. Moreover, indifference surfaces and tradeoffs presumably are "produced" by the various experiences affecting a person and, therefore, his value system. Thus, it is conceivable that given their experiences, second and third generation welfare families do have different and more sharply sloped indifference curves in the leisure-income space than the mean of other families. If so, response rates among that group may differ from those of other "more middle-class" individuals.[30]

The evidence from the Hausman and the New Jersey studies suggests that lower income groups—males in particular—respond as if they were strongly attached to market work. There were, however, sizable differences in work responses among the three ethnic groups studied in the New Jersey experiment, perhaps reflecting group taste differences.

If, as suggested above, the work ethic is "produced" by experience, then an FAP or other welfare program which alters group experiences could eventually change "tastes" as well as the behaviors that depend, in the short run, on various opportunity factors—support levels, marginal tax rates, and so on. By being "middle-class" in income or by having a secure income "to fall back on," recipients or their family members may become "middle-class" in tastes. Despite the author's doubts about the usefulness of this scenario, it represents an approach that bears objective investigation. If a secure income alters tastes in the expected direction, maintenance of a welfare population at some "middle-class" income level will eventually reduce the total real revenue used for welfare support, *ceteris paribus,* provided of course that marginal tax rates are not so high as to force all or most recipients to a "corner solution." In contrast, it is conceivable that "experience" with welfare will diminish the work ethic.

Finally, it is important to recognize that neither a "work ethic" nor a "leisure ethic" is preferable from an objective point of view. In other words, the economist qua economist cannot assert that the work ethic is "good" or "bad" without interjecting his own tastes or someone else's tastes into the analysis. Nor can he as a professional economist ascribe favorable or unfavorable connotations to the various taste patterns, such as those implicit in the words "lazy" and "ambitious." He can, however, examine the degree to which changes in institutions, opportunity factors, and, to some degree, tastes *will* influence observed behavior. Social scientists can also examine the degree to which various experiences alter tastes themselves—change the slopes of indifference curves in some dimension or another—and at what rate per unit time. Although these questions are probably more suited to the paradigms of other social scientists, the student of labor economics should be aware of these broader possibilities.

Notes to Chapter 2

1. Barry M. Goldwater, *The Conscience of a Conservative* (Shepherdville, Ken.: Victor Publishing Co., 1960), p. 74.

2. From a speech by President Lyndon B. Johnson, August 31, 1965, cited in *The Reader's Digest Treasury of Modern Quotations* (New York: Reader's Digest Press, 1975), p. 453.

3. Andrew Hacker, "Again the Issue of 'The Welfare State,'" *The New York Times Magazine*, March 22, 1964, p. 9.

4. Slope equals $\Delta L_i / \Delta w_i$, given $Y_o, \ldots, T$, or $\partial L_i / \partial w_i$. Elasticity equals $(\Delta L_i / \Delta w_i) \cdot (\overline{w_i} / \overline{L_i})$ or $(\partial L_i / \partial w_i) \cdot (\overline{w_i} / \overline{L_i})$ and is positive for the upward sloping portion of the curve and negative for the "backward bending" portion.

5. This is the common problem of nonhomogeneous labor—adding apples to oranges. Without a common denominator, we may have a delicious fruit salad, but little else.

6. Where the influence of racial, religious, or caste prejudices on work patterns is felt, the analysis becomes complex. At this stage, such complications are ignored. Discrimination is discussed in Chapter 9.

7. To be distinguished from Old Age and Survivor's Insurance (Social Security) which was originally designed as social insurance, not supplementary income. The program is still organizationally if not conceptually different from the program of Supplementary Security Income.

8. To be distinguished from Disability Insurance.

9. See Gordon L. Weil, *The Welfare Debate of 1978* (White Plains, N.Y.: Institute for Socioeconomic Studies, 1978), for a brief history of U.S. welfare and other transfer programs, as well as for some interesting information on the post-Nixon programs. Also see William J. Lawrence and Stephen Leeds, *An Inventory of Federal Income Transfer Programs* (White Plains, N.Y.: Institute for Socioeconomic Studies, 1978), for an annotated compendium of federal transfer (welfare) programs in 1978.

10. Address of President Richard M. Nixon on nationwide radio and television, August 9, 1969, 10:00 P.M. EST.

11. President's Address, August 9, 1969.

12. "Family Assistance Act of 1969," S.2986, 91st Congress, 1st Session.

13. AFDC is generally limited to female-headed families; AFDC(UP) includes male-headed families where the male head is unemployed.

14. "Family Assistance Act," p. 12.

15. "Family Assistance Act," p. 12.

16. "Family Assistance Act," pp. 23–29.

17. Readers should take the time to explain *in words* why this should be the case. They should also trace out the effect of lower marginal tax rates on the breakeven point and therefore on the number of persons who might seek support. The tradeoff between greater work incentives via lower MTRs for those on welfare and the number of potential recipients of support is of crucial importance to the success of any welfare reform effort. See in particular Frank Levy, "The Labor Supply of Female Household Heads, or AFDC Work Incentives Don't Work Too Well," *Journal of Human Resources* 14, no. 1 (Winter 1979): 76–97.

18. It is not coincidental that the attainable income line under high marginal tax rates is designated "FIX" in Fig. 2–4. With respect to shame coefficients, it is commonplace for people to argue that one "ought to be ashamed to take welfare." That statement expresses only one person's tastes about the utility of a dollar from one or another source. Moreover, the statement may emanate (1) from individuals whose w or Y_o from private sources is much higher than that available to welfare recipients, or (2) from individuals who receive income transfers via parity payments, preferential interest rates, low-cost or state-supported tuition, etc. While economists can and do take account of such attitudes and evaluate their consequences (particularly when these attitudes are institutionalized in the rules of social programs), economists—as scientists—cannot and should not be expected to judge the "rightness" or "wrongness" of the attitudes of the recipients or the "givers" in any particular case. Economic analysis does, however, help one to differentiate clearly between taste-related suggestions or reactions and those that are not based on one's personal tastes.

19. Leonard Hausman, "Potential for Financial Self-Support Among AFDC and AFDC-UP Recipients," *Southern Economic Journal* 36, no. 1 (July 1969): 60–66.

20. Note that the labor force participation rate of welfare mothers—the proportion of total recipients in the labor force times 100—varies from state to state.

21. Leonard J. Hausman, "The Impact of Welfare in the Work Effect of AFDC Mothers," in President's Commission on Income Maintenance Programs, *Technical Studies* (Washington, D.C.: U.S. Government Printing Office, 1970), pp. 83–100.

22. The elasticity of labor force participation with respect to support levels, $\partial LP/\partial Y_o \cdot \overline{Y}/\overline{LP}$, was found to be −0.37, while that for labor force intensity was −0.39. The elasticity of labor force participation with respect to marginal tax rates, $\partial LP/\partial t \cdot \bar{t}/\overline{LP}$, was −0.27. The tax elasticity of labor intensity, which includes an hours-of-work effect, was −0.43.

23. Harold W. Watts, "The Graduated Work Incentive Experiments: Current Progress," *Current Status of Income Maintenance Experiments*, reprint 73 (Madison, Wis.: Institute for Research on Poverty, 1971), pp. 15–21.

24. Institute for Research on Poverty and Mathematica, *Final Report on*

the New Jersey Graduated Work Incentive Experiment, ed. Harold W. Watts and Albert Rees (Madison, Wis.: Institute for Research on Poverty, 1977), vol. I–IV.

25. Institute for Research, *Final Report,* p. A-6.

26. A more sophisticated analysis employing intra-family substitution of market time and home time may explain this "puzzle." See Mark Killingsworth, "Must a Negative Tax Rate Reduce Labor Supply? A Study of the Family's Allocation of Time," *Journal of Human Resources* 11, no. 3 (Summer 1976): 354–65.

27. See the article by Harold Watts in Institute for Research, *Final Report,* as well as articles by Mortecai Kurz and Robert Spiegelman and by Terence F. Kelly and Leslie Singer in the same volume.

28. The interested reader should see *Journal of Human Resources* 60, no. 2 (Spring 1974), a symposium issue almost entirely devoted to the results of the New Jersey Graduated Income Experiment; M. Barth, G. Carcagno, J. L. Palmer, and Irwin Garfinkel, eds., *Toward an Effective Income Support System: Problems, Prospects and Choices* (Madison, Wis.: Institute for Research on Poverty, 1974); Joseph A. Pechman and P. Michael Timpane, eds., *Work Incentives and Income Guarantees: The New Jersey Negative Income Tax Experiment* (Washington, D.C.: The Brookings Institution, 1975); Peter H. Rossi and Katherine C. Lyall, *Reforming Public Welfare: A Critique of the Negative Income Tax Experiment* (New York: Academic Press, 1977); John L. Palmer and Joseph A. Pechman, eds., *Welfare in Rural Areas: The North Carolina–Iowa Income Maintenance Experiment* (Washington, D.C.: The Brookings Institution, 1978); Michael C. Keeley et al., "Labor Supply Effects and Costs of Alternative Negative Income Tax Programs," *Journal of Human Resources* 13, no. 1 (Winter 1978): 3–36; Irene Lurie, ed., *Integrating Income Maintenance Programs* (New York: Academic Press, 1975); and *Journal of Human Resources* 14, no. 4 (Fall 1979) for several articles on various aspects of the Gary income maintenance experiment.

29. For a contrast in policy positions, see Daniel P. Moynihan, *The Politics of a Guaranteed Income* (New York: Random House, 1973) and Martin Anderson, *Welfare* (Stanford, Cal.: Hoover Institute Press, 1978). Anderson summarizes the work incentive results of the various income maintenance experiments and several other studies.

30. The author doubts that there is such a chasm in attitudes between lower and higher income individuals, but the hypothesis exists and is ignored at one's intellectual peril.

3 | The Economics of Women's Liberation

A woman's place is in the home.　　　　American folk saying

Kinder, Küche, Kirche.　　　　German folk saying

The "proper" role of a woman, her "place in the home," her relative "valuation," "equal pay for equal work," "liberation," and sexual freedom have been the subjects of countless inquiries and treatises in recent years. The number of words written and spoken on these related subjects must rival the number delivered on any other "popular" topic, at least since 1900. This verbal barrage has accompanied (but not necessarily *caused*) a very substantial increase in female labor force activities—both in the Western world and, belatedly, to a lesser degree in the Eastern world. The reduction of time spent in the household and the secularly rising labor force participation (LFP) of married women, in particular, have been heralded, on the one hand, as harbingers of complete liberation ("by altering women's roles from that of semichattel to more complete independence or fulfillment, and by freeing women from household drudgery") and, on the other hand, as threats to society ("destroying the sanctity of society's crucial building block—the family").

Quite obviously, this text cannot consider all or even most of the multifaceted aspects of this tremendous social change and the arguments and philosophies surrounding it. Important insights may, however, be obtained by concentrating on one important change—the increasing labor force participation of women in contemporary America. Specifically, this chapter concentrates on recent experience in the United States and asks: What has caused the rising attachment of females—particularly married females—to the labor force? In the course of examining this question, we will have the opportunity to explore briefly several related questions and one important paradox. The paradox can be stated briefly by considering the expected effect of rising real income levels on leisure and household activities (usually regarded as superior goods). As family incomes rise, we would expect all family members to consume more nonmarket activities. Real levels of family (and husband's) income have been rising secularly in the United States, yet millions of married women have literally "poured" into the labor force in recent years. The question is, "Why?"

The Historical Record

The historical record, as indicated by census data, shows a secular increase in U.S. female labor force participation from 1890 through 1970—from 18.2 to 41.4 percent. By the late 1970s, participation was about 50 percent, although growth was not steady. As shown in Table 3–1, between 1890 and 1940, female labor force participation grew less than 1 percent per annum or about 1–2 percentage points per decade. The sharp acceleration after 1940 resulted largely from a change in the age composition of the female labor force, involving a very sizable increase in the proportion of 35-year-old and older women. Figure 3–1 shows that massive change and, in addition, reflects three other changes:

1. a secular growth in labor force attachment with each generation (cohort),
2. a sharp decline in participation for each generation in the childbearing years, and
3. a widespread, across-the-board increase in participation from 1960 to 1970.

In considering these three changes, it is useful to remember that the data for all females are heavily influenced by the behavior of married women. Indeed, the overall statistics are dominated by the "married

Table 3–1 *Female Labor Force Participation, 1890–1970 (Census Data)*

1970 (April)[a]	41.4
1960 (April)[a]	35.7
1950 (April)	29.9
1940 (April)	25.8
1930 (April)	23.6
1920 (January)	22.7
1900 (June)	20.0
1890 (June)	18.2

[a] Includes Alaska and Hawaii.
1950–70 includes 16 years of age and older.
1890–1940 includes 14 years of age and older.

Figure 3–1 *Changing Age Composition of Female Labor Force Participation (FLFP), 1890–1970*

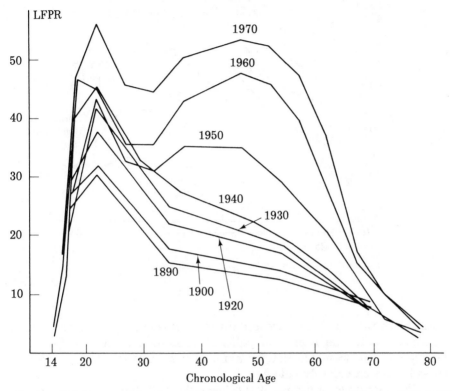

Source: U.S. Bureau of the Census, *Census Reports, U.S. Summary Volumes*, 1890–1970

women, husband present" category which represented 60.1 percent of all women and 72.4 percent of women 20 to 64 years old in 1970.

The secular growth in labor force attachment with each generation of women can best be seen by plotting participation by cohorts.[1] As shown in Fig. 3–2, each generation has experienced a higher age-specific participation rate. That evidence suggests that any factors inducing the overall growth are themselves "time-related," i.e., changing secularly. Despite the secular factors raising LFP, each generation shows a sharp decline in participation during the childbearing years. That hiatus from market activities, although not surprising, represents an important economic problem—an interruption in work life experience which has drawn attention to the "dual careers" (more accurately, multiple careers) of many modern women. Finally, the "across-the-board" participation increase in the 1960–70 period may represent the influence of several factors: a continuing surge of women 35 years and older entering the labor market;

Figure 3–2 *Participation Rates by Cohort up to 1970*

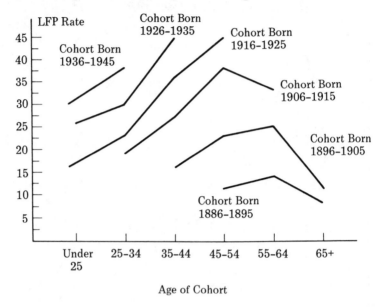

Age of Cohort

lower birth rates and/or increased divorce rates among younger women; and changes in the legal and political climate that are conducive to female participation. The determinants of these several changes are discussed more completely below.

Further understanding of the labor force choices made by women can be obtained by comparing the male to female participation rates in Table 3–2 and contrasting the participation patterns for single, divorced, and widowed women with those of the category "married women, husband present." Figure 3–3 shows the characteristic M shape in labor force participation for (all) women and for "married women, husband present." By contrast, the age-participation patterns for divorced women, single women, and widowed women more closely approximate the mesa-

Table 3–2 **Labor Force Participation Rates, 1970**
(Census Data)

All men, 16 years and above	76.6
All women, 16 years and above	41.4
Married women, husband present	39.2
Married women, husband absent	50.2
Single women	50.7
Divorced women	69.5
Widowed women	26.5

Figure 3–3 *Labor Force Participation Rates by Age for Men and Women by Marital Status Categories, 1970*

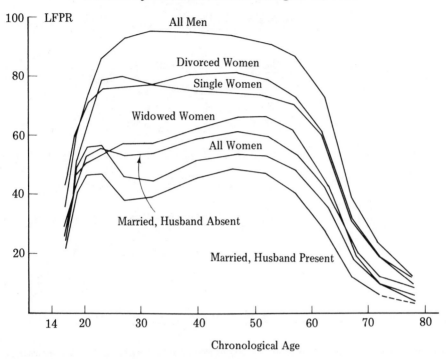

Source: U.S. Bureau of the Census, *Census of Population: 1970 Detailed Characteristics, Final Report*, PC(1)-D(1), *U.S. Summary* (Washington, D.C.: Government Printing Office, 1973), Table 216, p. 688.

or mound-shaped participation curve characteristic of (all) men. Note also the apparent influence of childbearing in the patterns for both "married women, husband present" and "married women, husband absent."

One final pictorial comparison is useful before we turn to more detailed analysis. Figure 3–4 shows the labor force participation pattern for three marital status groups: single men and single women, men and women with spouses absent, and men and women with spouses present. The similarity in participation rates for single men and single women is quite striking, and the "singles" pattern is not too different from that observed for "married men, wife absent." Note that the two most disparate patterns—in both level and shape—are the patterns for those who are coupled (or "commune-ized" in the terminology of Chapter 1). The influence of childrearing may be observed in three of the series: (1) married women, husband present; (2) married women, husband absent; *and* (3) married men, wife absent.

Figure 3-4 *Labor Force Participation—Presence or Absence of Spouse by Age and Sex, 1970*

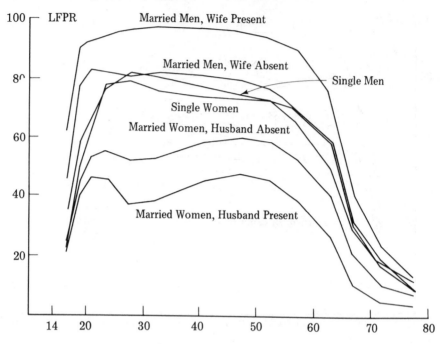

Source: U.S. Bureau of the Census, *Census of Population: 1970 Detailed Characteristics, Final Report*, PC(1)–D(1), *U.S. Summary* (Washington, D.C.: Government Printing Office, 1973), Table 216, p. 688.

We now turn from mere description and casual empiricism to a more precise analysis of women's participation.

The Household Sector, the Market Sector, and Comparative Advantage

Any economic analysis of female (or male) labor force participation must address itself to the question of comparative advantage in the household sector versus the market sector. In the absence of very substantial amounts of nonwage income (Y_o), husband-and-wife families must provide some time to the labor market to obtain claims on market goods. The family decision involves not only the division of total time between the market and the household, but also the division of time among household members. The family therefore faces the same economic question faced by two nations, and it will not surprise students of economics that the same general principle applies—that of comparative advantage. In the international case, each nation can maximize its total command over goods and services by specializing in producing those goods in which it has a comparative advantage and "trading" with the other nation. The same principle in modified form applies to family production. The modifications involve the recognition (1) that "trade" within the family is usually a communal as distinct from a market activity, and (2) that families worthy of the name can be thought of as having a common utility function. (The process of creating a common utility

Figure 3–5 *Comparative Advantage and the Allocation of Household Time. (More generally, the axes may be labelled "Household time intensive goods and services" and "Market time intensive goods and services." See note 23, Chapter 1)*

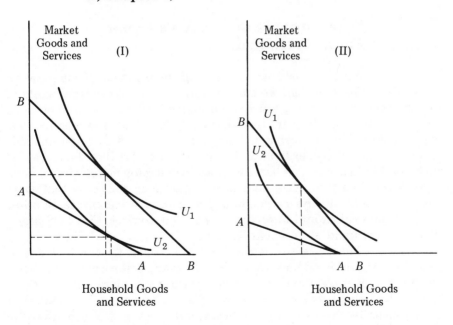

AA represents the production potential of member A

BB represents the production potential of member B

U_1, U_2, etc. represents the common utility surface

function is a continuous one—a "fact" to which any good marriage counselor will attest.)

With these two modifications, the family's economic problem becomes one of maximizing total command over both household and market goods, given the different productivities of family members (at least adults) in the market and in the household. Figure 3-5 shows the allocation and specialization necessary to maximize each party's contribution to family utility. As shown there, it pays the family as a unit to have each member specialize (allocate time and necessary goods inputs) in the area of his (or her) comparative advantage. This may involve—as in Fig. 3-5, II—a situation in which one member maximizes his (or her) contribution by not entering (or by dropping out of) the labor force. Note also that the greater the relative difference in the slope of the market-household productivity lines, the greater will be the likelihood that one partner (or person) will allocate his (or her) time largely to the household, while the other "specializes" in producing dollar income.[2] Given communal processes within the family, note that the distribution of market and household goods need not reflect productivity or "earnings" in either market.

Determinants of Women's Labor Force Activities

With the historical record and the principle of comparative advantage as background, we can turn directly to the determinants of the observed changes in participation and total hours of market work for women and ask: Why are the labor force activities of women increasing so rapidly? The proverbial person-on-the-street (POS) might find this question either foolish or too simple, and might assert that the increased participation has occurred because "most women (or more women) have to work these days to make ends meet." Except in the sense that some labor time must always be combined with natural resources or other forms of physical capital to produce goods and services, that POS assertion does not stand up to scientific scrutiny.

First, if "need" were the fundamental reason for the increase in participation, we would have to conclude from the historical record either (1) that the average American family has become more "needy" since 1890 and particularly since the late 1940s; (2) that the real earnings of males—usually the primary "breadwinners"—have declined over the past 30-70 years; and/or (3) that vast numbers of marriages have failed and the parties have not formed new husband-and-wife families. Actually, real family income and real hourly earnings for men have risen substantially over the period. Real earnings have declined from time to time, but the trend is strongly upward. Separation and divorce rates have risen, but they have not reached the epidemic proportions necessary to support the POS scenario. Pressing further, even if one concedes that women "have to work" in some sense, what explains the increase of work in the market versus work in the household?

Neoclassical economic theory suggests that the choice between more or less household work and market work depends (1) upon the market wage relative to the implicit productivity or "wage" in the household; (2) upon nonwage income; (3) upon the prices of complements and substitutes for market goods; and (4) upon tastes. Particularly important to the participation question is the ratio of the market wage to the implicit household wage. Following this general line of reasoning, Professors Cain, Bowen, Finegan, Mincer, Kosters, and others have isolated and measured the effects of several important influences.[3] Among these are:

1. husband's wage or potential income,
2. nonwage income,
3. small children in the household,
4. educational and earnings levels of women, and
5. the general rate (or level) of unemployment.

The studies indicated first, that the higher the husband's earnings, the lower is the wife's participation (at given levels for the other determinants, *ceteris paribus*). A similar conclusion was reached with respect to nonwage income. The easiest way to understand the similarity of the two results is to consider husband's earnings to be the equivalent of nonwage income (Y_o) and recognize the positive effect of Y_o on reservation wages: $\Delta W_o / \Delta Y_o > 0$. This reasoning leads us to expect the labor force participation of married women to fall as the real earnings of their husbands rise.[4] Indeed, this is what one finds as one looks across income groups (see Fig. 3–6, a). Not only is the opportunity greater for "well-heeled" women to emphasize the more pleasurable aspects of household activities and leisure, but the progressive income tax system imposes a higher marginal tax rate on women whose husbands "earn good money" than on women whose husbands do not. Thus, one would expect wives' labor force participation to fall as husbands' real earnings rise over the years.

Other powerful factors, however, have worked to more than offset the negative effects of rising male earnings. Among these are education and female earnings levels. Each cohort of women for the past 50 or so years has been better educated and has experienced higher real earnings potential than the previous cohort. Since most forms of schooling raise market productivity and earning potential more than household productivity, each cohort of females has responded by choosing a higher participation rate than the previous cohort. Moreover, Glen Cain found

Figure 3–6 *Selected Aspects of the Labor Force Participation of Married Women*

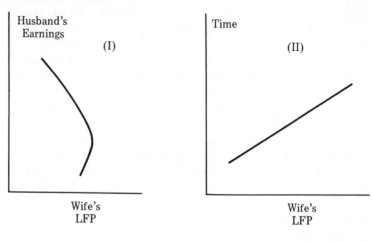

the "partial effect" of wives' earnings on participation, $\Delta LF_w/\Delta W_w$, to be about 1.5 times as strong as the negative effect of husbands' earnings on wives' participation.[5] Even the elasticity of wives' wage effect was found to be larger, absolutely, than the elasticity of husbands' wage effect on wives' participation.[6] Thus, as male and female earnings have risen at about the same rate in recent years, the net participation of married women—and therefore most women—has risen "on wage account."

Cain also examined the effect of increased schooling. As suggested above, increased schooling has altered market productivity relative to household productivity and it may alter the tastes of young women. Thus, in contrast to others, "schooled" women may have a stronger desire for what they might call "a meaningful career" or "an end to household drudgery." Cain found that schooling has a positive effect on participation. His finding may reflect taste effects, but also differences in earning potential not captured by the admittedly crude measure of earnings used in his study—the mean income of females employed full-time in the various SMSAs. In Cain's study, as in many others, it is simply difficult to isolate and identify a separate "taste effect."

It is much easier to show the effects on participation of the presence of children. Remember the hiatus indicated in Fig. 3–1. Cain's economic study found that a one percentage point increase in the proportion of husband-and-wife families having children under six years of age lowered the labor force participation of married women by 0.5 percentage points, a very strong effect. The magnitude of that effect and the sharp dip in female participation for all cohorts during the childbearing and childrearing years are eloquent testimony to the upward jump in the implicit value of household time when young children are present. It follows that lower birth rates among husband-and-wife families should lead to higher female participation rates. "On income account," increased divorce and separation rates should also raise female labor force participation. Finally, the available evidence from Cain and many other investigators indicates that married women, in particular, drop out of the labor force as general unemployment levels rise (and the potential payoff to market participation falls).

A Diagrammatic Representation of Women's Participation

One can easily diagram the empirical influences discussed above. For any given woman, W_o is fixed by her Y_o, the earnings of her husband (H_w), household factors, and tastes. Thus, her labor force choice can be plotted as shown in Fig. 3–7. At or above W_o, given Y_o, W_H, etc., the market wage exceeds the implicit household wage and the woman (and/or man) chooses to offer at least some time to the labor market.[7]

One can also picture (or plot) the distribution of entry or reservation wages for any group of women (or men), given their Y_o's, W_H's, etc. As market W_W's rise, for given levels of household productivity we would expect the ratio of market to household wages to exceed 1.0 for a larger and larger portion of the population. The solid lines in Fig. 3–8 show a hypothetical distribution of reservation wages for females and the cumu-

Figure 3–7 *The Reservation Wage and Labor Force Participation*

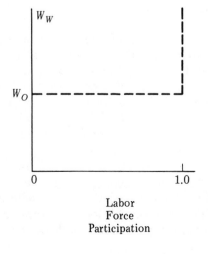

Where W_W is her market wage and W_O is the point where the ratio of the W_W to the implicit household wage equals 1.0

lative distribution of those wages. At any W_W (say, W_W^*), the labor force participation can be read either from the area under the distribution below W_W^* or more easily from the cumulative distribution, P^*. Changes in Y_0, W_H, U, etc., will shift the cumulative (and the frequency) distribution up or down (see the dashed lines) thereby raising or lowering the labor force participation rate.

Note that if the cumulative distributions for males and females have the same general shape and if the ratio of the market wage to the household wage is lower for women than for men, the men will be more likely to be in the inelastic upper tail of the LFP (cumulative distribution) curve than will the women. Under these conditions, one would expect much less constancy or inflexibility of labor force participation rates to wage changes among prime-age females. This is indeed what has been found by large numbers of scholars.

Other Possible Influences on Female Labor Force Participation

A number of other influences may alter or may have altered participation, although the available evidence is not as convincing as for the influences considered above. These include:

1. changes in the mix of U.S. industry and employment,
2. changes in attitudes toward "women working,"
3. mechanization of the household,
4. increasing numbers of young adults in institutions of higher education, and
5. changes in laws "protecting" women (i.e., laws excluding women from certain occupations, limiting hours, etc.).

It is quite likely that the movement of the U.S. economy away from agriculture and manufacturing and toward service industries (including government) has increased employment opportunities for women. The service sector offers more part-time work and more flexible hours, providing a better match with household employment. Changes in attitudes among male and female employers toward the employment of women (for example, in "nontraditional" jobs) may have reduced discriminatory hiring practices and, therefore, encouraged more participation. This influence on participation is difficult to find in the available evidence.[8] The increased mechanization of the American home may have led to a substitution of capital for labor time in "home production." In some instances, however, household mechanization (for example, the introduction of automatic washers and dryers, household freezers, and ice

Figure 3–8 *Shifts in Labor Force Participation*

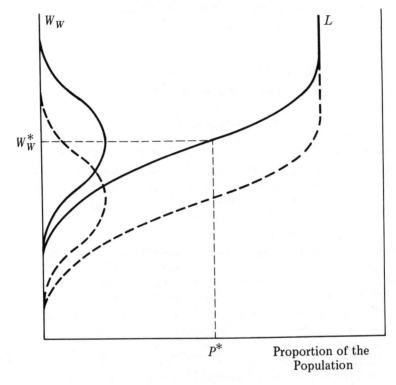

$$P^*$$

Proportion of the
Population

cream-making machines) may have raised the production of household time—usually the time of women—and, consequently, the level of the implicit household wage. The long-term growth of enrollment at institutions of higher learning and slower rates of labor force entry among young adults may have produced a substitution of older for younger persons in the labor force. Certainly, the largest surge in the labor force participation of married women 35 years of age and older was seen in the late 1940s and early 1950s, coinciding with the time during which young people in the smaller birth cohorts of the 1930s were coming of labor force age (16 years and older). The subsequent rapid growth of college enrollment and the high cash outlays required at that level of schooling may have induced a further increase in participation among mothers of college-bound youngsters. Lack of suitable family "panel" data and the difficulty of identifying the chain of causation have prevented economists from fully measuring the impact, if any, of these enrollment changes on female participation. Finally, the gradual removal of "protective" laws and regulations limiting women to particular occupations, activities, and hours may have widened employment choices and increased participation. It is not clear from existing evidence, however, whether these "protective" or choice-limiting laws and regulations ever had any substantial negative effects on participation.

Some Problems Associated with Increased Female Participation

As noted above, allocation of effort to the household and the market economy involves the same principle of comparative advantage as does the theory of international trade.[9] Participation in household activity, however, does not imply that women (or men) will devote themselves exclusively to the household. Indeed, exclusive household specialization has been declining. The higher labor force participation of women, however, has created some new and vexing social problems.

The first of these problems is related to the hiatus in participation during the childbearing and early childrearing years. As suggested above, historically, many women never entered the labor force. Those who did usually "dropped out" after marriage and/or childbirth and did not reenter. The present pattern involves labor force entry, a "drop-out" during the early childrearing years, and then reentry. Unfortunately, market-oriented skills and abilities developed in school and on the job depreciate or become obsolete during those childrearing years unless the market occupation and the household activities employ similar sets of skills. Professors Mincer and Polachek[10] among others have shown that this interrupted participation pattern creates serious schooling or training problems for young women. The anticipation of such a pattern, it is argued, has encouraged women (or girls) to prepare themselves for occupations that either are complementary to household work (e.g., teaching, nursing) or are expected to have low rates of depreciation and obsolescence (typing, keypunching, other clerical skills). It is clear that women whose occupations experience high depreciation rates and/or require constant updating (computer programming and most other professions) suffer substantial capital losses during the early childrearing period. Reentry often occurs at a reduced pay rate or in a less lucrative occupation. The affected women and the entire economy therefore suffer damages which could be avoided if the training bias and the capital losses could be eliminated or reduced. Day-care centers help, but the fundamental problem remains. The next chapter will treat the subject of the generation of human skills in greater detail.

A second and related problem is that of maintaining the quality of household production, especially the quality of the household's contribution to childrearing. If both adult family members are employed full-time, the role of parental guidance and training will change and the quality of childrearing may diminish even beyond the wishes of the parents. Unfortunately, current manpower policies and the presence of employment costs which depend upon *numbers hired* rather than *hours worked* induce employers to prefer full-time workers, male or female. Thus, some married women seeking to offer limited amounts of time to the market may be presented with a more dichotomous choice than they would have wished.[11] Altering manpower policies, effecting collective bargaining agreements, and otherwise creating incentives for employers to offer more part-time and more flexible work hours would help both to maintain and improve the quality of childrearing (perhaps by both parents) *and* to avoid the training bias and capital losses mentioned above. Although high labor force participation by both sexes seems to be the wave of the future, more flexible and adjustable hours could provide greater opportunity for families to raise both market income and the quality of household production, particularly in the rearing of the next generation.

Notes to Chapter 3

1. For a more complete discussion of this cohort technique, see Juanita M. Kreps and Robert Clark, *Sex, Age and Work* (Baltimore: Johns Hopkins University Press, 1975), pp. 10–12.

2. This "trade" model suggests that the gains from marriage (trade) will lead "unlikes" in productivity to attract and couple with each other. This "matching" tendency is muted, however, by the nature of the commune (family) itself, where the initial formation and the viability of the group depend, to some degree, upon similar tastes and similar productivities. See Chapter 1 for the role of love in this question.

3. Glen G. Cain, *Married Women in the Labor Force: An Economic Analysis* (Chicago: University of Chicago Press, 1966); William G. Bowen and T. A. Finegan, *The Economics of Labor Force Participation* (Princeton, N.J.: Princeton University Press, 1969); Jacob Mincer, "Labor Force Participation of Married Women," in Universities-National Bureau Committee for Economic Research, *Aspects of Labor Economics* (Princeton, N.J.: Princeton University Press, for the National Bureau of Economic Research, 1962), pp. 63–97; Marvin Kosters, *Income and Substitution Effects in a Family Supply Model,* reprint monograph P-3339 (Santa Monica, Calif.: The Rand Corporation, December 1966).

4. In *Income and Substitution Effects,* Kosters showed, however, that the effect of the husband's wages on the *amount of the wife's time offered* to the market has two elements—an income effect (as if W_H can be fully equated to Y_o) and a cross-substitution effect [whereby the wife's labor (household) time could be complementary or substitutable for the husband's labor (household) time]. To see the implications of Kosters's thinking heuristically, consider the effect on the wife's market hours of the workweek of the husband. The income effect could be expected to lead to a reduction in labor hours for the husband, but if the leisure (household) hours of the husband and wife were "gross comple-

ments in utility," higher labor force activity among wives would also induce higher labor force activity among husbands "on substitution account." See Thomas J. Kniesner, "The Full-Time Workweek in the United States, 1900–1970," *Industrial and Labor Relations Review* 30, no. 1 (October 1976): 3–15.

    5. Cain, *Married Women in the Labor Force*, p. 139.

    6. Cain's central regression results were as follows:

$$(3\text{-}1) \qquad LFP = \alpha + \beta_1 W_H + \beta_2 W_W + \beta_3 S + \beta_4 U + \beta_5 C + \epsilon$$

Results	β_1	β_2	β_3	β_4	β_5	R^2
Regression coefficient	−0.84	1.48	0.95	−0.56	−0.53	0.56
Standard error	(0.31)	(0.35)	(0.45)	(0.26)	(0.16)	
Elasticity at means	−1.31	1.49				

where

LFP = labor force participation rates in 1950 of "married women, husband present" in northern SMSAs of 250,000 and above,

W_H = median income (in hundreds of dollars) in 1948 of "male family head, wife present,"

W_W = median income (in hundreds of dollars) in 1948 of females who worked 50 to 52 weeks,

S = median years of schooling completed by females aged 25 years and older,

U = male unemployment rate (in percent), and

C = percent of husband-and-wife families with one or more children under six years of age.

    7. Remember that the *amount* of time offered also depends upon W_W, Y_o, etc. The participation rate is solely a reservation wage phenomenon. See H. Gregg Lewis, "Participacion de la Fuerza Laboral y Teoria de las Horas de Trabajo," *Rev. Facultad de Ciencias Economia* (May–December 1968): 49–63 and Yoram Ben-Porath, "Labor Force Participation Rates and the Supply Curve of Labor," *Journal of Political Economy* 81, no. 3 (May/June 1973): 697–704.

    8. Sex discrimination is discussed in Chapter 9.

    9. The similarity of the household and the market economy is illustrated more clearly in Russian than in English. Note the following definitions:

ХОЗЯИН	(n) master, boss, owner, proprietor, man
ХОЗЯЙНА	(n) mistress, proprietress, wife, missus
ХОЗЯЙСТВЕННОСТЪ	(n) thrift, economy
ХОЗЯЙНИЧАТЪ	(v) to keep house, to boss
ХОЗЯЙСТВО	(n) economy, household, economic system

    10. Jacob Mincer and Solomon Polachek, "Family Investments in Human

Capital: Earnings of Women," *Journal of Political Economy* 82, no. 2, pt. 2 (March/April 1974): S76–S108.

11. The graphically-minded reader will find it useful to depict for himself via indifference curve diagrams the utility loss which is implicit in the case where full-time work is the only alternative to household employment.

4 | The Economics of Human Capital

Ten Dollars Reward.

Ran away from the Subscriber, on the night of the 15th instant, two apprentice boys, legally bound, named WILLIAM and ANDREW JOHNSON. The former is of a dark complexion, black hair, eyes, and habits. They are much of a height, about 5 feet 4 or 5 inches. The latter is very fleshy freckled face, light hair, and fair complexion. They went off with two other apprentices, advertised by Messrs Wm. & Chas. Fowler. When they went away, they were well clad—blue cloth coats, light colored homespun coats, and new hats, the maker's name in the crown of the hats, is Theodore Clark. I will pay the above Reward to any person who will deliver said apprentices to me in Raleigh, or I will give the above Reward for Andrew Johnson alone.

All persons are cautioned against harboring or employing said apprentices, on pain of being prosecuted.

James J. Selby, Tailor.
Raleigh, N.C. June 24, 1824   26 St.

Up to this point we have not inquired into the source(s) of the skills that can be used in the productive process and that can influence wage rates and earnings levels. As the "mood quotation" above suggests, the process of skill acquisition and development has been a source of difficulties for people like William Johnson, Andrew Johnson, and James Selby. When the notice above appeared in *The Raleigh Star* on July 26, 1824, Andrew Johnson was sixteen years of age. The reward was never collected, and Andrew Johnson subsequently became the seventeenth president of the United States of America.

It is to the difficult process of skill acquisition and to the economics of that process that we now turn, concentrating on the following question: How can persons of limited means alter their stock of skills so as to raise future earnings and income levels?

A moment's reflection will suggest the historical importance of this simple question. When low-income individuals have found satisfactory answers, both income and self-respect have increased. Of greater current importance is the fact that many occupants of barrios, favelas, and ghettos (slums, by some of their many names) are still seeking answers to that crucial question.[1]

Indentured Servitude:
A Technique for Skill Development

Historically, those families that were able and willing to forego current consumption could provide (at least some) schooling, training, etc., for their young. When parents or other adult family members possessed specific productive skills, such skills often were passed on to the next generation. Farmers begat farmers, blacksmiths begat blacksmiths, machinists begat machinists, and so on. In addition to home instruction, tutors and teachers were available at market prices. Even the intrafamily skill transfers, however, involved "purchases" in the sense that costs in foregone output and/or foregone time were borne by the family in order to develop the requisite skills in the young. Indeed, this is the essence of any capital investment—that costs are borne now in the expectation of future returns. Hence, the term "human capital."

> Human capital represents a *stock* of skills and productive abilities— investments in man—from which income streams flow or can flow.

As John E. Cairnes noted, however, the situation of the common laborer and his children differs from that of families with large incomes and/ or with a stock of skills to transmit. In 1874, Cairnes wrote:

> . . . He [*the common laborer*] *is practically shut out from competition. The barrier is his social position and circumstances, which renders his education defective, while his means are too narrow to allow of his repairing the defect or of deferring the return upon his industry 'til he has qualified himself for a skilled occupation.*[2]

That Cairnesian view of class limits on socioeconomic mobility (i.e., the existence of "noncompeting groups") rests upon the inability of the poor *to finance* skill acquisition, *not* upon their *inability to absorb knowledge* or benefit from training. At its heart is the inability of the poor to borrow against the promise of higher future incomes—technically, *a capital constraint.* But even a cursory look at history—Western or Eastern, ancient or modern—suggests that the capital constraint identified by

Cairnes was not absolute. Borrowing did take place within families and extended families, but the recipients of the financial support and the training were usually expected to use their acquired skills for the welfare of the group providing the support. That expectation was policed and supported by the considerable force of family and social opprobrium. Indeed, such *tying arrangements* highlight further the difficulties connected with financing investments in human capital.

To arrive at the essence of the Cairnesian problem, we need an answer to the following question: Why did lenders in the past and why might prospective lenders *now* pass up opportunities for profitable investments in the development of human capital even when the returns on alternative investments in physical capital (land, buildings, equipment, stocks, bonds, etc.) were or might be substantially lower? The answer lies in the presence or absence of *collateral*—the ability or inability of the lender in the event of default to repossess the capital in which he has invested. Indentured servitude (and, in a different way, apprenticeship) eases this problem of collateral. By legally tying the indentured servant to his "master" for a period long enough for the master to recover his investment plus interest (i.e., establishing a legally enforceable property right), both the capital constraint and the collateral problem are reduced.

Figure 4–1 presents a graphic representation of the conditions under which a long-term servitude bargain "can be struck." If the present value of expected benefits, PV^B, equals or exceeds the present value of expected costs, PV^C, *for both parties* at time t_o, each would expect to gain. Thus, a *voluntary* servitude contract is possible—indeed, likely! Specifically, using the notation from Fig. 4–1, a contract is possible if

(4–1) $\qquad PV^B_{\text{Servant}} \geq PV^C_{\text{Servant}}$; that is, if

(4–2) $\qquad \displaystyle\sum_{t=1}^{T} \frac{W_t^*}{(1+r)^t} \geq \sum_{t=1}^{T} \frac{W_t}{(1+r)^t}$

$\qquad$ or alternatively, where $\dfrac{\displaystyle\sum_{t=1}^{T} \dfrac{W_t^*}{(1+r)^t}}{\displaystyle\sum_{t=1}^{T} \dfrac{W_t}{(1+r)^t}} \geq 1$

given "r" as a market rate of interest and T as the employment or job horizon of the servant, and if

(4–3) $\qquad PV^B_{\text{Master}} \geq PV^C_{\text{Master}}$; that is, if

(4–4) $\qquad \displaystyle\sum_{t=1}^{J} \frac{P_t}{(1+r)^t} \geq \sum_{t=1}^{J} \frac{S_t}{(1+r)^t}$

$$\text{or alternatively, where } \frac{\sum\limits_{t=1}^{J} \dfrac{P_t}{(1+r)^t}}{\sum\limits_{t=1}^{J} \dfrac{S_t}{(1+r)^t}} \geq 1$$

given "J" as the length of the period of indenture.[3]

Alternatively, one can solve the expected income and cost streams for the expected internal rates of return—r_S for the servant and r_M for the master. Such a procedure avoids assuming a particular market rate of interest. Equations (4–2) and (4–4) can be used to solve for these *internal rates of return* by setting the two sides of the respective equations equal to each other and solving for the relevant "r." Where the respective internal rates of return, r_S and r_M, equal or exceed market rates of interest (borrowing rates) and marginal rates of time preference for both parties, both parties would benefit *under conditions of perfect certainty with respect to the streams of costs and benefits.*[4]

Changing ethical standards, the problems of preventing fraud, and the costs of enforcing servitude contracts (particularly in view of the differing social stations and legal knowledge of the parties) led to a demise of explicit voluntary servitude arrangements in the Western world during

Figure 4–1 *The Economics of Indentured Servitude*

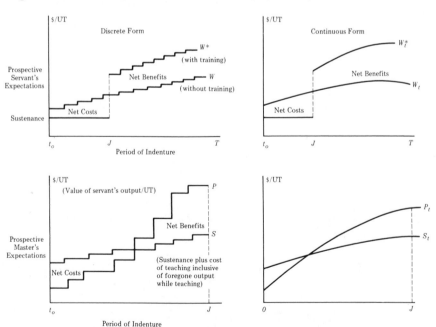

the 1800s. Nevertheless, other procedures for obtaining collateral and/ or tying individuals to long-term contracts have been devised. The enterprising reader should consider the differences and similarities between the older forms of voluntary servitude and the contractual arrangements for:

1. professional athletes,
2. graduate research and teaching assistants, and
3. federal employees undergoing training, particularly those in the military forces.

The more complex case of on-the-job training is discussed below.[5]

Alternatives to Voluntary Servitude: Apprenticeship

As suggested above, family apprenticeship arrangements have served in the past as an alternative to indentured servitude. Apprenticeship may also be a market phenomenon as distinguished from a family or communal one. Market apprenticeship arrangements are similar in some respects to voluntary servitude systems. For example, both apprentices and voluntary servants are expected to pay for the cost of their training (passage, etc.) out of the difference between the value of their output and their wages (subsistence costs) *during the training period or period of indenture* ($t = O$ to J). The master craftsmen (journeymen, "financiers," or masters) expect during that period to recover the cost of their time, tools, materials, and so forth, and to make at least a normal return.

Apprenticeship differs, however, from voluntary servitude in several important and related respects. Although the levels of earnings and productivity during the training period must be consistent with the interests of the contracting parties in each case, there is little *legal* support for apprenticeship arrangements. Masters are not bound by law to provide a particular level of skill during a particular (customary) period, nor are there low-cost legal means for assuring that apprentices will remain "attached" for the entire length of the apprenticeship period. The latter difference is important because the financier might expect to be recovering the largest portion of his costs plus interest during the latter part of the apprenticeship period. In contrast to the case of indentured servants, the public or *the law* will not bear any costs for maintaining the contract, and no one can be "cautioned against harboring or employing" runaways "on pain of being prosecuted." Legal actions between the parties are torts—within the civil law—with all the difficulties such cases may involve. Given a lack of legally established and presumably enforceable standards, apprentices must have some assurance that their training will meet a commonly accepted standard of competence so that the desired financial rewards and the status of journeyman will indeed be realized. Thus, because of the riskiness of the investment for both parties, institutional practices have developed to set the length of apprenticeship and to fix skill standards. In addition, institutional practices have developed which may (1) fix the wage level of apprentices (sometimes as an increasing percentage of the journeymen's rate); (2) test the competency of the apprentice before admission to journeyman's status; and (3) even regulate the wage level for journeymen. Finally, programs may be formally "registered," and the certification of competency may be buttressed by legal provisions. The more complex case of apprenticeship as an aspect of union wage policy is discussed later in this text.

In the absence of legal or trade union provisions, the problems connected with standards, competency, and so on, are handled in many ways. During the 1800s, for example, an apprenticeship system in Egypt was both sanctioned and enforced through family interconnections. A young man (often a craftsman's son) would be apprenticed to someone other than his father, almost always a friend of the family.[6] This arrangement provided first, a more unbiased system for assessing progress and competency than possible in a father-son relationship. The arrangement may even have helped to narrow any "generation gap" that may have existed. Second, the family-friendship connections helped both to enforce agreed upon or traditional compensation (rations, quarters, etc.) and training standards for the apprentice; and to insure that the apprentices would not "drop out" before completion of the training period. Elsewhere, other institutional arrangements have served the same general functions. See, for example, the certification standards of the Bureau of Apprenticeship, U.S. Department of Labor, as recommended by the Federal Committee on Apprenticeship.[7]

Alternatives to Voluntary Servitude: Specific On-the-Job Training

When the skill (productive potential) acquired in the training process is *specific* to the firm supporting (financing) the training, the problems connected with capital constraints, collateral, and expectations are fewer than in the cases discussed above. However, other complications and differences arise.

The specificity of the training itself raises the skill of the employee

Figure 4-2 *An Extreme Case of Firm Specific Training*

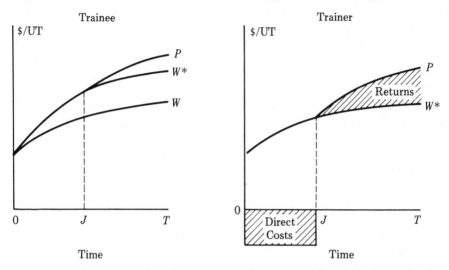

more in the "service" of his employer than in the "service" of any other employer. "Orientation," for example, represents specific training. Knowledge of the organizational structure of the firm, of the detailed rules and regulations or personnel procedures, and of the location of cafeterias, snack bars, toolrooms, bathrooms, and even water coolers presumably raises potential output only in that particular firm or location. The employee can therefore expect to be more productive and to earn a higher lifetime wage working for the employer who provided the training than for other employers. In this way, specific training provides its own collateral: the employer can expect to earn a return on his investment throughout the entire tenure of the employee rather than just during the training period. Indeed, it is precisely because an employer has "no hold" on an apprentice acquiring general training *after* the training period that the costs of investing in an apprentice have to be recovered *during* the training period. In the case of specific training, therefore, earnings of trainees do not have to be as low (relative to their productivity and to alternative earnings) as those of apprentices acquiring general as opposed to specific skills.

At the extreme, a person acquiring specific skills might pay little or none of the cost of his training during the training period. In such a case, the employer expects to recover his investment (including a normal return) subsequent to the training ($t = J$ to T). Figure 4-2 shows this extreme scenario. Such a case, however, is expected to be quite rare for the following reasons:

1. Subsequent to the acquisition of specific skills, both parties are in a position to impose costs on the other by severing their relationship. The employee, of course, will command lower wages in alternative employments, but the employer will be deprived of any returns he might receive subsequent to the training period $(P \geq W^*)$. Thus, specific training creates a *bilateral monopoly* situation. A "divorce," so to speak, is costly to both parties.

2. Given the nature of technical knowledge, it is quite difficult (costly!) to provide firm-specific training without providing some general training. The general training, of course, will increase the productive potential of the employee in alternative employments as well as in his initial employment.

It follows, then, that firms in which the trainee pays little or none of the cost of his training might expect a very large "demand" for the training program among the employees of the firm. It also follows that such firms may experience high turnover rates subsequent to training.[8] Raising the posttraining wage to reduce the turnover would, of course, lower the returns on the specific investment. These considerations led Gary Becker to suggest that one can expect the cost and benefits of firm-specific training to be shared by the parties both *during* and *after* the training period.[9] Obviously, the longer the expected tenure of the employee, the more likely a profit-maximizing (or cost-minimizing) firm would be to provide specific training for that employee.[10]

Alternatives to Voluntary Servitude: Subsidized Training or Schooling

Until now, our analysis of human capital development processes has concentrated on capital constraints, lack of collateral, and other aspects of the risks involved in human capital investments. Each of these considerations inhibits such investments unless the particular economic difficulties are eased by specificities, institutional or legal arrangements, etc. From a social point of view, limited opportunities for investments in skills may hamper the growth of the entire economy. Such limitations can lead to underinvestments in those individuals who possess great potential, can restrain social and economic mobility, and can ultimately lead to a segmented society. Such a society would have strong class overtones with class distinctions dependent upon access to skill development.[11]

It is obvious that the more an economy relies on technology and the more rapidly technology changes, the more serious will be the economic impact of the human capital problems cited above. Under conditions in which new human capital accumulation is difficult, existing knowledge and productive potential will depreciate and become obsolete.

> **Growth maximization
> requires
> $MSR_{HC} = MSR_{NHC}$**

The society will then experience an underinvestment in human capital relative to physical capital, and the growth of the economy will not be maximized. Indeed, such *opportunity losses* will occur whenever the marginal social rate of return (MSR) to investments in human capital (HC) is greater than the marginal social rate of return to investments in physical (nonhuman) capital (NHC). Constraints on either human or nonhuman capital that lead to different marginal social rates of return imply rates of economic growth that are suboptimal. Any position other than Z in Fig. 4–3 is a suboptimal investment position. The "have nots" in many nations have argued, at least implicitly, that national investment policies without subsidized schooling can or would lead to the social rate of return to schooling being higher than to investment in physical capital—i.e., to suboptimal growth rates.

In recent years, economists have attempted to estimate private and social rates of return to the two forms of capital. Such estimates, of course, were not available to the progenitors of the movement for public

Figure 4–3 *Optimal Social Investment in Human and Physical Capital*

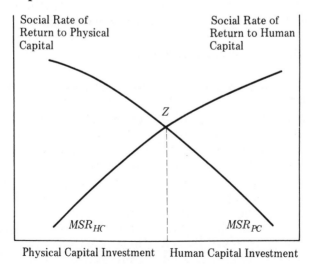

Social Rate of Return to Physical Capital   Social Rate of Return to Human Capital

MSR_{HC} Z MSR_{PC}

Physical Capital Investment   Human Capital Investment

Dollars of Investment per Unit Time

education. Nevertheless, the recent estimates give us an idea of the magnitudes that might have been involved. Becker, for example, estimated a private rate of return of 14.5 percent on investments in college education by native white urban males graduated in 1939. The estimates for such graduates in 1949 and 1958 were 13.0 and 14.8 percent, respectively. Becker also estimated a social rate of return of between 13 and 25 percent (closer to 13 percent after adjustment for quality) in contrast to an average social rate of return to corporate manufacturing investments of approximately 12 percent.[12] Adger Carroll and Loren Ihnen conservatively estimated a social rate of return to postsecondary technical training among 1959–60 graduates to be 16.7 percent. The private rate of return was estimated to be 23.9 percent.[13] The distinction between private and social rates of return will be further discussed below.

Regardless of the scientific support or lack of support for their position, the human capital "have nots" in a political democracy represent a political force of considerable moment. Even in nondemocratic nations or "limited democracies," the political power of the uneducated, untrained, or "shirtless ones" is substantial. Given an awareness of capital constraints and a widespread desire for upward economic mobility in many Western nations, it is not surprising that subsidized public education attracted and continues to attract much public support. In the United States, for example, groups as diverse as the Quakers, the Populists, the International Ladies' Garment Workers Union, the National Association of Manufacturers, the Catholic "social actionists," and the American Federation of Labor have supported subsidized schooling. Nor is it surprising that public support for education and technological sophistication appears to be positively correlated in most areas of the world. For example, one of the first acts of the revolutionary Communist government in the Soviet Union was to institute widespread public education for the "workers and peasants" as the base for construction of a modern economy.

The American movement for subsidized education was not limited to elementary and secondary education. It also supported the creation of a large number of land-grant colleges and universities, together with other public institutions of higher learning. In the opinion of many, the provision of subsidized training for the sons (and later daughters) of farmers and mechanics was a conscious attempt to relax capital constraints and change curricular offerings toward "practical" studies. A similar effort led to the establishment of publicly supported rural schools in Denmark, Holland, and elsewhere.[14]

In general, these approaches at all levels support (subsidize) schooling from general tax revenues and represent nothing less than the establishment in each country of a new *social contract*—one involving nonmarket reallocations of income among families and across generations.

A reasonably complete understanding of the reasons for and the usefulness of this social contract involves an awareness of the potential gains
in social productivity discussed in this chapter and the conditions under
which income transfers have minimal negative effects discussed in Chapters 1 and 2.[15]

We turn now to a direct examination of subsidized schooling. Figure
4–4 represents a simplified view of the schooling process, considering
initially only pecuniary returns and assuming that the individual (or
his family) pays the total cost of the schooling. W_2 and W_1 represent
the relevant expected income streams with and without training, respectively, given that the student is not employed during the schooling period
(t_0 to t_4 inclusive). Area A represents foregone earnings, including a gradual improvement in productivity while in school. Area B represents those
direct or out-of-pocket costs attributable to schooling,[16] and area C represents the net pecuniary benefits flowing (or more correctly, expected at
t_0 to flow) from the investment in schooling. According to Theodore
Schultz, in 1956 foregone income (area A) represented about 60 percent
of the cost of a high school or college education in the United States.[17]
Note that if area B is very large relative to mean family incomes, relatively few students may be able to meet the capital requirements of
schooling. Under such circumstances, the rate of return to this form of
training could be very high without a commensurate (supply) response
by prospective students. This argument, of course, is one presented by
the supporters of "free public education." Remember, however, that although B or some sizable portion of it is borne by the public under "free
public education," A is the larger share of the opportunity costs.[18]

Figure 4–4 *Costs and Returns to Investments in Schooling*

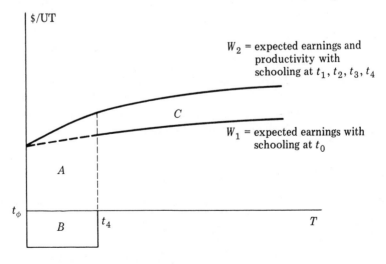

Several additional aspects of subsidized schooling require detailed consideration:

1. the nonpecuniary benefits and costs of schooling,
2. the public benefits and costs of schooling, and
3. the external (or neighborhood) effects of schooling.

Nonpecuniary Benefits and Costs

Ideally, in estimating the private benefits and costs of schooling (or in calculating internal rates of return), one would like to incorporate all benefits and costs, including nonpecuniary ones. Certainly, schooling (and education more generally) often provides benefits to the individual that are not easily translated into dollar amounts, including those attributes of mind and manner that we associate with a well-educated person.[19] There are also psychic costs—particularly around exam time—which are not generally quantifiable in monetary form. Among the largest of the psychic costs may be a growing "social distance" between the person undergoing schooling and those friends and associates whose "life styles" have not been so altered.

Although such benefits and costs cannot be quantified often or easily, it does not follow, as some might suggest, that measurement of pecuniary benefit/cost (B/C) ratios is so limited that it cannot be used for the analysis of individual school choices or of the efficiency of schooling decisions. Awareness of the role of nonpecuniaries in schooling serves, rather, to warn against incomplete or naive use of pecuniary B/C or rate of return ("r") calculations. If, for example, one is willing to specify the sign (or direction) of the net nonpecuniary benefits or costs, one can consider a calculated B/C ratio or a pecuniary "r" as a maximum or minimum. Similarly, if a particular schooling activity results in a low pecuniary "r" or a B/C ratio < 1 in the presence of net nonpecuniary benefits, one can use the pecuniary analysis to estimate the monetary value one would have to attach to the nonpecuniary benefits before the measured B/C ratio would be ≥ 1 and/or before "r" would be commensurate with returns in alternative investments. This "monetizing" of benefits allows a more precise consideration of the opportunity costs of nonpecuniaries.

Public Benefits and Costs of Schooling

Subsidized schooling, of course, implies public costs. Three measures are often delineated, as follows:

1. the social B/C ratio $= \left(\dfrac{PV_B}{PV_c}\right)_s$ or $r_s =$ the social rate of return,

2. the public B/C ratio $= \left(\dfrac{PV_B}{PV_c}\right)_p$ or $r_p =$ the public rate of return, and

3. the private B/C ratio $= \left(\dfrac{PV_B}{PV_c}\right)$ or $r =$ the private rate of return.

The three measures are often confused—particularly the social and public measures—by those who have only a nodding acquaintance with human capital theory.

Figure 4–5 shows the relevant areas of costs and benefits. The private B/C ratio or rate of return, as noted above, measures the expected usefulness of the investment to the individual investor, given the costs he expects to bear and the benefits he expects to receive. In principle, it is the private rate of return or private B/C ratio which should influence his behavior. The social measure relates the expected future productivity of an investment to the expected social costs, including individual as well as other costs and benefits. In contrast to these two very useful calculations, the public measure compares public expenditures now with public revenues later. Whether expressed as $(PV_B/PV_C)_p$ or as r_p, this measure merely catalogues or summarizes the *periodicity of transfer payments among the population.* The measure includes subsidies and other expenditures among the "costs" (including income tax exemptions for students) and may include increased future taxes, reduced unemployment compensation payments, and reduced welfare costs among the "ben-

Figure 4–5 *Social, Public and Private Benefits and Costs of Subsidized Education*

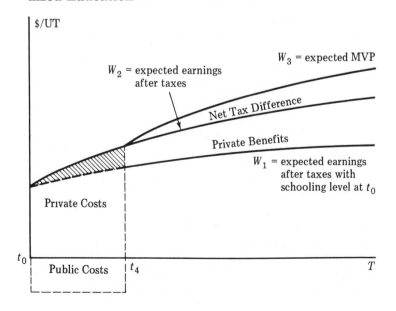

efits." Such public calculations *are not germane* to questions about the social efficiency of an educational investment. Those questions are addressed properly by the social and not the public measure.

Public benefit/cost or rate of return calculations make some sense when governmental activities yield "public goods" (e.g., in the case of defense or environmental protection). In such cases, the public as a whole is buying (or investing in) a public good over time. Public B/C calculations for education or schooling, however, merely amount to measuring the way in which the existing taxation-expenditure system transfers resources among the body politic at various points in time. The use of public B/C calculations in such instances has little or no economic content and certainly cannot be used as a guide to public policy.

External (or Neighborhood) Effects of Schooling

Finally, we come to the question of *externalities*—costs and benefits in pecuniary and/or nonpecuniary form that are created by the investment and flow to persons other than the individuals or public bodies involved in the investment process. These are "third-party" benefits and costs. Although externalities are difficult to isolate and measure, the values of external benefits and costs belong, in principle, in the social B/C or r_s calculations. To the degree that an investment in schooling (regardless of financial arrangements) reduces real costs and/or increases benefits for third parties, the investment is more socially profitable than it would appear from private calculations or from social calculations which overlook these externalities. Certainly, the polemicists for and the founders of public education—such as Thomas Jefferson—anticipated large external benefits from schooling via the connection between political democracy and a literate population. One does not, however, have to adopt the philosophy of eighteenth century liberalism to support the presumption that schooling may contain positive externalities. Consider, for example, the difficulties of establishing supermarkets with their lower real distribution costs in geographic areas with (say) 85–90 percent rates of illiteracy. Consider also the possible externalities to biological, medical, and other research at various universities. In thinking about the example of beneficial university research, one should remember that if all of the benefits of schooling (or research) are captured by the student, researcher, or institution, there are no externalities.

Finally, it is useful for the reader to remember that foregone income represents not only the earnings potential prior to schooling, but also the value of additional productive potential generated during each period in school (see the cross-hatched area in Fig. 4–5). In empirical work, it has often been convenient for researchers to use the earnings stream of each schooling level as an estimate of the foregone earnings of the next higher level. Such a practice understates the "true" opportunity cost or foregone income if productivity and potential earnings rise in each time period as a result of schooling.

Expected Rates of Return and Schooling Decisions

If individuals making schooling or curricular decisions are seeking to maximize their wealth or income streams, one can expect from human capital theory that their decisions will be functionally related to expected private rates of return or private benefit/cost ratios. Thus, one is led by theory to assume that individuals compare the expected alternative lifetime earnings streams flowing from various schooling or curricular decisions and, moreover, that individuals choose the stream or set of streams with the highest expected return. That "lifetime" conception has been challenged by Richard Freeman,[20] who argues that the required information is not readily available to or obtainable by the decision maker—say, the average college student—at any "reasonable" cost. Instead, Freeman suggests that students or prospective students are apt to use beginning salaries as *proxies* for the various levels of lifetime earnings. Following this approach, Freeman argues that whenever beginning salaries for particular occupations are high compared with salaries or beginning salaries in other occupations, *ceteris paribus*, one should expect a larger proportion of students to opt for those particular curricula or courses of study. A similar argument applies when the starting salaries of college graduates are high or low relative to the average salary level of high school graduates. Using his "realistic" proxy for lifetime earnings streams, Freeman was able to construct a model of college and curricular enrollments that articulates quite well with the flows into American colleges and universities and into various curricula. That model and several other approaches to the demand for schooling and human capital are developed in Chapter 8.[21]

Notes to Chapter 4

1. See, for example, *Child of the Dark: The Diary of Carolina Maria de Jesus*, trans. David St. Clair (New York: E. P. Dutton & Co., 1962), in which life in a Brazilian slum (favela) is pictured in all its dehumanizing detail. Note that Carolina's verbal skills, together with her sensitivity and dedication to life itself, helped to raise her and her family above the subsistence level and out of the favela.

2. John E. Cairnes, *Some Leading Principles of Political Economy Newly*

Expounded [1874] (New York: Augustus M. Kelley, 1967), pp. 65–66.

3. In continuous form, the same dual conditions apply:

$$\int_{t=0}^{T} W_t^* e^{-rt}\, dt \geq \int_{t=0}^{T} W_t\, e^{-rt}\, dt \text{ and}$$

$$\int_{t=0}^{J} P_t\, e^{-rt}\, dt \geq \int_{t=0}^{J} S_t\, e^{-rt}\, dt.$$

Note that these conditions imply that both

$$\int_{t=0}^{T} (W^* - W)_t\, e^{-rt}\, dt \text{ and} \int_{t=0}^{J} (P - S)_t\, e^{-rt}\, dt \geq 0.$$

4. Servitude contracts were often used to finance passage to colonial America, and the same analysis applies in this case. Transport expenses take the place of training costs to the financier (ship owner?), "J" remains the period of indenture (perhaps beginning at the time of landing), and the comparison of earnings or income streams involves one in the "Old World" and one in the "New." Given the knowledge of the day and the normal vagaries of everyday life, some distribution of capital gains and capital losses is to be expected for both servant and master (financier).

5. To further examine the role of collateral, property rights, and ethical standards in conditioning the ways in which skills are or can be developed, the reader should examine the training of slaves. Certainly, financing the acquisition of job-related skills (or greater physical prowess via better food, health care, etc.) by slaves provides its own collateral. In the event of default, slaves could be foreclosed upon and subsequently sold at a price equal to the present value of their expected future productivity less maintenance costs. Thus, although banks might refuse or hesitate to lend money to poor freemen for skill enhancement (unless physical capital were used as collateral), the same banks might readily provide funds for numerous purposes on the strength of slave collateral. Even these loans, of course, were not riskless. An owner who allowed the condition of his slaves to deteriorate (e.g., in the antebellum American South) was not only a poor master in the eyes of the slave, but also a poor risk for the bank. See any good "Negro history" for examples, or see Harriet Beecher Stowe, *Uncle Tom's Cabin, or Life Among the Lowly,* abridged (New York: World Syndicate Publishing Co., 1938), or Robert Evans, "The Economics of American Negro Slavery," *Aspects of Labor Economics* (Princeton, N.J.: Princeton University Press, 1962), pp. 184–243. Conscientious readers may also wish to work out for themselves the various reasons for differences in the training of slaves in ancient Greece and Rome compared with slave training in the antebellum American South. The same human capital model can be applied, but the extent of training differed substantially. The question is, "Why?"

6. This information, provided by several Egyptian students, is from *The El Gabarti Diaries.* The precise reference has eluded the author, but a system so conceived would make economic sense.

7. Martha F. Riche, "An Assessment of Apprenticeship," *Monthly Labor*

Review 87, no. 2 (February 1964): 143–48, and *Code of Federal Regulations,* vol. 29, chap. 5, pt. 521, 1976.

8. A similar phenomenon may occur in governmentally supported general training programs where it pays the individual to undergo training, but not necessarily to enter the occupation for which he has been trained. The reader might wish to investigate portions of the U.S. Comprehensive Employment and Training Act (CETA) program (initially labeled Title I) or similar governmentally subsidized training programs in other nations from this point of view.

9. Gary Becker, *Human Capital: A Theoretical and Empirical Analysis with Special Reference to Education* (New York: Columbia University Press, 1964).

10. See Walter Y. Oi, "Labor as a Quasi-fixed Factor," *Journal of Political Economy* 70, no. 6 (December 1962): 538–55, for further elaborations of specific training. Consider, for example, the role of specific training in Japan where employees appear to be married to their firms for life. Training in economic activities in which employment is irregular and high turnover is expected (e g., contract construction) provides a sharp contrast.

11. One might reasonably apply the terms, "the haves" and "the have nots," to those with and without access to human capital development opportunities. These expressions, however, predate the economics of human capital. During the 1800s, economists and social philosophers were inclined to trace income differences to the ownership of physical assets, stressing the distinctions between the rentier, the bourgeois, and the proletarian classes. Recent human capital analysis supplements these earlier explanations, demonstrating that the distribution of human capital is also an important determinant of the distribution of income. The linkage between the distribution of human capital and the distribution of income is discussed further in Chapter 13.

12. Gary Becker, *Human Capital: A Theoretical and Empirical Analysis with Special Reference to Education,* 2d ed. (New York: National Bureau of Economic Research, 1975), pp. 194–209.

13. Adger B. Carroll and Loren A. Ihnen, "Costs and Returns for Two Years of Postsecondary Technical Schooling: A Pilot Study," *Journal of Political Economy* 75, no. 6 (December 1967): 862–73.

14. See Theodore W. Schultz, *Transforming Traditional Agriculture* (New Haven, Conn.: Yale University Press, 1964), particularly chap. 12, for a brief analysis of this widespread movement.

15. The reader is urged to work out the conditions for widespread acceptance of this social contract, and to compare these conditions with those required for acceptance of a social contract involving widespread redistributions of income to the poor for purposes other than education (e.g., welfare payments).

16. The reader is urged to work out for himself whether room and board expenses at college belong in area B.

17. Theodore W. Schultz, *Investment in Human Capital; the Role of Education and of Research* (New York: The Free Press, 1971), pp. 79–101.

18. As suggested above, the use of public funds to offset capital constraints and maximize social rates of return is accepted among individuals of varying political and economic persuasions. Note that Nobel Prize winner and leading conservative economist Milton Friedman implicitly accepts these arguments in his plan for schooling vouchers. Calling for subsidies of students directly rather

than of school systems, his plan is not pointed toward reducing public support for schooling. Rather, it is intended to encourage competition for students between the public and private school systems, thereby improving the quality of both systems and permitting greater variance in the mix of offerings. See Milton Friedman, *Capitalism and Freedom* (Chicago: University of Chicago Press, 1962), pp. 83–107.

19. Note that the Russian expression for a well-educated man, ЛИБЕРАЛЪНЫЙ ЧЕЛОВЕК (liberal'nii chelovyek), implicitly pays homage to the value of the liberal arts.

20. Richard Freeman, *The Overeducated American* (New York: Academic Press, 1976).

21. To test your understanding of human capital theory, consider the following question:

A few years ago, a leading bank placed the following sign in each of its branches:

> You're not worth what you earn,
> You're worth what you save.

Explain why the message on the sign is analytically incorrect in general, but why it nevertheless may be correct from the vantage point of a lending institution. (In answering the question, it will be useful to examine how banks determine net worth.)

5 | *The Economics of Minimum Wages*

If a $3.00 minimum wage is good, isn't a $100 minimum wage better?
Anonymous

In this chapter, we turn to an analysis of minimum wages and similar wage regulations. It is not our intention to determine whether wage minimums are "good" or "bad" in some abstract sense, but rather to trace out the results of wage minimums concentrating on the question: What are the effects of increased minimum wages both on the employment and income levels of individuals affected by the legislation and on the national economy?

This general question contains several others:

1. Under what economic conditions will a minimum wage increase be a "shell game," providing an aura of governmental assistance to underprivileged or poorly paid workers without actually having any economic effect?
2. Under what economic conditions will a minimum wage increase actually damage the employment and income prospects of the intended beneficiaries?
3. Under what economic conditions will a minimum wage increase both the welfare of poorly paid workers and national economic welfare?

Under particular economic conditions, all three of the outcomes suggested in questions 1–3 are possible. Analysis of the effects of minimum wages therefore requires an evaluation of the requisite conditions. A prerequisite to that evaluation is an understanding of the demand for labor services and an understanding of labor market structures.

The Demand for Labor Services

In the absence of slavery and/or communal systems for organizing production and distribution, employers rent labor time for use as one of several inputs in the production process. The demand for labor time (or labor service per unit time) is therefore a derived demand, having its origin in the technology of the various firms desiring labor services, in the demand for the goods or services produced by the respective firms, and in the availability and price of other inputs.

Neoclassical economic theory represents the technological factors behind labor demand in a *production function,* say

(5–1) $X = f(L,K)$

where X represents physical output per unit time, and L and K represent inputs of labor and capital services, respectively, per unit time.

The Cobb-Douglas function is among the most useful of the available specific production functions:

(5–2) $X = TL^\alpha K^\beta$

where $0 < \alpha < 1$, $0 < \beta < 1$ and where X, L, and K are as defined above and T is a parameter > 0.

Specifically, T represents "the state of the productive arts" extant in a given firm. It is possible that two firms employing the same inputs of labor and capital, for example, could produce different amounts of X because the firms differ in technology (knowledge). Note the distinction here between *technology* and *capital.*

The Cobb-Douglas formulation emphasizes also the multiplicative interaction of inputs in the production process. Unlike other possible formulations of the production function that involve fixed production coefficients (fixed combinations of inputs), the Cobb-Douglas implicitly allows for substitutions among the various inputs in producing X. The restrictions in Eq. (5–2) on the magnitudes of α and β insure that the firm is operating in the "second" or "economically relevant" phase of the production function, in which all inputs experience *diminishing marginal productivity.*[1.]

Diminishing marginal productivity of labor exists when the positive marginal product of labor, $\Delta X/\Delta L$, *declines as L increases,* given that technology and the quantities of other inputs remain constant. Thus, increasing L will increase output at a decreasing rate. A similar pattern applies to K and any other variable input included in a Cobb-Douglas type of function. Although there are other production functions available, the Cobb-Douglas will serve our purposes in this chapter.

Figure 5-1 *The Marginal Product of Labor in the Economically Relevant Range of the Production Function*

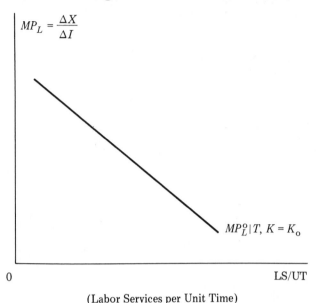

(Labor Services per Unit Time)

Following the discussion above, the marginal product curve for labor services (MP_L) can be shown as a downward sloping function of labor inputs (Fig. 5–1).

The *value* of the marginal addition to output (i.e., marginal value product, or MVP) also depends on the price of the product. Wherever the price of the product, P_x, is fixed to the firm by product market competition, then $MVP_L = P_x \cdot [\Delta X/\Delta L]$. This measure is also called the value of the marginal product (VMP_L) or marginal revenue product (MRP_L) by some economists. Where the firm is a product market monopolist, $MVP_L = MR \cdot [\Delta X/\Delta L] = \Delta(X \cdot P_x)/\Delta X \cdot [\Delta X/\Delta L]$ rather than $P_x \cdot [\Delta X/\Delta L]$ where MR is marginal revenue.[2] This formulation for monopoly takes into account the effect of the firm's increased output on the market price(s) of its product(s). Readers will find it useful to prove for themselves that MVP_L for a monopolist is always smaller than (to the right of) the MVP_L for a competitor, *ceteris paribus*.

We can now picture the firm's task of choosing the desired amount of labor per unit time. Assuming that the firm is a competitive buyer of labor (i.e., that the firm faces a completely elastic supply of labor at the prevailing market wage), the firm will use labor up to point E in Fig. 5–2. At that point, the wage, W (or cost per unit of labor input), is equal to the marginal value product. No firm seeking to maximize profits or minimize costs that is free to do so would employ less labor than L_o

Figure 5–2 The Competitive Firm's Determination of Labor Inputs

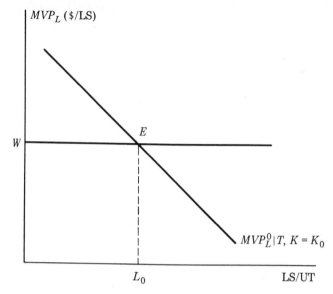

because in such a case, MVP_L would exceed the additional labor costs. The firm would not be maximizing its potential returns. Beyond L_o, the additional value of output (additional revenue) would not "justify" the additional costs.

Beyond Marginal Product

The discussion above captures the essence of simple marginal productivity theory. Indeed, many textbooks and other expositions stop after it has been demonstrated that under competitive labor market conditions, labor inputs will be paid the value of their marginal contributions to output. Such a limited presentation suggests "ivory towerism" or "unrealism" to many individuals, and also leaves the impression that MVP_L is identical to the demand curve for labor. This impression is inaccurate and can lead to serious confusion and policy errors.

To show the relationship between MVP_L and the demand for labor, D_L, let us trace out the effect of a lower wage on the amount of labor demanded by a firm. Consider via Fig. 5–3 a decline in the price of labor services from W_o to W_1. Given K and T, it will pay the firm to expand output *toward* L_1. In the process of doing so, however, the marginal value product of capital, MVP_K, will increase, reflecting the use of more labor with the existing *stock* of capital. At a constant price for capital services, it will then pay the firm to increase its use of that input, acquir-

Figure 5–3 *The Demand Curve for Labor and Internal Equilibrium*

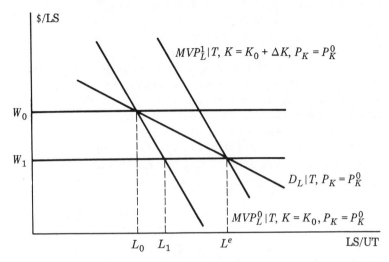

ing new capital stock or renting additional capital services. More generally, it will pay the firm to increase the use of any input that is complementary to labor. (An input is complementary to labor if $[\Delta X/\Delta L]/\Delta I > 0$ with X and L as defined above and I representing any nonlabor input.) As K increases, MVP_L will shift outward, raising the labor use "target" beyond L_1. The use of even more labor again affects the productivity of capital, etc. This iterative process—which may take some time—leads the firm to L^e rather than to L_1. At L^e, the firm has reached a new *internal equilibrium*. Both more labor and more capital services will be used than at the initial equilibrium, but the input proportions will have moved in the direction of the input that has become relatively cheaper—i.e., $(L/K)_e > (L/K)_o$. Moreover, the new equilibrium will be characterized by the condition in Eq. (5–3) just as the old equilibrium was. At any equilibrium, the marginal product per dollar of any input must be equal to the marginal product per dollar of any other input.

(5–3) $$\frac{MP_L}{W} = \frac{MP_K}{P_K}$$ where P_K = the cost per unit of capital services.

More generally,

(5–4) $$\frac{MP_L}{W} = \frac{MP_K}{P_K} = \frac{MP_o}{P_o} = \frac{1}{MC}$$

where *"o"* designates other inputs and *MC* represents marginal costs.

Alternatively stated, allocative or internal equilibrium is defined as a position from which the firm cannot gain further by changing input amounts or combinations, given input prices.

This entire adjustment process is captured in the demand curve for labor. Not only does the demand curve represent the different rates of labor use the firm wishes to obtain at differing wage levels, but it is also a locus of cost-minimizing points reflecting the internal adjustment of input proportions to the relative prices of all variable inputs. As Fig. 5–3 indicates, D_L is crossed at each point by MVP_L curves specific to different amounts of other inputs. It follows then that MVP_L can be considered as a "demand curve" for labor services only in the shortest of runs, a time period during which the use of other inputs has not or cannot be altered to achieve internal equilibrium. Formally, then,

(5–5) $MVP_L = h(W\,|\,K,\, 0,\, T,\, P_K,\, P_o,\, \ldots)$ and

$D_L = f(W\,|\,T,\, P_K,\, P_o,\, \ldots)$ where *"o"* represents other inputs.

Minimum Wage Effects in Competitive Labor Markets[3]

Competitive labor markets are defined as labor market areas (1) in which there are a large number of firms (perhaps producing different products) seeking the labor services of a large number of persons; (2) in which no single demander or supplier of labor has any effect on the market wage; and (3) in which the various parties have reasonably complete knowledge of workers' skills, employment conditions within the various firms, and market wages. By considering labor services to be homogeneous (or by adding up the different services in productivity units recognized by all demanders), we can diagram such a market in Fig. 5–4. The horizontal scale of the "market" diagram is obviously larger than that of the individual demand and supply diagrams, as is the scale of the individual (firm) demand diagram relative to that for individual supply.

Under competitive conditions, each demander and each supplier of labor is a "price taker." Each individual worker and each firm sees demand and supply, respectively, as infinitely elastic at the going wage. All parties adjust their respective desires to that price (and make other adjustments necessary to keep firms and households in internal equilibrium).

The "going wage," however, is not static. Although no single demander or supplier has any particular influence on the market price, the sum of their respective desires and actions determines that price. The vicissitudes of life on both sides of the market—deaths, illnesses, natural disasters, product price and other input price changes, new family

Figure 5–4 *A Competitive Labor Market*

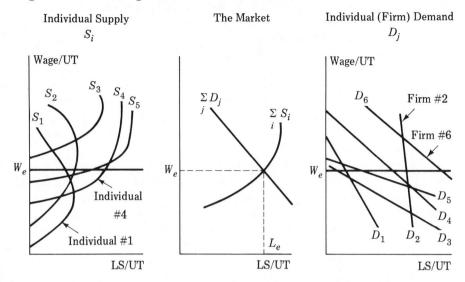

formations and disformations, changes in the number of persons coming of labor force age, migration, immigration, etc.—constantly shift the individual and firm curves and therefore the market supply-and-demand curves.

We are now ready to use the competitive model to investigate (anticipate? predict?) the effects on employment and incomes from the establishment of, or from an increase in, the minimum wage. Throughout the analysis, we assume that the market is for low-skilled workers. (We suggest that, etymologically, the term "unskilled worker" is a non sequitur.) Moreover, we assume that enforcement costs are low enough and penalties for disobeying the minimum wage statute high enough that we can ignore any enforcement problems.

Consider at the outset a minimum wage that is lower than W_e in Fig. 5–4. Such a statutory minimum will have no immediate economic effect since it will not be in the interest of any party to pay or accept so low a wage. A noneffective minimum could, of course, become effective as a "wage floor" if D_L were to shift down and/or if S_L were to shift out for any reason. Note parenthetically that effective minimum wages, which are usually expressed in "nominal amounts" and are not "indexed" (tied to an index of living costs or average product prices), can and do become ineffective with time.

A minimum wage, which is totally or largely ineffective, however, may have substantial political and even economic benefits to legislators and other public officials. Where there is among the populace some vague moral commitment to a fair wage, a "social minimum" in Reder's words,[4] public officials will earn political "chits" by declaring their support for such a standard. Indeed, were they to oppose such a standard, they would alienate some individuals who might otherwise be political supporters. In this regard, it is of interest to note that national and state minimum wages in the United States appear to have been ineffective in most areas most of the time. In a similar fashion, the massive increase in the formal minimum (or base) wage in the Soviet Union during the late 1950s was an increase from a previously ineffective level. The new minimum merely institutionalized the wage level that had been generated by labor market forces.[5]

In any economic-political system that covers a number of labor markets, however, a largely ineffective minimum wage may be effective in some low-paying areas. Such areas may be characterized by relatively more abundant supplies of low-skilled labor, by lower living costs, and by lower compensations for nonpecuniaries. In such cases, *real wages* may be equal across geographic areas even though *money wages* are not—i.e., the labor markets may be in geographic equilibrium. Under such conditions, the general moral commitment to "fair wages" is buttressed by the economic interest of those in and committed to the high (money) wage areas.

We can best examine the influence of effective minimum wages by considering a "case" in which the minimum is effective everywhere. Figure 5–5 shows the impact of such a universally effective wage under competitive market conditions. Note that the labor market at W_M is

Figure 5–5 *An Effective Statutory Minimum Wage in a Competitive Labor Market*

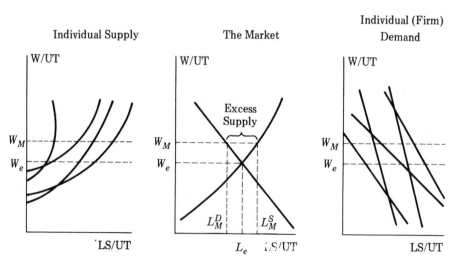

characterized by excess supply, $L_M^S > L_M^D$, and that actual employment is lower and desired employment is higher than under unrestricted competition. Under the impact of the higher minimum, employers will raise capital-labor ratios and the ratio of other inputs to low-skilled labor. Note that this input change *does* NOT *mean that efficiency has been raised.* Moreover, given the input substitution possibilities among the various firms, the composition of low-skilled employment among firms will also change. Changes in input proportions, of course, take time, a point to which we will return later in this chapter when discussing the results of empirical studies.

The precise way in which the available employment is rationed among those desiring such employment cannot be explained by this simple model. To understand that aspect of minimum wages, one needs to consider the specifics of personnel policies (which may be related to on-the-job training), seniority arrangements (perhaps under union contracts), the influence of labor costs per head compared with labor costs per unit time, and so on. We will address these issues in Chapter 7.

Although our model predicts that employment and output will be lower under the new minimum than under competitively generated wages, it also predicts that not all persons lose. Those low-skilled workers who remain employed—particularly those who remain employed on a full-time basis—gain at the expense of other low-skilled workers. In addition, however, low-skilled workers as a group may gain if the market elasticity of demand for low-skilled labor < 1.0. With an elasticity in this range, all low-skilled workers could gain *if* the reduced employment were shared proportionally or *if* the employed gainers compensated the losers.

When the minimum is effective in only some of the competitive labor markets covered by the law, theory predicts that labor costs and total costs will increase in these markets, that some workers will earn higher incomes, and that employment will be reduced in the low (money) wage areas. Moreover, theory predicts that the payoff to new investment in low-wage areas will diminish, leading one to expect, *ceteris paribus,* less movement of economic activity from higher to lower (money) wage

Table 5-1   *Elasticity of Demand for Labor*
$\lambda = (\Delta L^D / \Delta W) \cdot (\overline{W} / \overline{L}^D) =$ Percent Change in Labor Demanded per Percent Change in Wage

Value	Employment (L^D)	Total Labor Cost and Total Labor Earnings $(L^D \cdot W)$
$0 < \lambda < -1$	↓	↑
$\lambda = -1$	↓	—
$-1 < \lambda < -\infty$	↓	↓

areas. Thus, in the United States, one might have labeled the minimum wage historically as an economic attack on the American South and other low-wage areas (Indian reservations?). Alternatively, but with equal validity from an analytical viewpoint, one might credit the minimum with helping to prevent "the runaway shop" and preserving employment in the high-wage areas. From a national viewpoint, the minimum wage under these conditions prevents economic mobility and reduces potential employment and output for the nation as a whole.

In considering further the "competitive case," we need to recognize that statutory wage minimums are usually not universal in coverage. Any disemployment produced in the covered sector may result in a supply shift that reduces wage levels in the uncovered sector. Moreover, some persons may choose to drop out of the labor force rather than shift to uncovered (often very low-paid and/or intermittent) work. The interactions between the covered and uncovered sectors are complex, depending upon the demand-and-supply elasticities in the two sectors, as well as the proportions of the disemployed who move to uncovered employment and who drop out of the labor force. Finally, by raising the relative cost of low-skilled labor, effective wage minimums also inhibit efforts at job simplification (in the covered sector) and opportunities for on-the-job training. The latter effect has been explicitly recognized by the U.S. Congress, which has provided "subminimum pay" for some apprentices, trainees, and student-workers.[6]

Minimum Wage Effects in Monopsony Labor Markets

Neoclassical theory leads us to expect different minimum wage effects in monopsony labor markets. Etymologically, monopsony means "single buyer," but the term (model) as it is used in economics includes all market structures in which the employment decisions of a single buyer or group of buyers have a discernible effect on the market wage(s). The employment decisions of any large buyer or group of buyers must take account of the influence of their own actions on the market wage level (and therefore on their own labor costs), a "burden" not placed on employers in competitive labor markets.

For convenience, we will first trace the effects of minimum wages under monopsony in the "pure" or single buyer case. Initially, we need to identify differences in supply costs relative to those under labor market competition. Because the supply curve seen by the monopsonist is upward-sloping (and because all labor times are assumed here to be equally productive), increased employment by the monopsonist will raise his marginal labor costs $(MC_L$ in Fig. 5–6). Equating MC_L with MVP_L will lead the monopsonist to employ fewer labor services (L_z) at a lower wage (W_z) than under competition. Monopsonists will therefore produce less output than would have been produced under competition, *ceteris paribus*. This social loss or output effect of monopsony is analogous to the "dead weight" loss under product market monopoly. Figure 5–6 also shows that the supply price of L_z units of labor services will be W_z. Thus, monopsony is characterized by the following relationship:

(5–6) $$MVP_L = MC_L > W_L$$

in contrast to that under competition:

(5–7) $$MVP_L = MC_L = W_L.$$

Although the monopsony firm is in internal equilibrium, workers are not receiving the value of their marginal contribution to output; total labor cost and income is $(L_z \cdot W_z)$ rather than $(W_e \cdot L_e)$. Indeed, the area $(W_e - W_z) \cdot (L_z)$ is properly called *exploitation*. Monopsony, therefore, not only has a negative income or output effect, but also transfers income from workers to employers. In this "pure" case, however, the term *exploitation* has no pejorative connotations. Our hypothetical monopsonist is motivated by the same cost-minimizing or profit-maximizing desires as are competitive buyers of labor. The actions of the monopsonist result solely from the market structure in which he finds himself rather than from an "evil" intent or an attempt to "sweat" the workers. This situation contrasts with that in which groups of employers consciously coordinate their employment and pricing policies and in which it is presumed that the exploitation is intentional, analogous to a combination in restraint of trade in the product market.

Note also that the neoclassical word "exploitation" differs from the Marxist word "exploitation." Because all value is created (and "belongs

Figure 5–6 *Comparison of Monopsony and Competitive Labor Market Conditions*

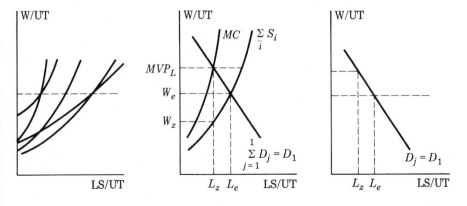

> "When I use a word," Humpty Dumpty said in rather a scornful tone, "it means precisely what I intend it to mean, neither more nor less."
>
> "The question is," said Alice, "whether you can make words mean different things?"
>
> "The question is," said Humpty Dumpty, "which is to be master, that's all?"
>
> ***Through the Looking Glass***
> **Lewis Carroll**

to") labor according to doctrinaire Marxists, any income claimed by employers represents exploitation. Some exploitation might take the form of lengthening the workday, workweek, and workyear while not altering the earnings (or subsistence wage) of labor—a "sweating" of workers by management. Under this variant, income is transferred from worker to employer *and* total output and income is *increased* by employer power. Remember that neoclassical exploitation implies a reduction in total output. It is not surprising, therefore, that the word "exploitation" has generated such confusion and argumentation. As Lewis Carroll suggested (see insert), any word can mean different things. Unless we are aware of its multiple meanings, the *word* will become our master, and we will become or remain perplexed and often angry.

Figure 5–7 *Minimum Wage Effects Under Monopsony*

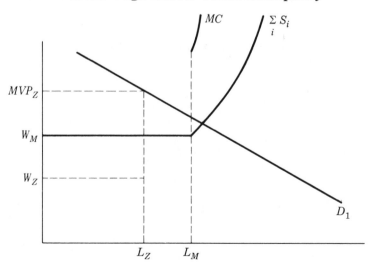

Consider now the change in the monopsonist's supply and marginal cost curves resulting from an effective, enforced minimum wage. Figure 5–7 shows these new relationships. Equating MVP_L with MC_L under the new condition leads the monopsonist to raise employment (to L_M) *and* wages (to W_M), as long as W_M falls between W_Z and MVP_Z. Indeed, if the authorities fixing W_M were omniscient, they could set W_M at what would have been W_C, thus eliminating all dead weight losses and all exploitation.

To predict an increase in employment as the result of an increase in wages appears to many persons to contradict common sense. That counterintuitive result can be explained by recognizing that one *market imperfection,* monopsony, which has led to a reduction in output is being countered here by another imperfection, the minimum wage, leading the monopsonist to act *as if* he were a competitor. Thus, he behaves as if he were facing an infinitely elastic supply curve.

The model developed above probably should be called the *plain, old-fashioned monopsony model.* It is characterized by the assumption that "the company" has no knowledge of the underlying supply curves of various individuals, but sees only the market curve. If, however, the employer knew or could estimate the minimum supply price for each separate unit of labor service, he would act instead as a *discriminating monopsonist.* If his knowledge of the individual supply curves were perfect or complete, the market supply curve and his marginal cost curve would be synonymous. There would be no dead weight loss under perfectly discriminating monopsony: L_e would be demanded and exploitation would be represented by the total area between W_e and the supply curve. By proving these several propositions for themselves, readers will be able to demonstrate that they understand the essence of the monopsony analysis.[7]

To summarize, effective minimum wages that counter monopsony power will raise earnings, employment, and output (except in the case of a perfectly discriminating monopsony). The productivity of the economic system will increase and the distribution of income will be more equal than under unrestrained monopsony.

It follows then that neoclassical theory provides *several sets* of hypotheses concerning the primary and secondary effects of minimum wages on employment and earnings. We now turn to empirical investigations testing these hypotheses.

Empirical Studies of Minimum Wage Effects

Competitive or Monopsony Markets?

Because market structure is crucial in determining the effect of minimum wages, we must now ask: Can we characterize labor markets as largely competitive or monopsonistic? Our answer to this question will be restricted largely to American labor markets, the locale of many, if not most, empirical studies. The methods employed in those studies, however, are applicable to labor markets anywhere in the world.

For many years, radicals, liberals, progressives, labor unionists, and farmer-labor advocates in the United States argued explicitly and implicitly that American labor markets could be characterized as monopsonies. Indeed, the U. S. Congress appears to have agreed with this interpretation in the National Labor Relations Act of 1935 (also known as the Wagner Act). Section 1 of that act, one of the cornerstones of American labor and collective bargaining law, reads in part:

The inequality of bargaining power between employees who do not possess full freedom of association or actual liberty of contract, and employers who are organized in the corporate and other forms of ownership association substantially burdens and affects the flow of commerce, and tends to aggravate recurrent business depressions, by depressing wage rates and the purchasing power of wage earners in industry and by preventing the stabilization of competitive wage rates and working conditions within and between industries.[8]

In addition to asserting some of the contemporaneous "underconsumptionist" doctrines, that legislative declaration clearly presumes widespread monopsony power. The Wagner Act goes on to encourage the formation of labor unions to counter such monopsony power. Unions will be discussed in Chapter 10.

Despite legislative and other public and private declarations that American labor markets are or have been monopsonistic, there have been only a few direct empirical investigations of that contention. The seminal analyses have been those of Robert Bunting, who used old age and survivor's insurance (social security tax) data as a base.[9] These data permitted Bunting to define 1774 labor market areas in the United States as of March 1948—by county and related groups of counties—and to calculate employment concentration ratios. The ratios measured the proportions of low-skilled and semiskilled employment concentrated in the largest firm or firms for all market areas. Among these ratios were one for the largest firm (a "pure" monopsony would measure 1 or 100 percent), the largest four firms, the largest ten firms, and the largest thirty firms. Bunting found relatively few instances in which *any* of the concentration ratios exceeded 50 percent, suggesting that the overwhelming proportion of American labor markets cannot reasonably be characterized as monopsonistic. Because of certain data and conceptual questions, Bunting's study is not "definitive" (to use his words). Nevertheless, it strongly suggests that monopsony is a limited or isolated phenomenon rather than a general one.

Casual empiricism also suggests that monopsony has been limited in recent years, at least since World War II. The availability of good roads and other forms of low-cost transportation, the widespread owner-ship of automobiles, high rates of literacy, and the observed migration of large numbers of persons throughout the country (many with low income levels and little human capital) indicate that both sufficient re-sources and sufficient information are available to permit a choice of labor market areas for individuals who might otherwise feel "trapped" in monopsony markets. Thus, even if some monopsonies, measured by concentration ratios, exist or continue to exist in remote areas (e.g., in areas devoted to mining, fishing, or lumbering), the extent of any monop-sonist's or monopsony cartel's power to keep wages low will be limited.[10] A folk expression in eastern Kentucky (a mining region) asserts that young Kentuckians learn their particular "3Rs" in school—"Readin', Ritin', and Route 23." Route 23 runs directly north to Columbus and Toledo, Ohio and to the Ann Arbor–Detroit urban complex in Michigan. Traffic on Route 23 would limit any monopsony.

It is not surprising, therefore, that many modern American labor economists assume generally that labor markets are competitive. The presumption that labor markets are monopsonies, however, remains in the public consciousness, particularly in union circles and in the legisla-tures. The situation may represent a classic "cultural lag." Note that the Fair Labor Standards Act (FLSA; or the "Wage and Hours Law") was initially enacted in 1938. Let us now turn to detailed evidence on the actual effects of the wage minimums in the United States.

Regional Effects

The earliest studies on the impact of the FLSA were those conducted by the original administrator of the act. In his report to the president after the imposition of the $0.25 per hour minimum in 1938, the adminis-trator noted that fewer than 0.05 percent of workers in industries affected by the law lost their employment for reasons probably traceable to the act. The effect seemed to be very small. In considering the import of the study, note first, that the relevant measure is not the effect on all covered employment, but the proportional effect on low-skilled workers. Note also that the initial report was made two weeks after the imposition of the act, a time frame necessarily involving a very short-run demand elasticity. According to the report, however, the workers who were af-fected were largely in the South and in very low-wage industries—specifi-cally pecan shelling, tobacco stemming, lumbering and bagging, cotton seed crushing, and manufacturing of seamless hosiery and cotton garments.[11] Most of these industries reacted by substituting machinery for labor. A supplementary Bureau of Labor Statistics survey of ten independent stemmeries from 1935 to 1940 showed that there had been a major shift to stemming by machine and that employment *and* wages had risen in the ten companies. Unfortunately, econometric techniques were not yet widely available and the state of the business cycle was not held constant in this analysis. A similar study by the U.S. Department of Labor on the effect of the $1.00 minimum instituted in 1955 showed some negative employment effects, particularly in sawmills and seamless hosiery mills.[12] In the affected industries, employment rose in some mills while falling in others over the first two years after the imposition of the act. Note that the data reflect actual employment changes, not changes from the employment level which might have been expected had not the minimum been imposed. Again, lack of econometric sophistication and computation skills necessarily limited the analysis.

Other early studies found some of the effects that we would postulate from the competitive model, although rapidly increasing real and money wage levels and monetary inflation made the statutory wage ineffective after a short time.[13] In general, these early studies support the hypotheses suggested by competitive labor market theory *and* the proposition that the early effects were concentrated largely if not entirely in low-skill-intensive industries in the South.

Youth Employment and Unemployment

Later research attention in the United States has been directed toward the effect of minimum wages on young people. Efforts in this direction were stimulated during the 1960s and 1970s by the growth in unemployment levels of youths, particularly among nonwhites. Table 5–2 shows the increases in the federal statutory minimum and Fig. 5–8 plots the general minimum against the levels of youth unemployment from 1950 to 1978. Moreover, the ratio of youth unemployment rates to adult rates grew during this period.

Several studies considered the possible effects of the various minimums both on employment and unemployment levels. In the words of Juanita Kreps, who wrote one of the major summary articles in the field,[14] all the analyses were characterized by a "simple theory, but complex proofs." The statistical or specification problems were legion, involving the following:

1. statistically satisfying approaches by which to capture the effects, if any, of the temporally fixed minimums given the secularly rising level of money wages,
2. statistically satisfying approaches by which to capture the effects, if any, of long-run versus short-run elasticities of demand (involving both the effects of anticipations and lags),
3. statistically satisfying approaches by which to capture the effects, if

Table 5–2 *Federal Minimum Wage Changes*[a]

Effective Date	Nonfarm Workers		Covered Farm Workers
	Covered	Newly Covered	
October 24, 1938	$0.25	$ —	$ —
October 24, 1939	0.30	—	—
October 24, 1945	0.40	—	—
January 25, 1950	0.75	—	—
March 1, 1956	1.00	—	—
September 3, 1961	1.15	1.00	—
September 3, 1963	1.25	—	—
September 3, 1964	—	1.15	—
September 3, 1965	—	1.25	—
February 1, 1967	1.40	1.00	1.00
February 1, 1968	1.60	1.15	1.15
February 1, 1969	—	1.30	1.30
February 1, 1970	—	1.45	—
February 1, 1971	—	1.60	—
May 1, 1974	2.00	1.90	1.60
January 1, 1975	2.10	2.00	1.80
January 1, 1976	2.30	2.20	2.00
January 1, 1977	—	2.30	2.20
January 1, 1978		2.65	
January 1, 1979		2.90	
January 1, 1980		3.10	
January 1, 1981		3.35	

[a] Source: Bureau of Labor Statistics, *Youth Unemployment and Minimum Wages*, bulletin 1657 (Washington, D.C.: U.S. Government Printing Office, 1970), p. 11, Table 15, and Employment Standards Administration, U.S. Department of Labor, *Minimum Wages and Maximum Hours Standards under the Fair Labor Standards Act*, submitted to U.S. Congress, 1977, p. 3.

By June 1, 1964, almost all employees in manufacturing, mining, construction, transportation, and communication were covered by the national minimum wage. Roughly three-fourths of the employees in finance, insurance, and real estate were covered by that date, only one-third of those in retail trade, and less than one-third of those in service and miscellaneous industries. All employees in agriculture and domestic service were excluded. Subsequent amendments extended coverage to domestic service, to part of agriculture, and to enterprises with smaller annual gross revenues, and further reduced the list of specific exceptions to the law.

Figure 5–8 *Youth Unemployment and Increases in the Basic Minimum Wage, 1950–1978*

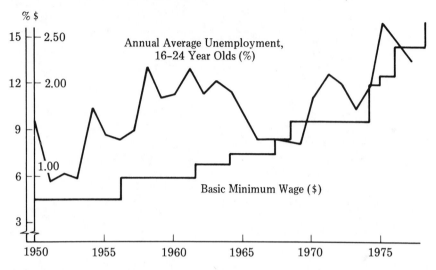

Sources: Table 5-1 and *Employment and Training Report of the President* (Washington, D.C.: Government Printing Office, 1978), Table A-6, p. 192.

any, of the gradually widening coverage of the minimums and the related impacts, if any, on the remaining uncovered sectors, and

4. statistically satisfying approaches by which to capture the effects, if any, of the rapid increase in the youth population (reflecting the "baby boom" of the 1940s and 1950s) and to observe the interactions, if any, of this supply effect with the secularly rising minimum wage levels.

Given these statistical and specification problems together with "poor data" (with respect to the detailed questions being asked), it is not surprising that the studies have not all reached the same conclusions. Nevertheless, the weight of the evidence appears to support the existence of a sizable disemployment effect, particularly among nonwhite youths, but an effect muted over time by the effects of inflation and by dropouts from the labor force. A study by Thomas Moore showed that during the 1950s and 1960s minimum wage effects could be felt as much as thirty months after the initial wage change.[15] A 1978 study of the minimum wage in Quebec also indicated sizable disemployment effects among young men and women.[16]

The effect of minimum wages on unemployment as distinct from disemployment is less clear. As suggested above, such an effect may be masked by transfers to the remaining uncovered sectors or by dropouts from the labor force—a type of "discouraged worker effect." The linkage of wage minimums to increased crime, prostitution, drug pushing, etc., has been suggested but never satisfactorily examined in an empirical analysis. Quite obviously, data problems abound in those areas of inquiry.

The studies as a whole, however, support the presumption that the minimum wage narrowed the range of options available to young Americans precisely at the time when large numbers of them poured into the labor force and into secondary schools and colleges. If choice was indeed limited, one must conclude that the minimum wage actually *structures* the labor force/employment/schooling experiences of youth in a particular way. Such structuring induces young people to participate exclusively in schooling until they drop out, "flunk out," or graduate, at which time they are expected to be exclusive participants in the labor force (employed or unemployed) or exclusive participants in the household sector. Moreover, such structuring appears to be occurring despite clear evidence of a desire on the part of many youths *not* to specialize in either schooling or labor force activities. About one-half of the American teenage labor force (14–19 years of age), for example, were both in school and in the labor force as long ago as 1960. The proportion was even higher for the 18–19-year-old group.

Consider briefly the human capital consequences of such structuring. As noted in Chapter 4, human skills of various types are acquired through a great many experiences. Some skills are probably acquired best (at lowest cost) in schools and others on the job. Among the latter may be work force discipline, a range of interpersonal accommodations, and an understanding of the constraints and "second best" solutions always encountered in what sociologists and educators call "the world of work." To the degree that foreclosing of work opportunities inhibits the acquisition of these useful skills and understandings at an early age, it raises both the opportunity cost of acquiring the skills (at a later age) and the rate of job turnover. Perhaps it was the awareness of these more subtle effects that led the U.S. Congress to exempt trainees from the statutory minimum wage. Note, however, that informal training of the type discussed here is not unique to *formal* apprenticeship or O-J-T programs.

Throughout this chapter, we have explicitly assumed that services are a completely variable input in the production process, that information about market wages and skills is widely available on both sides of the market, and that, in most circumstances, competitive labor markets prevail. Such assumptions appear to fit the low-skilled labor market, which is most affected by wage minimums. They may not, however, fit the markets for less homogeneous and/or higher-skilled categories of labor quite as neatly. Nor may they always characterize the low-skilled labor market.

In Chapters 6 and 7, two of the assumptions made above are relaxed: the assumption that information about skills and wages is readily (cheaply) available, and the assumption that labor is a completely variable input. Relaxing those two assumptions allows us to examine the economics of job search and to consider segmented labor markets.

Notes to Chapter 5

1. Where $(\alpha + \beta) = 1.0$, production possesses no economies or diseconomies of scale. Doubling all inputs will merely double output.

2. MR $\equiv$ marginal revenue $= P_x(1 + \eta)$ where P_x is the market price of the product and η represents the elasticity of product demand.

3. For the seminal work in the area, see George Stigler, "The Economics of Minimum Wage Legislation," *American Economic Review* 36, no. 3 (June 1946): 358–65.

4. Melvin Reder, "The Theory of Occupational Wage Differentials," *American Economic Review* 45, no. 5 (December 1955): 833–52.

5. For a detailed discussion of how market forces operate under that supposedly regulated labor market, see Robert M. Fearn, *An Evaluation of the Program for Reducing the Workweek in the USSR*, CIA/RR ER 61–13 (Washington, D.C.: Central Intelligence Agency, March 1961), and *An Evaluation of the Soviet Wage Reform, 1956–62*, CIA/RR ER 63–22 (Washington, D.C.: Central Intelligence Agency, August 1963).

6. *29 Code of Federal Regulations 519–22 and 527–8* (Washington, D.C.: U.S. Government Printing Office, July 1, 1976).

7. It will also be useful for readers to construct for themselves a geographic model involving two regions, each containing a covered and an uncovered sector. By assuming an initial equilibrium between regions and markets (money wage differences equalizing for nonpecuniaries) and by assuming monopsony and/or competition in the covered markets, one can derive a set of employment-wage predictions from each separate set of conditions. Moreover, one can examine the expected effect of the wage minimums on regional and sectoral movements of labor and capital.

8. Public Law 198, 74th Congress, 29 U.S. Code, Secs. 151–166, Act of July 5, 1935.

9. Robert L. Bunting, *Employer Concentration in Local Labor Markets* (Chapel Hill: University of North Carolina Press, 1962), and "A Note on Large Firms and Labor Market Concentration," *Journal of Political Economy* 74, no. 4 (August 1966): 403–5.

10. Governmentally created and maintained monopsonies and/or monopsonies produced by limited understanding of the "outside world" may, of course, still exist. Some, but certainly not all, American Indian reservations may fall into this category. The apartheid system in South Africa might also be analyzed as a governmentally maintained monopsony cartel.

11. For an excellent summary of the various industry and regional effects, see John M. Peterson and Charles T. Stewart, Jr., *Employment Effects of Minimum Wage Rates* (Washington, D.C.: American Enterprise Institute for Public Policy Research, August 1969). Also see George Macesich and Charles T. Stewart, Jr., "Recent Department of Labor Studies of Minimum Wage Effects," *Southern Economic Journal* 21, no. 4 (April 1960): 282–85.

12. Norman J. Samuels, "Plant Adjustments to the $1.00 Minimum Wage," *Monthly Labor Review*, 81, no. 10 (October 1958): 1137–42.

13. See particularly Peterson and Stewart, *Employment Effects*.

14. For three good summaries, see Bureau of Labor Statistics, *Youth Unemployment and Minimum Wages*, bulletin 1657 (Washington, D.C.: U.S. Government Printing Office, 1970), chap. 2; Juanita M. Kreps, "Youth Unemployment and Minimum Wages," *Nebraska Journal of Economics and Business* 10, no. 1 (Winter 1971): 14–21; and Steven P. Zell, "The Minimum Wage and Youth Unemployment," *Economic Review*, (Research Dept., Federal Reserve Bank of Kansas City, Mo.) January 1978:3–16.

15. Thomas G. Moore, "The Effect of Minimum Wages on Teenage Unemployment Rates," *Journal of Political Economy* 79, no. 4 (July/August 1971): 897–902.

16. Pierre Fortin, "Une Evaluation de l'effet de la Politique Québécoise du Salaire Minimum sur la Production, l'emploi, les Prix et la Repartition des Revenus," mimeographed (Quebec: Ministry of Labor and Handicrafts, June 1978).

6 | *The Economics of Job Search*

It's not what you know, it's who you know . . .   Anonymous

Ask, and it shall be given you; seek, and ye shall find; knock and it shall be opened unto you: For everyone that asketh receiveth; and he that seeketh findeth; and to him that knocketh it shall be opened.   Matthew VII, 7–8

In the previous chapter, we assumed that each prospective or actual employee and employer possessed substantial knowledge about the wage levels, skills, and conditions of employment prevailing in the relevant labor market. Using that assumption, we could argue, along with Adam Smith, that the range of real wages for each skill level would be narrow, differing only by the implicit value of the nonpecuniaries associated with various employments. Note that our conclusion did not require that we assume "perfect knowledge." Wherever a substantial amount of knowledge exists or is easily (cheaply) acquired and wherever individuals are free to seek their own interests, the simple yet powerful models developed in Chapter 5 provide us with considerable understanding of the market process. They also provide us with hypotheses that are susceptible to empirical verification or refutation (e.g., those concerning the impact of minimum wages on employment in competitive labor markets).

Where information about jobs, wage rates, and skills is limited and/or costly to obtain, however, conventional labor market models may be less than satisfying guides to understanding and predicting labor market phenomena. That, of course, was precisely the concern of the antimarginalists of the post-World War II period who saw conventional theory as "unrealistic." Regardless of the validity of their charge, an examination of the implications of highly imperfect information is useful in understanding labor market activities.

The first part of this chapter considers employee search. A set of related questions are examined:

1. How do prospective employees search for employment (jobs)?
2. What search techniques "pay off" for job seekers?
3. Can the various techniques be examined in terms of the principles of economics?
4. What are the labor market implications of these search techniques on wage distributions, on the distribution of jobs among available applicants, etc.?

In the second part of the chapter, comparable questions are asked about employer search. Finally, the implications of imperfect knowledge for the entire labor market are discussed.

Employee Search

Where useful labor market information is limited and costly to obtain, labor market information becomes an economic good. The acquisition of that good—with its attendant benefits—requires the expenditure of time and market resources, as does the acquisition of any other economic good.

Let us consider a prospective employee searching for information about employment opportunities. By definition, we already know that he expects a market earnings level greater than his reservation wage, that he is *in* the labor force, and that he is unemployed. Assume, first, that the prospective employee faces not a single potential wage offer, but a distribution of potential wage offers. Indeed, this assumption is "realistic" in the sense that all wage surveys and labor market studies indicate some variance in earnings within labor markets even for narrowly defined occupational groups. Assume further that the prospective employee *does not know* the details or the value of each potential job offer, but that he does know (or has a relatively accurate idea of) the mean and variance of the offer distribution, μ and σ^2, respectively.[1] See Fig. 6-1.

Does our hypothetical job seeker search under these conditions for some "best job" or does he simply take any offer, subscribing to the philosophy that "a bird in the hand" is preferable to search? If he does seek to locate some "best offer," how does he know when to stop searching? How does he know what the "best offer" actually is? George Stigler viewed our searcher's decision problem as just another variation of the economic calculus, suggesting that he would continue to search (collect job offers) until the expected marginal benefits from further search were

Figure 6–1 *An Offer Distribution of Wages*

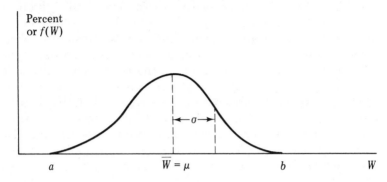

equal to the expected (or known) marginal search costs.[2] Stigler reasoned that the expected wage from the first search is the mean wage and that the maximum expected wage offer would increase with additional searches. Because of the shape of most offer distributions, however, the probable additional gain (additional income stream) from each additional search diminishes. Search therefore exhibits diminishing marginal benefits. Where job offers are normally distributed and storable, the marginal calculus yields an optimal number of searches, N_o in Fig. 6–2, from which the searcher selects the most advantageous wage (or net employment benefit). If offers are not storable, the marginal cost of search includes, in principle, the highest wage offer previously received as well as the

Figure 6–2 *The Stigler or Order Statistical Model of Optimal Search*

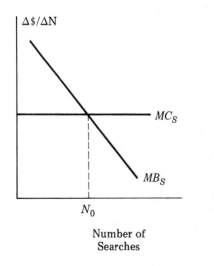

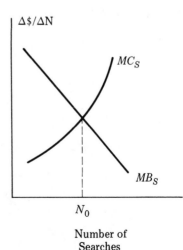

direct costs of search. Stigler and others have observed labor market behavior that is consistent with this "order statistic" scenario, notably the job interview process of prospective college graduates and of various professionals.[3] Moreover, many individuals appear to "shop" for consumer durables (including automobiles) in the same way, collecting "N" offers and prices before deciding on the most advantageous one.

Most employee search, however, is not of the "order statistic" type. A wide spectrum of empirical studies suggests that prospective employees search *sequentially*. They seek a job which meets some minimum criteria—a "good job"—and reject immediately any job offer that fails to meet that standard.[4] This behavior can be explained in part because many job offers are not "storable" or have only short term "storability." The criterion separating "good jobs" from "bad ones," however, can also be traced to an economic calculus. Technically, the criterion or "critical wage" for each searcher is determined by solving the expected benefit-cost calculus for the wage, W_c, at which the marginal cost of search is equal to the marginal benefits: $MC_s = MB_s$ (expected values). Figure 6–3 shows the location of the critical wage in a hypothetical distribution with "α" representing the probability of accepting any (and each) employment (wage) offer. Aldon Turner[5] neatly summarized and contrasted some of the differences and implications of both order statistic and sequential search. His summary is excerpted and paraphrased in Table 6–1.

The necessity of labor market search also produces labor market behaviors that would not be anticipated or explainable by simpler, adequate information labor market models. First, sequential search implies that prospective job seekers will resist downward wage adjustments and/or will shun "low-wage" jobs even while unemployed as long as some

Figure 6–3 *Sequential Search and the Critical Wage*

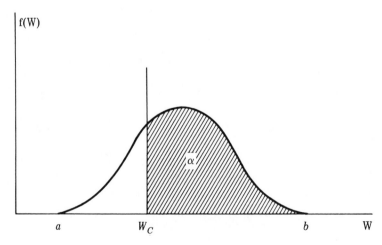

Table 6-1   *Implications of Order Statistic and Sequential Search under the Assumption That Costs and Offer Distributions Are Invariant across Searchers*

Implication	Order Statistic	Sequential
1. Implies a critical wage	No	Yes
2. Implies an optimal number of searches	Yes	No
3. Bothered by offer evaporation	Yes	No
4. Implies a short time period in which offers are gathered	Yes	No
5. Implies a refusal to apply for possible offers	Possibly	Yes
6. Implies a willingness to allow offer evaporation and to remain unemployed	No	Yes
7. Implies a positive correlation between the number of offers obtained and the value of the accepted offer	No[a]	No
8. Implies the following distribution of the number of offers solicited	Point (N_o)[a]	Geometric

[a] In 7, no correlation will exist because the number of offers under these conditions is invariant—at the optimum number (N_o)—across individuals (see 8), making the concept of correlation meaningless. Wherever the number of offers solicited varies among searchers because of differences in cost or offer distributions, the order statistic model implies a strong positive correlation.

support level (Y_o) is available and as long as the expected offer distribution does not change. Thus, where sequential search rather than order statistic search is the rule, wage adjustments are apt to be "sticky" downward. It follows that the wage flexibility implicitly assumed in our conventional models may not be forthcoming *in the short run*. This downward wage rigidity implication of search is also important in understanding voluntary (and/or frictional) unemployment. Moreover, with some further elaborations, the sequential search phenomenon helps to explain cyclical (or business cycle) unemployment (discussed further in Chapter 12). Second, the range of search analyses indicates that the more imperfect the information concerning wage offer distributions, the wider will be the variance of wage rates for particular occupations in given labor markets.[6] Third, because MB_s represents the present value of future earnings, search will be longer in an order statistic process or the critical wage will be higher in a sequential process the longer the expected job tenure. Thus, critical wages will be lower and/or search will be less extensive for casual or short-term jobs in comparison with more permanent ones, given skill levels and the same MC_s's for the two types of jobs.

Until now, job search has been considered as a unidimensional process. In fact, it is multidimensional, involving numerous techniques and approaches. For example, search may be formal or informal. Formal search involves the use of market or purchased inputs in the search process—for example, public and private employment services, want ads, union hiring halls, etc. Informal search includes activities such as acquiring information from friends and relatives, direct applications at the "plant gate," plant visits, etc. Much evidence indicates that informal sources—particularly information from friends and relatives—are especially effective in the job search process.[7] Contrary to popular expectations, these apparently chaotic, unorganized information search processes usually pay off for the searcher at very low cost in time and resources per "unit" of useful information.

One reason for the "efficiency" of informal search can be found in Albert Rees's distinction between extensive and intensive search.[8] According to Rees, one can search extensively [i.e., search for more wage or job offers (Ns), more price quotations, etc.] or one can search intensively (i.e., acquire detailed information about the many nuances of given employment situations). Formal search is largely an extensive method and provides very little useful (or trusted) information about the important details of the workplace itself—the nature of the supervisory staff, the compatability of the workforce, the incidence of accidents, the seniority system, and so on. Informal search provides not only the data obtainable by formal search, but also valuable (and trusted) information about the conditions of the workplace. Search among most workers, therefore, is informal and sequential, although the higher-cost formal and order statistic approaches are also used in some cases.[9]

Summarizing the implications of the job search process, we have the following conclusions:

1. Under sequential search, wages tend to be "sticky" downward in the short run. Downward adjustments in the critical wage for each individual depend upon a downward shift in the offer distribution expected by that individual. Order statistic search has no such implication.
2. In general, formal search methods are usually not good substitutes for informal methods. Formal methods, however, may be superior for certain sets of workers. For example, where the searcher and his friends and relatives have a truncated view of the actual offer distribution (say, because of immigrant or minority status), the searcher may find formal search to be *relatively* more attractive. Indeed, where information is truncated by color, race, religion, national origin, or class, the usually efficient and low-cost methods of informal search tend to maintain the existing distribution of jobs by color, race, etc.
3. The longer the expected job tenure, the greater the length of the search process (under order statistic search) and the higher the critical wage (under sequential search). Search for casual jobs will therefore tend to be less extensive (on the part of the prospective employee) and critical wages for such jobs will be lower.

4. Measured unemployment *resulting solely from job search* is a voluntary and productive economic process, not a loss of productive output for individuals and society. Such unemployment can be called *frictional unemployment* or *search unemployment*. The role of sequential search in cyclical and structural unemployment is discussed in Chapter 12.

Employer Search

Employers also face the problem of acquiring useful information about prospective employees. In a manner similar to that used by employees, prospective employers have alternative search methods. As Stigler suggests, wages and search costs are substitutes. A firm can "match the market" by paying the going wage and simultaneously use measuring and testing devices to select the most qualified employees. Alternatively, the firm may "cream the market" by paying substantially above the going rate and laying off those workers who do not meet exacting performance standards during a trial period. Given that some of the firms in a market area use the two approaches outlined above, firms that pay below the average (going) market rate will experience lower worker quality, higher turnover of experienced personnel, or both.

In addition to recognizing the general proposition that for employers wages and search costs are substitutes, we ask in this section: Is there an equivalent for employers of the three classifications of search for employees: order statistic versus sequential search, formal versus informal, and extensive versus intensive search? The answer is "Yes" in each case.

As noted above, competitive demanders of labor are faced both with a "going" or average market wage and with a schedule of wage-search tradeoffs. They are also faced with a vaguely identified distribution of prospective quality among the available labor force by occupation. The cost-minimizing (or profit-maximizing) employer will seek to maximize the quality of his recruits from the actual or expected distribution of skill via the marginal calculus in the equation:

(6–1)
$$\frac{\Delta MP_R}{\Delta W_s} = \frac{\Delta MP_R}{\Delta C_1} = \frac{\Delta MP_R}{\Delta C_2}$$

where MP_R represents the expected marginal product (skill level plus other attributes) of each recruit, W_s represents the starting wage, and the C's represent the marginal costs per recruit of the various search techniques; all figures are expressed in present values.

Employers could conceivably search in an order statistic fashion, interviewing N_o applicants for each position and then choosing from among them. They will tend to do so wherever the prospective employees will not "evaporate" during the negotiating period. Where worker evaporation is rapid, employers will search sequentially, accepting the first employee that meets a (minimum) standard of competence.

Employers using either order statistic or sequential search experience strong inducements to use "cheap screening devices" rather than more costly testing and performance measures. To avoid investigating each prospective employee in detail, hiring standards are established that reduce the number of applicants to "manageable" proportions. As Rees notes: "Within the narrowed field, extensive search can be conducted through the most appropriate channels."[10]

This process of fixing an acceptable standard is analogous to fixing a critical wage, but it also fixes the standard by proxy. Where the population is composed of disparate but easily identifiable subgroups (races, colors, sexes, distinctive religious groups, education levels) and where such characteristics are correlated with skill levels, race, color, sex, religious preference, educational attainment, etc., may be used as a (or the) screening device. Indeed, where there are two easily identifiable groups with different mean levels of skill (as in Fig. 6–4) and downward rigid wages, a random selection from among the highest-skill groups will often minimize search costs. "Statistical discrimination" of this type results from informational deficiencies and the attempt to minimize search costs rather than from a dislike of, hatred toward, or desire to harm the members of group B (in Fig. 6–4).

Screening techniques would have no economic value if wages were flexible downward (so that lower-skilled persons could bid into the market and change hiring standards) or if the two groups were equally skilled. Figure 6–5 presents minority and majority groups whose skills are equal in the sense that any line "S_o" will divide each distribution into equal

Figure 6–4 *"Statistical Discrimination"*

Skill Level

Figure 6–5 *Equal Skill Distributions Among Majority and Minority Groups Within a Given Population*

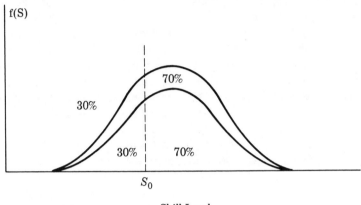

Skill Level

relative parts. Screening by majority or minority status under such circumstances can play no economic role. Screening techniques therefore involve prejudgment or prejudice (if one prefers), but should be carefully distinguished from labor market discrimination (discussed further in Chapter 9).[11]

From various labor market studies, we have considerable evidence regarding the substitution of wages for search costs and employer search methods. In the Chicago labor market study published in 1970, Rees and Shultz found for employers that:

> *By far, the most important informal source in all occupations is employee referral.* [Consider the high benefits and low search costs of that approach.] *Three of our establishments . . . paid bonuses to present employees for referrals who were hired; in one case, the bonus was $50 per hire. Several employers listed employee referrals as their preferred source of recruitment. The few cases in which employers told us that they preferred not to use referrals were cases in which they were trying to upgrade their work forces or in which they were having difficulties with cliques.*[12]

In addition, Rees and Shultz sought to measure those differences in $\sigma / \overline{X}$ for certain narrowly defined occupations that could be traced to search cost tradeoffs. Their calculations indicated that a hypothetical firm employing half its typists through employment agencies and half through want ads would pay $0.18 per hour less than the labor market average given the age, seniority, and experience of the typists. Most of this effect ($0.14) was related to want ads. Other studies have traced the wage-labor turnover tradeoff with considerable success.[13]

Awareness of the economics of search and the wage-search cost tradeoff among employers helps us to understand labor market phenomena for which we previously had little explanation. For example, an awareness of search costs forces us to distinguish between statistical discrimination, motivated by desires for cost minimization, and overt labor market discrimination, motivated by distastes. It also follows from the search models that the screening criteria actually employed will change as the labor market "tightens" or "loosens"—that is, as the relative costs and expected benefits of search change for employers (and prospective employees). Note, therefore, that employment and wage opportunities for minority or disadvantaged workers may improve or deteriorate across the business cycle without any change in the degree of discrimination. Note also that improvements in the amount of human capital possessed by minority (or immigrant) workers may not generate the same income streams and yield the same rate of return as does human capital among majority (or native) workers if screening itself depends upon majority (or immigration) status. Screening literature suggests that the low-cost social "solution" to such problems would be to alter information flows and not simply to prohibit "discrimination."[14]

Within those firms and occupations that expect job tenure to be short (e.g., contract construction, casual labor, convenience restaurants, seasonal farming), employers will be much less willing to bear "up front" recruitment costs and will attempt to contract out search to agencies, labor market brokers, or organizations specializing in finding (providing) part-time workers: union hiring halls, labor contractors, crew bosses, etc. Thus, in such employments, labor will be almost entirely a variable cost—an input cost that depends solely upon output levels. Hirings and layoffs will be closely correlated to expected output or sales levels. For other occupations, fixed recruitment costs (and other "up front costs") will be borne by employers in the expectation of future returns. In these occupations or activities, labor becomes a "quasi-fixed" factor of production (to use the term coined by Walter Oi).[15]

Finally, as suggested above, extensive search by employers will often be coupled with an initial screening criterion (or qualifications level) in those employment areas where skills are heterogeneous and where it is costly to ascertain the skill level of each candidate for employment (e.g., a candidate must have a Ph.D. in economics and at least two years of teaching experience or equivalent, and have demonstrated an ability to develop a research program in some aspect of macroeconomics).

Dual Labor Markets, Search Theory, and Public Policy[16]

In the late 1960s and the 1970s, a number of economists turned their attention to a particular labor market "anomaly"—the simultaneous existence of "good" jobs and "bad" jobs in the same labor market area, the apparent rigidity of that arrangement, and the limited mobility of persons between the two sectors. "Good" jobs are defined by the investigators as high-wage, long-tenure positions with opportunities for advancement. "Poor" jobs lack these attributes. Moreover, dual labor market theorists argue that conventional, neoclassical analysis does little to explain (or help us to understand) the apparently persistent tracking of particular persons (blacks, women, etc.) into poor jobs. To the degree that such tracking takes place, they argue, human capital development programs intended to improve employment prospects and income levels for the poor and minorities will fail or will "succeed" only at very high costs.

Most dual market theorists examine duality (or market segmentation more generally) from either a Marxist or an institutionalist perspective. In the Marxist variant, the emergence of separate and disjoint market segments is seen as endemic to capitalism and as part of the process by which capitalists (and their class allies) divide the proletariat into competing and conflicting groups. Successful segmentation thus obscures the underlying common interests of workers and postpones concerted action by the proletariat to alter or overthrow the capitalist system. This explanation of duality is perhaps most clearly enunciated by Michael Reich, D. M. Gordon, and R. C. Edwards.[17] Institutionalists regard most labor market phenomena, including duality, as dependent upon and traceable to "the rules of the workplace," the perceived needs of large and perhaps bureaucratic corporations and unions, the growth of property rights in jobs (e.g., seniority systems), and similar forces, including government regulations. Such rules, regulations, and institutions effectively structure labor markets just as they structure product markets and interpersonal relationships. As suggested earlier in this chapter, much of the neoclassical explanation of duality may be found in the economics of search, in truncated and high-cost information, in statistical discrimination, and so forth.

Both the segmented labor market and the neoclassical explanations of dual markets "predict" that poor jobs will be concentrated among immigrants, racial and ethnic minorities, and similar categories of workers. For this and other reasons (including the scope of the problem), it is difficult to test empirically which of the several explanations best explains the phenomenon of duality. Because of the difference in paradigms, it is particularly difficult to test the Marxist variant against the other two.

The various explanations, however, offer very different predictions of the future in capitalist economies and have very different public policy implications. The most extreme Marxist explanation (as well as some of the less extreme "models") suggests that under capitalism (private ownership of the physical means of production) labor markets will become more and more segmented over time. The Marxist solution to the inequities of such developments and the economic losses ("contradictions") involved in future segmentation is the eventual elimination of capitalism. Institutionalists do not "predict" future segmentation or duality. Rather, their work suggests that solutions to observed social inequities and inefficiencies can be had, if desired by the public, via institutional changes, new laws and regulations, etc. Among these might be changes in union hiring hall practices or in the procedures and emphases of public employment services. As noted above, neoclassical analysts trace duality (and segmentation) to informational imperfections in *any* labor market (whether the participating firms are capitalist or socialist), provided only that the firms are seeking to minimize input (labor) costs per unit of output and that information is costly. Neoclassical economists also trace segmentation to human capital problems—noncompeting groups, capital constraints, etc. It is not surprising, therefore, that these economists look to the development of low-cost search methods as a way to improve earnings and employment prospects for the unemployed and those in poor jobs. That emphasis may be separate from or in conjunction with programs for skill development.

Although both the neoclassical and the institutional approaches are "optimistic" in the sense that they look toward improving job opportunities and earnings levels, nothing in the neoclassical approach implies that such improvements are easy to obtain. At the current level of understanding, for example, neoclassical search analysis contains little hope for improvement via formal search methods (e.g., national employment service actions, computer job matching, etc.)—approaches often recommended to raise the employment and earnings status of those "trapped" in poor jobs. Neoclassical analysis does suggest that indirect and/or informal approaches may be very productive. For example, the activities of churches and other civic groups in welcoming newcomers and introducing the poor (and others) into the social mainstream may have very high social rate of return. The gain, however, will not be dramatic or easily identified. A similar phenomenon may exist in newly integrated schools because school experiences increase the exposure of the (formerly segregated) students and their parents to a wider network of informal information.

One can also conclude from the search analysis developed here and the human capital theory discussed in Chapter 4 that lower-cost information flows may be required if returns to human capital investments are to be maximized, particularly for minorities and others outside the stream of informal information. Presumably, this is an important part of what labor polemicists and others are seeking when they call for the enactment or implementation of "comprehensive manpower programs." Nevertheless, actually discovering and/or developing low-cost search techniques consistent with the market process is not a simple task. (See footnote 14 for an example of a governmentally supported program that inadvertently improved labor market information.) To the degree, however, that existing public or private institutions constrain or inhibit the development of low-cost search techniques, *ceteris paribus,* both neoclassical and institutional economists would favor institutional changes if the necessary changes could be accomplished at relatively low direct costs. The change in institutions sought by Marxists, of course, is in a different qualitative dimension.

Finally, it is important to recognize that despite the particular slant of the initial investigator or investigators, widespread concern with dual markets has required all labor economists to probe more deeply into the fundamental nature and workings of labor markets and has improved our collective understanding. Another form of segmentation—internal versus external labor markets—is discussed in Chapter 7.

Notes to Chapter 6

1. $\mu = \int_a^b wf(w)dw \simeq \sum_{i=1}^{M} \frac{W_i}{M}$ and $\sigma^2 = \int_a^b (W - \mu)^2 f(W)dW \simeq \sum_{i=1}^{M} (W_i - \mu)^2/M$ where M is the number of potential or possible wage offers in a noncontinuous distribution.

2. George Stigler, "Information in the Labor Market," *Journal of Political Economy* 70, no. 5 (October 1962): 94–105.

3. To the best of the author's knowledge, the term "order statistic search" was first employed by Aldon A. Turner in "An Empirical Investigation of Search Techniques Used by Job Searchers" (Ph.D. diss., North Carolina State University, 1972).

4. See, in particular, H. L. Sheppard and A. H. Belitsky, *The Job Hunt: Job-Seeking Behavior of Unemployed Workers in a Local Economy* (Baltimore: Johns Hopkins University Press, 1966), and Turner, "Job Searchers."

5. Turner, "Job Searchers."

6. George Stigler, "The Economics of Information," *Journal of Political Economy* 69, no. 3 (April 1961): 213–25, and Stigler, "Information in the Labor Market."

7. See, in particular, Sheppard and Belitsky, *The Job Hunt;* Melvin Liure and E. Rayack, "Racial Differences in Migration and Job Search: A Case Study," *Southern Economic Review* 33, no. 1 (July 1966): 81–95; W. H. Miernyk, *Inter-Industry Labor Mobility* (Boston: Northeastern University Press, 1955); and G. P. Shultz, "Recent Research on Labor Mobility," in *Proceedings of the Fourth Annual Meeting* (Chicago: Industrial Relations Research Association, 1951).

8. Albert Rees, "Information Networks in Labor Markets," *American Economic Review* 56, no. 2 (May 1966): 559–66.

9. Turner, "Job Searchers," and J. J. McCall, "The Economics of Information and Optimal Stopping Rules," *Journal of Business* 38, no. 3 (July 1965):

300–17, showed sequential search usually to be the more efficient search approach.

10. Rees, "Informational Networks," p. 560.

11. For representative statements of screening models, see McCall, "The Economics of Information"; A. A. Alchain, "Informational Costs, Pricing and Resource Unemployment," in *Microeconomic Foundations of Employment and Inflation Theory*, ed. E. S. Phelps (New York: W. W. Norton and Co., 1970), pp. 27–52; E. S. Phelps, "The Statistical Theory of Racism and Sexism," *American Economic Review* 62, no. 4 (September 1972): 659–61; P. Gayer and R. S. Goldfarb, "Job Search, the Duration of Unemployment and the Phillips Curve: Comment," *American Economic Review* 62, no. 4 (September 1972): 714–17; and R. L. Peterson, "Economics of Information and Job Search: Another View," *Quarterly Journal of Economics* 6, no. 1 (February 1972): 127–31.

12. Albert Rees and George Shultz, *Workers and Wages in an Urban Labor Market* (Chicago: University of Chicago Press, 1972), p. 200.

13. See, in particular, S. J. Nickell, "Wage Structure and Quit Rates," *International Economic Review* 17, no. 1 (February 1976): 191–203.

14. For a description of the policy consequences of this distinction, see Donald D. Osburn, *Negro Employment in the Textile Industries of North and South Carolina*, research report 1966-10 (Washington, D.C.: Equal Employment Opportunity Committee, November 1966), and Phyllis Wallace and Maria Beckles, *Negro Employment Patterns in the Textile Industry*, research report 1966-11 (Washington, D.C.: Equal Employment Opportunity Committee, November 1966). A special example is provided by Richard Robbins, "An Evaluation of Publicly-Supported Mobility of Low Income Rural Residents" (M.A. thesis, North Carolina State University, 1967), which examines the success of a subsidized mobility program sponsored by the North Carolina Fund. In order to relieve the "manpower shortage" in urban industrial centers, job seekers from largely rural areas were provided with mobility assistance and information and moved to the Greensboro–High Point–Winston Salem area. To be eligible, the applicants had to be unemployed or earning less than $1,200 a year in the "home area." The experiment, supported by the U.S. Department of Labor, has been viewed as a failure by some observers because a sizable proportion of the migrants returned home after a brief stay in the urban area. The high return rate among the participants, who were largely black or American Indians, was ascribed to a desire to return to their home surroundings, extended families, tribes, etc. Robbins was unsatisfied with this explanation and found, upon investigation, that most of the returnees went home to positions that approximately matched their money earnings in the urban area. Robbins demonstrated that "down home" employers had found a cheap screening mechanism for competent workmen via the mobility project, a mechanism previously unavailable. The cost to employers—most of whom were white—of ascertaining the competency of individual nonwhite workers had previously induced the use of racial screening practices. Those costs, however, were lowered substantially by the mobility project. Thus, the subsidized mobility program opened employment opportunities and raised incomes both for those who stayed in the new area and those who returned.

15. Walter Y. Oi, "Labor as a Quasi-fixed Factor," *Journal of Political Economy* 70, no. 6 (December 1962): 538–55.

16. For a comprehensive discussion of segmentation and neoclassical theory covering both dual and internal labor markets, see Glen Cain, "The Challenge of Segmented Labor Market Theories to Orthodox Theory," *Journal of Economic Literature* 14, no. 4 (December 1976): 1215–57.

17. Michael Reich, D. M. Gordon, and R. C. Edwards, "A Theory of Labor Market Segmentation," *American Economic Review* 63, no. 2 (May 1973): 359–65.

7 | *The Economics of Internal Labor Markets*

*The internal labor market, governed by administrative rules, is
to be distinguished from the external labor market of conventional
economic theory where pricing, allocating, and training decisions
are controlled directly by economic variables. These two markets
are interconnected, however, and movement between them occurs
at certain job classifications which constitute ports of entry and
exit to and from the internal labor market. The remainder of the
jobs within the internal market are filled by the promotion or
transfer of workers who have already gained entry. Consequently,
these jobs are shielded from the direct influences of competitive
forces in the external market.*

Peter Doeringer and Michael Piore,
Internal Labor Markets and Manpower Analysis[1]

The quotation above not only defines internal and external
labor markets, but also suggests that "conventional" neoclassical analysis
may have limited applicability. It is to the nature of internal labor markets and to their linkages with the external market that we turn in
this chapter. The discussion is centered around the following three questions:

1. How do internal labor markets work?
2. To what degree is the existence of the internal market itself determined by external economic forces and to what degree is the internal
market institutionally determined?
3. To what degree are internal market processes influenced by changes
in external markets?

Questions 2 and 3 are obviously interrelated, and they will be addressed
together later in the chapter.

Promotion, Job Tenure, and Job Ladders

Internal labor markets are usually characterized by elaborate internal promotion and transfer systems depending at least in part upon seniority or tenure and possessing a limited number of entry and exit ports. Figure 7–1 provides a representative example of such ports and job ladders. Doeringer and Piore in their seminal work in internal markets noted:

> *The rules governing internal labor allocation and pricing accord certain rights and privileges to the internal labor force which are not available to workers in the external labor market. The internal labor force, for example, has exclusive rights to jobs filled internally, and continuity of employment, even at entry ports,*

Figure 7–1 *A Representative Internal Job Structure—Job Ladders and Entry Ports*

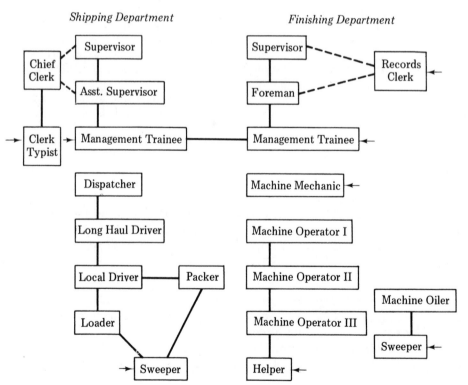

is protected from direct competition by workers in the external labor market. The phenomenon of internal markets is thus closely akin to the problems which other authors have identified as "industrial feudalism," "the balkanization of labor markets" and "property rights" in a job.[2]

Internal labor markets exist, according to Doeringer, Piore, and many other analysts, in both unionized and nonunionized firms and plants. Indeed, nonunion firms or establishments sometimes have more elaborate internal market structures than unionized firms—for example, the detailed rules and regulations concerning promotion, transfer, etc., in American governmental agencies.

One can trace the existence of internal labor markets and their varied natures to a number of causes. One interpretation argues that the internal market characteristics emerge from work experiences in the enterprise itself or in particular sets of enterprises, and are therefore specific to the nature and structure of the enterprise, the industry, and the union (if any). Explicit or implicit rules governing interpersonal relationships on the job and property rights associated with specific jobs grow over time to accommodate the experiences and desires of the employers and employees, *and* are conditioned strongly by the institutional framework within which the activities are embedded. Understanding observed patterns therefore requires an appreciation both of the institutions themselves and of the unique or distinctive history of the given industrial area and/or geographic vicinity. Probing into history and institutional structure is, of course, the essence of the institutionalist method of analysis. A second, not quite disjoint, analytical approach is to concentrate on the explanatory factors suggested by neoclassicial theory that are common to all enterprises. That methodology leads one to concentrate on the economics of search and the economics of training as the primary influences accounting for the presence and nature of internal markets. A third approach looks to the nature and stage of the current class struggle to understand the elaboration of internal markets—an approach suggested by Michael Reich, D. M. Gordon, and R. C. Edwards in their analysis of dual labor markets noted in Chapter 6.[3] That Marxist approach will not be further explored here, but a synthesis of the neoclassical and institutional approaches is presented below.

Labor as a Quasi-fixed Factor

Professors Oi, Becker, and Mincer in separate works[4] have demonstrated that the presence of recruitment, training, and other "up front" costs converts labor from a totally variable factor into a "quasi-fixed factor" (Oi's terminology). Their analyses indicate that the total expected cost of labor contains both variable and fixed components. In Eq. (7–1), fixed recruitment costs *(H)* and training costs *(K)* are added to the present value of wage costs, $\sum_{t=1}^{T} W_t(1 + r)^{-t}$. Total income is represented by Eq. (7–2) where

$$(7\text{–}1) \qquad \phi = \sum_{t=1}^{T} W_t(1 + r)^{-t} + H + K$$

$$(7\text{–}2) \qquad Y = \sum_{t=1}^{T} (M_t + \Delta M_t)(1 + r)^{-t}$$

M_t = marginal value product at time t and ΔM_t is some positive function of K, i.e., $\Delta M_t = g(K)|g' > 0$. That is, increased productivity is produced under conditions of increasing marginal costs. Setting $Y = \phi$ shows that each employer at equilibrium earns a periodic rent on his investment in search and training, the size of that rent (ρ) for each employee being

$$(7\text{–}3) \qquad \rho_i = \frac{H_i + K_i}{\sum_{t=1}^{T} (1 + r)^{-t}}$$

Note from the discussion in Chapter 4 that ΔM, the acquired skills, must be firm-specific.

For the employer at equilibrium, $\rho = M^* + \Delta M^* - W^*$ where the *'s denote long run values. ρ represents a wedge between MVP_L and W_L, and it is to this rent that neoclassical approaches look for an understanding of internal markets and for the degree to which insiders are "protected" from outside competition.

A More Complete Neoclassical Model of Entry Ports and Job Ladders

Consider the hiring and training decisions of a firm seeking to maximize profits or at least minimize costs. With the aid of modern neoclassical analysis, three "models" can be developed to illustrate the forces behind the hiring and training decisions of the firm. First, a decision-making rule for internal training can be presented. Second, a decision-making rule for internal promotion (transfer) and training versus the hiring of an already skilled outsider can be specified. Third, a decision-making rule for internal training in firm-specific skills versus the hiring and training of an outsider with similar skills can be elaborated.

Decision Rule for Internal Training of a New Employee

Following the quasi-fixed factor and the human capital analysis already developed, one would expect employers to train their new employees if the present value of expected future benefits to the employer (Y) is no less than the expected future cost (ϕ). Thus, training can be expected to occur if $(Y - \phi) \geq 0$. A simple way of looking at that decision-making process is presented in Fig. 7–2. More precisely, training will be profitable if:

(7–4)

$$\overbrace{\sum_{t=1}^{J} (M_t + \Delta M_t - W_t)(1 + r)^{-t}}^{\alpha} + \overbrace{\sum_{t=J+1}^{T} (M_t^s - W_t^s)(1 + r)^{-t}}^{\beta} \geq$$

$$\overbrace{\sum_{t=1}^{J} C_t(1 + r)^{-t} + R}^{\gamma}$$

where

M_t = the marginal value product in the tth period (with the superscript "s" representing the presence of the desired skills),

Figure 7–2 *Managerial Decision Process: Training for a New Employee*

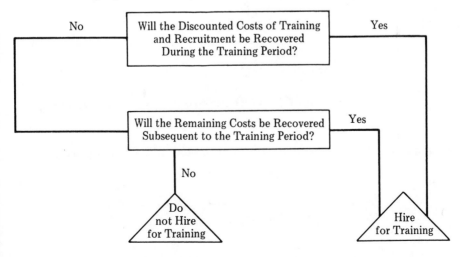

C_t = the firm's cost in the tth period = $(M'_t + \Delta M'_t - M_t - \Delta M_t) + K$ = the opportunity cost of potential output plus direct training costs (K),

W_t = wage (or compensation) payments in the tth period,

R = recruitment costs,

r = an appropriate discount rate,

J = the length of training period,

T = the tenure of the employee, and given that $\Delta M_t = f(C_t)$ where $f' > 0$, i.e., skills are produced at increasing costs.

All these values are those expected by the employer at the outset of the hiring-training period (at t_o).

For the newly hired employee to be trained "at company expense," the wedge between M and W (i.e., α and β) must be sufficient to cover both recruitment and training costs (γ). The implications for monopsony are obvious. If no monopsony exists and if the training is not specific to the firm, $M^s_t = W^s_t$. Under these conditions, any firm-borne training and recruitment costs will be reimbursed by the employee during the training period $(\alpha \geq \gamma)$. The payment of these costs may come about via a lower training rate, $W_1 \ldots W_j$, via payment of C_t or R by the employee, or via some combination of the two. This particular variant of the decision rule may be appropriately labeled *apprenticeship*, considered in less precise terms in Chapter 4.

Decision Rule for Internal Promotion and Training versus the Hiring of an Already Skilled Outsider

The decision rule in this instance is as follows:

(7–5) $(Y - \phi)_I \geq (Y - \phi)_O$
          given that $(Y - \phi)_I \geq O$

and given that I and O designate insider and outsider, respectively.

More specifically, the insider will be promoted and trained only if

(7–6)

$$\overbrace{\sum_{t=1}^{J} (M_t + \Delta M_t - W_t)_I (1 + r)^{-t}}^{\alpha} + \overbrace{\sum_{t=J+1}^{T_I} (M^s_t - W^s_t)_I (1 + r)^{-t} -}^{\beta}$$

$$\overbrace{\sum_{t=1}^{J} (M_t^s - W_t^s)_0(1+r)^{-t}}^{\gamma} \quad - \overbrace{\sum_{t=J+1}^{T_O} (M_t^s - W_t^s)_0(1+r)^{-t}}^{\partial} \geq$$

$$\overbrace{\sum_{t=1}^{J} C_t(1+r)^{-t} - (R_o - R)}^{\ell}.$$

R now represents the cost of hiring a replacement for the insider in his original position. If tenure expectations are equal $(T_l = T_O)$, if skills are general (as they presumably are in this case),[5] and if labor markets are competitive, β, γ, and ∂ are each equal to O since marginal value product is equal to the respective Ws. Equation (7–6) then becomes

(7–7) $$\sum_{t=1}^{J} (M_t + \Delta M_t - W_t)_l(1+r)^{-t} \geq \sum_{t=1}^{J} C_t(1+r)^{-t} - (R_o - R)$$

We have, therefore, a result similar to that above. A rational firm will institute an internally financed training and promotion program in general skills only if the differential in recruitment-search costs and/or earnings relative to productivity during the training period exceeds the discounted value of the training costs.

Because recruitment-search costs for skilled workers can often be expected to be greater than for less skilled workers, we would generally expect $(R_o - R)$ to be positive. Positive values of $(R_o - R)$, of course, induce internal promotion and training, *ceteris paribus*. Where existing institutions create lower R_o's relative to R, even to the point where $(R_o - R) < O$, entry ports could be open even at relatively high skill levels.

This model articulates well with the operations of the unionized construction industry. Under the usual hiring hall arrangements, the skills of journeymen are general and are guaranteed by the union. Thus, R_o is quite low and $(R_o - R)$ may be negative. Internal training and promotion can be expected to occur *only* if younger or inexperienced employees are willing to self-finance skill acquisition *during* the training period. If our model fits that industry, we should observe multiple entry ports and the virtual absence of an internal market. This is indeed what we find in much of the construction industry. Moreover, we find standardized apprenticeship arrangements in some, but not all, locals.

Looking even more closely at the unionized construction industry and other industries with hiring halls (e.g., longshoring and entertaining), it seems likely that the hiring hall had its origin in the irregular employment patterns of those industries and in the high R_o's which probably existed in the absence of hiring halls. The alternatives for management to use of the hiring hall are first, to maintain a steady work force, paying $W_t > M_t$ during the "off season" to avoid the recurrent R_o's,[6] or second, to find some other cheap screening and recruiting device.

The U.S. advertising industry at the professional level also appears to fit this model. Account executive skills are not firm-specific, however unique the executives may be in creativity. Given the ready availability of information about various account executives, R_o may be close to or even less than R. Moreover, the industry's labor market is highly competitive. It is not surprising, therefore, that firms appear to have very limited internal markets at these professional levels and that considerable lateral movement exists between firms.

Despite the cases noted above, internal training may exist in some firms where that training appears to include general skills. The explanation for this may lie in the fact (mentioned in Chapter 4) that it is difficult to provide specific training without also raising general skills. Under such conditions,

$$(7\text{--}8) \qquad \sum_{t=J+1}^{T_I} (M^s - W^s)_I (1 + r)^{-t} > O$$

Thus, the insider will be trained and preferred to any already trained "apparently equivalent" outsider provided that

$$(7\text{--}9) \qquad \sum_{t=1}^{J} (M_t + \Delta M_t - W_t)_I (1 + r)^{-t} + \sum_{t=J+1}^{T_I} (M_t^s - W_t^s)_I (1 + r)^{-t} \geq$$

$$\sum_{t=1}^{J} C(1 + r)^{-t} - (R_o - R)$$

The reader will find it useful to draw for himself the appropriate managerial decision diagrams—similar to Fig. 7–2—for Eqs. (7–6), (7–7), and (7–9).

Decision Rule for Promotion and Specific Skill Training of Insiders versus Recruitment and Specific Skill Training of Outsiders

By a simple elaboration of the analysis developed above, a decision rule for firm specific training can be established. Figure 7–3 shows the general managerial decision process. In a manner similar to that given in Eqs. (7–4) and (7–5) above, the important factors influencing the decision are developed in the equation:

$$(7\text{--}10) \qquad \sum_{t=1}^{J_1} (M_t + \Delta M_t - W_t)_1 (1 + r)^{-t} + \sum_{t=J_1+1}^{T_1} (M_t^s - W_t^s)_1 (1 + r)^{-t} -$$

$$\sum_{t=1}^{J_2} (M_t + \Delta M_t - W_t)_2(1+r)^{-t} - \sum_{t=J_2+1}^{T_2} (M_t^s - W_t^s)_2(1+r)^{-t} \geq$$

$$\sum_{t=1}^{J_1} C_{t1}(1+r)^{-t} - \sum_{t=1}^{J_2} C_{t2}(1+r)^{-t} - (R_2 - R)$$

where the insider is represented by "1" and the outsider by "2." One or the other will be afforded specific training, usually accompanied by subsequent promotion or transfer. The insider will get "the nod" from management if Eq. (7–10) holds. If not, the outsider will be preferred, provided, of course, that $(Y)_2 \geq (\phi)_2$. For either party, the acquisition of firm-specific skills creates monopsony power (and a periodic rent for the employer) during the periods $(T_1 - J_1)$ or $(T_2 - J_2)$, respectively. Now if the tenure, training time, and training costs of the two candidates are equal $(T_1 = T_2, J_1 = J_2, C_{t1} = C_{t2})$ and if competitive wages are paid during the training period (J), the insider will be preferred for training if $R_2 > R$, provided, of course, that the employer expects to earn at least "r" from training the insider. Where the outsider is preferred, an

Figure 7–3 *Managerial Decision Process: Training an Insider or an Outsider in Firm Specific Skills*

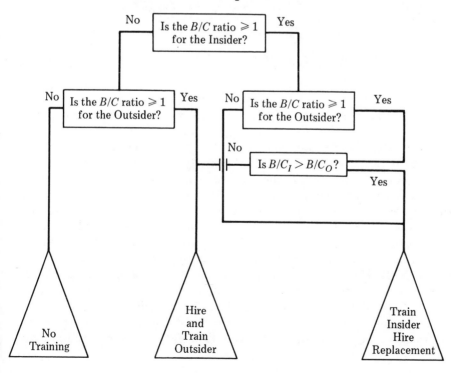

entry port can be expected at that job level. Note that the comparison may be between a specific (known) insider (or insiders) and an expected value for outsiders.

Insiders will have decided advantages over outsiders if their expected tenure is longer $[E(T_1 > T_2)]$ and if their expected training time is shorter $[E(J_1 < J_2)]$, *ceteris paribus*. It seems reasonable to surmise that these considerations account for the care taken by firms to select for training-promotion employees committed to or loyal to the firm. Even loyal employees, however, may be "passed over" by a rational employer if they are too advanced in age or have learning disabilities. Generally speaking, one would expect management to select from among both outsiders and insiders, *ceteris paribus*, on the basis of the largest $(T - J)_i$'s, $i = 1s, 2s$.

Despite the obvious advantages of insiders with lower recruitment-search costs and longer tenure expectations, outsiders can compensate and thereby compete successfully in a number of ways. First, as suggested above, the larger $(T - J)_2$ is relative to $(T - J)_1$, the more management will prefer the outsider, *ceteris paribus*. Thus, we should observe some older insiders being "passed over" for younger outsiders and, more likely, younger insiders. Moreover, the same phenomenon should exist, our model suggests, if $C_2 < C_1$, $J_2 < J_1$, and/or more generally if the following equation holds:

$$(7\text{--}11) \qquad \sum_{t=1}^{J_2} \{(M' + \Delta M' - M - \Delta M)_2 + K_2\}(1 + r)^{-t} < \sum_{t=1}^{J_1} \{(M' + \Delta M' - M - \Delta M)_1 + K_1\}(1 + r)^{-t}$$

Wherever external training or work experience is more complementary to firm-specific training than prior internal training or work experience, one would expect the firm to prefer the outsider. Such instances may (and probably do) include job categories and training programs that require high levels of general skills. Usually acquired outside the firm, those general skills would complement the specific training, lowering both direct and indirect training costs. Management trainees and accountants in a large, specialized firm provide examples of this phenomenon. Moreover, if the external training or experience is easily (cheaply) ascertained, the possession of such training may serve to lower R_2 relative to R. That "credentials effect" also strengthens the competitive position of "accredited" outsiders relative to their "nonaccredited" competitors.

In general, then, the probability of an entry port for each job category "*j*" should depend upon the cost-benefit tradeoffs for outsiders versus those for insiders. Specifically, the probability of an entry port, $p(EP)_j$, is expressed in the following equation (the signs expected are indicated above the equation):

$$(7\text{-}12) \qquad p(EP)_j = p\left(\overset{+}{\dfrac{C_1}{C_2}}\left[\text{or }\dfrac{K_1}{K_2}\right], \quad \overset{-}{\dfrac{T_1}{T_2}}, \overset{+}{\dfrac{J_1}{J_2}}, \overset{-}{\dfrac{R_2}{R}}\right)$$

Moreover, as has been suggested in the literature of labor economics, $(R_2 - R)$ may change systematically over the course of the business cycle as the sellers (or buyers) bear more or less of the search costs. Thus, it follows from the analysis above that internal labor market behavior can be expected to be influenced by changes in external markets, but the question of "how much?" still remains unanswered.

The outcome of the specific skills bargain is not easy to predict for either management or employees and for insiders or previous outsiders. The development of specific skills creates a bilateral monopoly in which either side can impose costs on the other side by severing their employment relationship. Moreover, the threat point (the point at which either side can earn as much outside as inside the employment "marriage") changes as relative wages change across the cycle and as relative productivities change. Thus, accurate predictions of future Ms and Ws are probably impossible. We know that at the outset of specific training, it pays both the employer and the employee to strike what each considers to be a long-term bargain, sharing both the costs and the returns from firm-specific training. Moreover, as Oi noted in his seminal article on quasi-fixities,[7] the economic rent $(M - W)$ cushions the impact of the business cycle on workers with firm-specific skills. Layoffs of such workers will not occur or will occur less frequently (or severely) than will layoffs of workers without firm-specific skills. The incidence of unemployment, therefore, is connected not with skill itself, but with skill specificity. Unemployment will be discussed further in Chapter 12. It is consistent with this analysis that the long employment tenures expected, for example, in leading Japanese firms and the concept of the Japanese firm as a type of extended family are particularly conducive to firm-financed training of workers, both in specific and in general skills.

Assessment of the Neoclassical Approach to Internal Labor Markets

Despite the fact that the neoclassical decision-making model articulates well with casual observations of various labor markets, many of these phenomena can be explained by institutional factors. Alternatively, institutional factors can supplement and/or interact with the economic factors described. For example, the analysis above considered only the opportunity set and motivations of employers and individual employees, but the collective desires of employees for a wage-promotion-training structure that is not "arbitrary" may lead to constraints on individual decision making. Certainly, the establishment of an agreed upon framework for such decisions is one important function of a union or even for employees' associations which do not formally engage in collective bargaining. Such efforts are usually justified not by profit or rate of return maximization, but by an appeal to "fairness" or "equity." Many nonunionized as well as unionized enterprises have well-developed wage structures involving systems of job classifications and matrices of pay grades and pay steps within grades. Despite the origin of these structures (many are based initially on labor market surveys), the existing wage differentials acquire over time an aura of respectability or fairness and are thus resistant to change—even if external labor market conditions change the market pattern of relative wage rates or if internal costs (e.g., training costs) change.

At the present stage of research into internal markets, it is simply not possible to specify the approximate (or average) extent to which internal markets reflect institutional compared with external market influences. For example, recent empirical studies in the United States indicate that job tenure is one of the more important factors in determining earnings levels.[8] The linkage of wage rates to tenure may reflect the workings of an internal investment process such as that envisioned in a neoclassical model (O-J-T). Alternatively, it may represent the workings of a system of job rights developed over time, buttressed by feelings of equity ("seniority *should* govern in promotions") and institutionalized in job classification or promotion systems. Clearly, in short periods of time and/or in strongly unionized enterprises, institutional structures might sharply limit or channel the effects of changing economic factors. Modern neoclassical economists suggest, however, that the institutions and the institutional forms themselves may be developed in response to economic opportunities and pressures. The neoclassical theory of institutional change, however, is only in an embryonic stage.

Internal Labor Markets and Market Segmentation

The decision rule approach employed in this chapter to examine internal markets may also be used to examine other forms of labor market segmentation—e.g., dual labor markets. A brief example will suffice.

Consider a firm seeking to employ someone from the external market to fill a job "with a future," say for rung one on a "tall" promotion ladder. Note that this decision already involves the decision not to transfer internally (i.e., to have an entry port). The employer must know how to choose from among various job applicants, and all of the search considerations discussed in Chapter 6 are relevant. Chief among these is the expectation that information about the skills of particular applicants will be limited and costly to obtain. If, in addition, race, sex, national origin, ability to speak a particular language, etc., are believed by the employer to be low-cost proxies for skill, then the probability of the applicants obtaining a "good job," p(GJ), will depend upon the group to which he or she belongs, given downward rigid wages. Thus, we have the equation:

$$(7\text{–}13) \qquad p(GJ)_B = p\left(\overset{+}{\frac{C_W}{C_B}}\left[\text{or}\ \frac{K_W}{K_B}\right],\ \overset{-}{\frac{T_W}{T_B}},\ \overset{+}{\frac{J_W}{J_B}},\ \overset{+}{\frac{R_W}{R_B}}\right)$$

where "W" and "B" represent (say) easily identified racial characteristics. The expected signs are indicated above the equation. Note that access to "poor jobs" may not include the human capital-related determinants, C and J, and T may also be an unimportant factor for such jobs. If general skills are complementary with firm-specific training and if there have been or are systematic differences by race in access to general skill training (e.g., racial segregation, unequal schools), segmented markets by race will tend to emerge *without* labor market discrimination (also see Chapter 9).

A Policy Note

Quite obviously, the presence of segmented markets (internal, dual, or whatever) raises important policy questions from the standpoints both of equity and of efficiency. Judged against the ethical standards common to many individuals around the world, labor market segmentation implies unequal opportunities for personal development and advancement, an indefensible situation. Many if not most people would argue that such inequalities should be removed. In addition, segmentation can imply inefficiencies in job placement such that the total output and income of a society could be greater under alternative arrangements. Yet, it is usually very difficult to achieve political agreement on labor market policies related to these issues.

Policy disagreements often do not appear to be based on differences in objectives or in visions of an ethical society or an efficient economy. Disagreements hinge in large part upon how segmented markets are understood and "explained." If, for example, segmentation is seen as resulting largely (or solely) from unequal access to maximum skill development (often in public institutions) with the effects being exacerbated by the economies of labor market search, the suggested "solutions" often will be to equalize access to human capital and to develop lower cost methods of communicating information about individual competencies. If segmentation is seen as largely an institutionally determined phenomenon, a range of possible public programs may be suggested—special training programs, quotas, affirmative action programs, other legislative changes in trade union and employer practices, etc. Many of these programs involve changing "the rules of the workplace" to conform with socially specified (rather than locally specified) norms. If, as some of the more radical economists suggest, the practice of segmentation is another phase in the continuing class struggle between employers and workers (a divide-and-conquer tactic), none of the approaches suggested by neoclassical or (neo)institutionalist thinking will resolve the problem.

Obviously, the policy debates on this topic in the United States and around the world are complicated by our collective inability to answer more precisely the question raised above: To what degree is the existence of the internal market itself determined by external economic forces and to what degree is the internal market institutionally determined? To date, we also have been unable to give a satisfactorily complete answer to the analogous question: To what degree are segmented markets, in general, determined by market forces such as recruitment-search costs, training costs, etc., and to what degree is segmentation a product of institutional influences and constraints that are not amenable to benefit/cost considerations?

Obviously, more knowledge in this area of inquiry would help in developing "appropriate" public policy. As Chapters 6 and 7 indicate, some understanding is now available, but identification and interpretation problems are considerable. Consequently, the guidance afforded to policy makers by academicians is, although increasing, quite limited.

Notes to Chapter 7

1. Peter B. Doeringer and Michael J. Piore, *Internal Labor Markets and Manpower Analysis* (Lexington, Mass.: D. C. Heath & Co., 1971), p. 2.

2. Doeringer and Piore, *Internal Labor Markets*, p. 2. That work also cites two intellectual precursors: Arthur M. Ross, "Do We Have A New Industrial Feudalism," *American Economic Review* 48, no. 5 (December 1958): 914–15, and Frederick Meyers, *Ownership of Jobs: A Comparative Study,* Institute of Industrial Relations Monograph Series (Los Angeles: University of California Press, 1964).

3. See Glen Cain, "The Challenge of Segmented Market Theories to Orthodox Theory," *Journal of Economic Literature* 14, no. 4 (December 1976): 1215–57, for a more complete description of the relative emphasis of different researchers employing the institutionalist and the Marxist approaches.

4. Walter Y. Oi, "Labor as a Quasi-fixed Factor," *Journal of Political Economy* 70, no. 6 (December 1962): 538–55; Gary Becker, *Human Capital: A Theoreti-

cal and Empirical Analysis with Special Reference to Education (New York: Columbia University Press, 1964); and Jacob Mincer, "On-the-Job Training: Costs, Returns and Some Implications," *Journal of Political Economy* 70, no. 6, supplement (October 1962): 50–79. Alvin M. Cruze in "Determinants of Curriculum Offerings in the North Carolina Community College System." (Ph.D. dissertation, North Carolina State University, 1972) applied these ideas to the demand for curricular offerings. A modification of his approach forms the basis for the model of entry ports and job ladders presented below.

5. This case can be modified to represent a current outsider who was formerly employed and trained in the firm-specific skills of that establishment or plant. The reader should assess the implications of that case.

6. In some agricultural areas of the United States experiencing seasonal employment patterns, public welfare payments and certain public perquisites may act to maintain the work force in the geographic area during the off-season. Such arrangements, of course, transfer the costs which otherwise would be borne by private employers to the general taxpayers. The arrangements also maintain lower "on-season" wages than would have been the case in the absence of such public welfare or "charity."

7. Oi, "Labor as a Quasi-fixed Factor."

8. For examples of tenure effects on earnings, see David N. Hyman and Robert M. Fearn, "The Influence of City Size on Labor Incomes," *The Quarterly Journal of Economics and Business* 18, no. 1 (Spring 1978): 63–73, and Howard Birnbaum, "Career Origins, On-the-Job Training and Earnings," *Southern Economic Journal* 42, no. 4 (April 1976): 587–99.

8 | The Demand for Human Capital

The beginning is the most important part of the work. . . . Let early education be a sort of amusement; you will then be better able to find out the natural bent. Plato, *The Republic, Book I*

This chapter concentrates on the question: How do individuals decide on the amount and type of schooling or training they wish to acquire? Note that this demand for a *stock of skills* is not the equivalent of the demand for labor time considered in Chapter 5. First, the labor time desired is a *flow*—a schedule of time desired by employers or prospective employers with respect to various wage rates (or prices per unit of time). Second, labor demand presupposes some set or sets of skills. Third, labor demand is derived from production functions and market conditions. In contrast, the demand for schooling or training is the desire to enter and/or undergo a process through which skills are acquired (more properly, "developed"). The question is, "Whence do these desires originate?"

Certainly, one can undergo schooling or training in order to achieve a *flow of current utility or satisfaction.* Learning to paint, reading Shakespeare, and/or examining the nuances of nuclear physics may be immediately rewarding and very "soul-satisfying." In such cases, the demand for training or schooling per unit time is analytically equivalent to the demand for any other good. Hence, the expression "the demand for schooling *on consumption account.*" Generally, however, schooling or training is sought not for current consumption, but to acquire skills from which *subsequently* may flow higher levels of productivity, income, or utility. This is the "investment demand" which sets schooling and training apart from other purchased "commodities." Because schooling and training are generally undertaken in the expectation of future returns, the way in which those expectations are formed becomes an important focus of analysis.

We have already alluded to investment demand in Chapter 4 while developing benefit/cost and rate of return analysis. Another part of the question—that related to O-J-T and firm-specific skills—was considered in Chapters 6 and 7. Indeed, we are led by those discussions to the expectation that the higher the internal rate of return on the marginal increment of investment, the more human capital acquisition—schooling, training, etc.—is desired. Moreover, those analyses lead us to expect, in the absence of capital constraints and other barriers, that the rate of human capital acquisition will be sensitive to changes in costs (or expected costs) and in expected future benefits. Even where constraints exist (provided that they are not omnipotent), acquisition should still be positively related to the expected rate of return, although response rates could be small.

The "practical" question then becomes: How do individuals assess or estimate the costs of and particularly the returns to such long-term investment decisions, given all the informational inadequacies and market structures discussed above? Current costs of schooling or training should be relatively easy to estimate. Estimation of future benefits is more difficult, however, if only because relative compensation levels can be expected to change over time (with changes in the demand for factor inputs, commodities, etc.). Thus, any such estimate is subject to some, even considerable, error. Imagine, for example, the possible errors in estimated returns to training in the making of buggy whips shortly before the advent of the automobile.

These considerations suggest the possibility of capital gains and losses in the human capital investment process similar to those experienced by investors in physical capital. Rates of return actually experienced by the investor may turn out to be greater than or less than market rates. Alternatively and more precisely stated, the market value of the acquired human capital (if there were a *stock* market for those skills) would be greater or less than the cost of acquiring the skills. It follows that with the freedom to choose careers and occupations comes the risk of capital losses (and the possibility of capital gains) on the investment in the requisite training programs.[1]

Such risks are fewer or absent in traditional and totalitarian societies, where career training decisions are not often within the control of the individual or his family. Capital constraints and the strong forces of social opprobrium in traditional societies serve to maintain schooling and occupational distributions intergenerationally. Under such circumstances, youths may even be chided for seeking to "rise above their station." In totalitarian or slave societies, schooling and occupational choices are largely or entirely the prerogative of the state (or, in decentralized slave societies, of the owner). Our inquiry, therefore, is restricted to societies and economies that allow a degree of individual freedom in career development.

Lifetime Income Maximization

Many economists see the choice of schooling, curricula, and/or occupations within the context of lifetime income maximization. Given an expected rental rate per unit of human capital, each individual is expected to divide his available time (in each time period) between earning, learning, and leisure so as to maximize lifetime income (or wealth). Because foregone income is a function of previous learning and because skills acquired early in life can be expected to "bear fruit" over an entire lifetime, these life cycle theorists expect leisure, household activities, and especially schooling to predominate early in life. As learning and (therefore) potential earning power increases, the opportunity cost of further learning increases. Moreover, given a finite lifespan, the expected present value of future returns diminishes as an individual ages. This simple scenario suggests that there is a point in each life cycle at which specialization in learning and household activities is no longer optimal. Moreover, that point varies among individuals as age, former human capital acquisition, and abilities (among other characteristics) vary. Earnings profiles reflect these "state variables" as well as various human capital decisions. Rather elegant "optimal control" formulations have been developed to model these life cycle patterns and to generate testable hypotheses about the determinants of schooling and worklife patterns, including optimal retirement ages.[2] See Fig. 8–1 for a graphic representation of these approaches as they are applied to schooling and the end of schooling specialization (t^*). In a simple model of learning, earning and leisure, t_0^* and t_1^*, represent two possible points at which specialization in household activities (leisure?) and the production of human capital

Figure 8–1 *Characteristic Optimal Paths of Human Capital Accumulation*

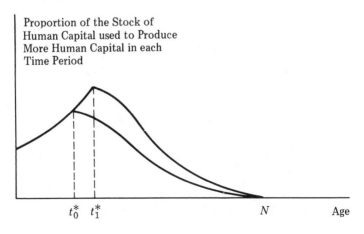

Proportion of the Stock of
Human Capital used to Produce
More Human Capital in each
Time Period

t_0^* t_1^* N Age

(schooling) ends. The differences in t^*'s result from some difference in the "state variables"; e.g., native ability, nonwage income and the like. The proportion of the stock used to produce more human capital may also be expected to differ from person to person.

In general, life cycle approaches presuppose that each individual selects from among the many alternative income paths open to him the particular path that maximizes the present value of expected income (or, more broadly, expected utility). Usually, the individual is assumed to face a given rental rate per unit of human capital which does not or is not expected to vary over time. Moreover, life cycle models characteristically involve only "one type" of human capital.

The "unrealism" of these approaches has given pause to some scholars and certainly would raise doubts concerning the "usefulness" of the models among laypersons. In considering this objection, however, one must remember that all scientific inquiry involves simplification—that is, all scientific models are "unrealistic" in some sense. As Albert Einstein is purported to have said:[3] "Everything should be made as simple as possible, but not simpler." In science, the "proof of the pudding" is in the predicting. Life cycle models, however "unrealistic," have been useful in predicting the characteristics of school enrollment, labor force entry, and the general shape of earnings streams through time.[4]

Because life cycle models usually assume only one type of human capital and one rental rate, and because the future is often assumed to be known, the questions to which the model have been applied have been limited. The assumption of a known future is particularly troublesome. Other investigations of choice in these areas, however, have introduced special assumptions concerning the ways in which future income streams are estimated. Two such models are discussed below: one is based on peer patterns and one on beginning salaries.

Occupational/Schooling Choices and Peer Patterns

Several researchers have suggested that young people, in particular, form expectations concerning future labor force, earnings, and unemployment patterns from the experiences of their older "peers."[5] Casual empiricism suggests that there may be considerable mileage in this formulation. As the poet Longfellow wrote:

> *Lives of great men all remind us*
> *We can make our lives sublime,*

> *And, departing, leave behind us*
> *Footprints on the sands of time.*[6]

Indeed, the literature on "role models," "idols," and so on is massive. It is with peer patterns in mind, for example, that many socially conscious people in the United States advertise and otherwise popularize black role models in order to stimulate maximum upward mobility among socially and educationally deprived black youngsters. Although casual evidence of the efficacy of such approaches is readily available,[7] precise formulations giving rise to testable hypotheses are difficult to find.

A study by Solomon Polachek[8] attempts to apply the peer pattern approach to occupational choices among females. He argues that female (as opposed to male) occupational choice should reflect the "expected" hiatus in labor force participation experienced by many, indeed most, married women during the early childrearing years (see Chapter 3). If in making schooling and occupational choices, young women accept the observed labor force participation patterns of older females as indicating the likely pattern for themselves, they can be expected to select occupations with the following characteristics:

1. little (expected) depreciation or obsolescence in skills over time,
2. high complementarities between market skills and household skills, and
3. little or no O-J-T.

Thus, one would interpret enrollment in preparatory curricula for "typical female jobs" (typists, key punchers, secretaries, nutritionists, home economists, nurses, teachers, etc.) as reflecting conscious and utility-maximizing choices. This model and similar ones based on peer patterns explain part of the observed difference in enrollment and occupational patterns by sex. If taken literally, however, models based on "peer patterns" would imply little or no change over time in curricular and occupational distributions. We know from recent observations, however, that such changes are occurring—sometimes at very rapid rates—all over the world. Thus, although such an approach helps us to understand some of the difference between male and female curricular and occupational choices, it does not articulate well with recent changes in both labor force participation and female "penetration" into nontraditional curricula and occupations. In a word, peer pattern studies may help us to understand what has been—no mean accomplishment—but not to anticipate what will be. The approach below, while not concentrating on the dimensions of choice by sex, does point toward future changes as distinct from past patterns of development.

Schooling/Occupational Choice and Relative Salaries

This approach, pioneered by Richard B. Freeman,[9] begins with the assumption that individuals—particularly young people—cannot and therefore do not estimate lifetime earning streams in the manner assumed by the life cycle or rate-of-return models. Nor are peer patterns assumed to be particularly relevant to schooling and career choices.

A Freeman-type approach assumes that schooling and curricular choices are dependent upon the relative salary structure observed by the student or prospective student at or around the time in which he is making his curricular and career decisions. Alternatively stated, this approach assumes that current salary levels are used as proxies (or cheap screening devices) for unavailable (and unattainable) future income streams or estimated rates of return. Where beginning salaries of "schooled" occupations relative to those of "unschooled" occupations are sizable and/or growing, a Freeman-type analysis predicts that more young people will opt for continuing their schooling, *ceteris paribus.* That conclusion is not surprising. Note, however, that the decisions are not lifetime- or peer-related. Indeed, the "shortsightedness" of the assumed decision-making process gives rise to several implications not present in the lifetime or peer models. In particular, the responsiveness of curricular demand for well-paying occupations implies, *ceteris paribus,* that relative salaries will fall when the cohort of trainees "hit the market" after completion of their training. The implied lag structure can give rise under certain "realistic" circumstances to cycles of "over- and undersupply" in particular occupations.

Figure 8–2 traces out such a scenario, one closely approximated by some of Freeman's empirical work. For example, assume an initial equilibrium in the market for college graduates (at ZC) such that the earnings differential between college graduates and high school graduates $[(Z - P)/P]$ is just sufficient to maintain the existing pattern of labor supply. Thus, the pecuniary marginal rate of return to schooling is just enough to maintain relative flows into the respective training programs and occupations. Now, assume an increase in the demand for persons with college training. The initial short-run effect will be to raise Z to Z'. If this increase is used by prospective college enrollees as a cheap screening device for the (unavailable) rate of return or change in the rate of return, one would expect *enrollment* in the demand-related curricula to respond positively. Given a long training period (say, 3–6 years) for such occupations, skill margins will fall only after the larger number of graduates pour into the labor market and wages may fall with a lag. Where rates are downward rigid or sticky, short-term unemployment will emerge. Thus, unemployment will grow, and/or entry wages and skill margins will fall. The supply adjustment eventually alters

Figure 8–2 *Response to Increased Demand for Skills Acquired by Schooling: A Cobweb Scenario*

(I)

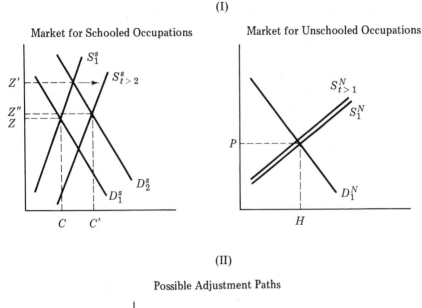

Market for Schooled Occupations   Market for Unschooled Occupations

(II)

Possible Adjustment Paths

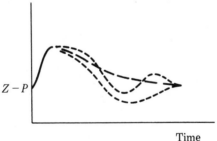

Time

relative wage levels, discouraging entry into the training programs or curricula. Figure 8–2, II shows various possible adjustment paths. Further exogenous shifts in demand can, of course, alter or complicate the adjustment paths.

These demand-oriented models fit well the enrollment patterns observed during a number of recent periods of occupational shortages and gluts in the United States. Among these was the shortage of engineers and physicists after Sputnik I during the 1960s and the subsequent glut. A similar shortage-and-glut situation for zoologists and other specialists in environmental studies was experienced in the early 1970s. Note that one can trace both these patterns to an exogenous policy change in federal expenditure patterns and requirements.

It is not clear, however, whether the apparent fall in the rate of return to *all* college training in the 1960s and early 1970s can be explained by a similar model. In his book, *The Overeducated American,* Freeman argues this case, but the jury is still out on the issue. In particular, an alternative and more complex explanation of the "overeducated" phenomenon has been advanced by James Smith and Finis Welch.[10] Simply stated, they argue that the reduction in the rate of return (and beginning salaries) for college graduates is traceable both to a supply shift in the college occupations (see Fig. 8–3) and to a decline in the relative quality of education imparted during the "baby boom" college years of the 1960s. In Fig. 8–3, demand curves are shifted out equally for both occupations. The narrowing of the wage differential comes from the relative population shift into college-trained occupations.

Note that for different occupations, either the Freeman or the Smith-Welch scenario could be the correct one. Both analyses agree that the ratio of beginning salaries can play an important, if not crucial, role in schooling and training decisions.

Figure 8–3 *A Supply-related Reduction in Rates of Return to Schooling**

Market for Schooled Occupations   Market for Unschooled Occupations

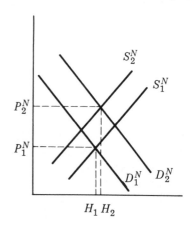

*Note also that a rapid growth in the student-instructor ratio, *ceteris paribus,* implies a reduction in the "addition" to marginal product obtained through education; so that educational attainment is systematically overstated by conventional measures; i.e., graduates, years of school completed, etc.

Practical Lessons for Career Choosers, Guidance Counselors, and Others

We argued above that career choice involves a risk of capital loss, one not usually deductible from income or other taxes. Moreover, it follows that the more narrowly trained the individual, the greater the risk of a capital loss in rapidly changing modern economies. Mean (or average) occupational salaries, *ceteris paribus*, will contain compensating differentials for such risks if these risks are or can be foreseen. For example, structural iron workers engaged in building highrises are paid relatively more than those employed at ground level. There are also occupations in which the mean earnings levels reflect a large possibility of a small income, but a very small possibility of an extremely large income flow—e.g., acting, professional sports, and so forth.

Where the risks are unpredictable, however, occupational earnings patterns will not normally reflect the risks of the investment. That is the position in which American engineers and zoologists found themselves during the "gluts" in their respective occupations.

The existence of both expected and unexpected risks suggests the following three practical rules for young (or old) persons in their career training choices:

1. Be cognizant of the built-in risks in each career choice.
2. Be aware of the linkages between the various occupations (common skill sets) in order to minimize any seen or unforeseen losses. Such an awareness often comes from a broadly based liberal arts or general education, which can become a tool for reducing potential capital losses as well as providing some consumption benefits.
3. Choose occupations whose nonpecuniary aspects are personally pleasing. Indeed, the best of all (labor market) worlds is to be paid well for something one would do, if it became necessary, for much less. Choosing an occupation that "turns you on" can yield a considerable nontaxable rent in personal satisfaction, even if relative salaries change to one's pecuniary detriment.

Note that the predictive models developed above explain the choices of individuals *on the margin* in their schooling and career choices. Those *intramarginal* individuals who receive considerable personal satisfaction from their work and their training can be affected, but not "destroyed," by even sizable changes in relative compensational levels. As Adam Smith asserted in 1776, ". . . it is the whole of the advantages and disadvantages of various employments of labour . . ." that is of importance in labor market and career choice.

Notes to Chapter 8

1. In some nations (e.g., the United States), gains and losses on physical (nonhuman) capital are afforded special income tax treatments. This preferential treatment does not usually extend to gains and losses on human capital.

2. Thomas Johnson, "Time in School: The Case of the Prudent Patron," *American Economic Review* 68, no. 5 (December 1978): 862–72; James Heckman, "A Life Cycle Model of Earnings, Learning and Consumption," *Journal of Political Economy* 84, no. 4, pt. 2 (August 1976): 511–44; William Haley, "Human Capital: The Choice between Investment and Income," *American Economic Review* 63, no. 5 (December 1973): 929–44; Yoram Ben-Porath, "The Production of Human Capital and the Life Cycle of Earnings," *Journal of Political Economy* 75, no. 4 (July/August 1967): 352–65.

3. An extensive search of "famous quotations" failed to unearth the precise source of this quotation. Even if Albert Einstein were not the author, he would have endorsed the sentiment because it represents the essence of scientific investigation.

4. T. D. Wallace and L. A. Ihnen, "Full-time Schooling in Life Cycle Models of Human Capital Accumulation," *Journal of Political Economy* 83, no. 1 (February 1975): 137–55; William J. Haley, "Estimation of the Earnings Profile from Optimal Human Capital Accumulation," *Econometrica* 44, no. 6 (November 1976): 1223–38.

5. Juanita M. Kreps, *Sex in the Marketplace: American Women at Work* (Baltimore: Johns Hopkins University Press, 1971); Juanita M. Kreps and Robert Clark, *Sex, Age and Work* (Baltimore: Johns Hopkins University Press, 1975).

6. Henry Wadsworth Longfellow, *The Poetical Works of Henry Wadsworth Longfellow* (The Psalm of Life) (Boston: Houghton Mifflin Co., 1882), p. 13.

7. During the early period of public school integration in the state of Virginia, the author participated in a tutorial program for the first group of black youngsters to be integrated into the "white" school system. For a while, the tutorial program languished. A few visits from highly successful black professionals, however, had a strong positive effect on student interest in the tutorial program and a discernible influence on student performance in their new schools.

8. Solomon Polachek, "Differences in Expected Post-Schooling Investment as Determinants of Market Wage Differentials," *International Economic Review* 16, no. 2 (June 1975): 451–80. See also Jacob Mincer and Solomon Polachek, "Family Investments in Human Capital: Earnings of Women," *Journal of Political Economy* 82, no. 2, pt. 2 (March/April 1954): S76–S108 for estimates of the influence of labor force intermittence on female earnings.

9. Richard Freeman, "Overinvesting in College Training," *Journal of Human Resources* 10, no. 3 (Summer 1975): 297–311; "The Decline in the Economic Rewards to College Education," *Review of Economics and Statistics* 59, no. 1 (February 1977): 18–29; "A Cobweb Model of the Supply and Starting Salary of New Engineers," *Industrial and Labor Relations Review* 29, no. 2 (January 1976): 236–48; *The Overeducated American* (New York: Academic Press, 1976).

10. James P. Smith and Finis Welch, *The Overeducated American: A Review Article,* monograph P-6253 (Santa Monica, Calif.: The Rand Corporation, November 1978).

9 Discrimination in Employment, Earnings, and Human Capital

The Lord spoke to Moses and said, Speak to the Israelites in these words: When a man makes a special vow to the Lord which requires your valuation of living persons, a male between twenty and sixty years old shall be valued at fifty silver shekels, that is shekels by the sacred standard. If it is a female, she shall be valued at thirty shekels.
Leviticus XXVII, 1–5

On the sixth day, the Empress [Elizabeth of Russia] had the child [Anne] baptized and brought me an order from the Cabinet for the sum of sixty thousand rubles. (A considerable discount from the 100,000 awarded her for the birth of Paul.) She sent the same amount to the Grand Duke, which further increased his satisfaction.
Catherine the Great[1]

Women in this country still make fifty-seven cents for every dollar men make, and 80 percent of us are in low-paying jobs.
Marlo Thomas, 1979[2]

The quotations above could suggest that females are paid less (and therefore "valued" less) than equally competent males, i.e., males with equivalent marginal value products. Alternatively, they could suggest that women are somehow inherently or otherwise inferior (in productive potential) to males and are therefore paid less. Certainly, the seeming constancy of the "value" of females to that of males for over 3,000 years is startling. Similar differences in valuation or earnings by age, race, color, religion, national origin, and so on can and have been observed in many nations. Quite naturally, the observations have given rise to allegations of discrimination, and it is to the topic of discrimination that we now turn. Specifically, we seek an answer to the following question: To what degree do observed earnings differences (and therefore different relative valuations) between groups reflect discrimination for or against the members of the group(s)? Alternatively stated, the question becomes: How can we tell whether discrimination actually exists, and if it does, how can we measure its relative effect?

One might assert naively that discrimination in employment or earnings always exists (against some persons or groups) unless such discrimination is forbidden by law. The naiveté of that assertion results either (1) from an implicit faith in the ability of the law and law enforcement mechanisms to prevent discrimination (in a low-cost manner); (2) from a failure to take account of labor market pressures to end discrimination when it is present; and/or (3) from a failure to define discrimination carefully. Preventing discrimination by law may be extremely difficult and/or costly especially in view of the complexity of labor markets and the difficulty of identifying discrimination. In Chapter 7, for example, we considered the way in which imperfect and costly information, differential search costs, and tenure expectations—among other factors—can lead to employment selection on the basis of sex, race, etc. In those cases, cheap screening devices (statistical discrimination) can and will yield positive returns to profit-maximizing employers under less-than-full employment conditions (and in the presence of downward wage rigidities and search costs). In addition, we know that wage differences at full employment can and do reflect skill differences, differences in search costs, returns to specific human capital, and so forth. To that list must be added earnings (or income) differentials based on transport or commuting costs, locational peculiarities, and the cost of living. Thus, earnings or wage differences emerge from many causes, and at the outset, we need to define discrimination so that it is identifiable as a separate phenomenon. We shall use the following definition: Discrimination (economic discrimination) refers to differences in treatment (in wages, employment, schooling, etc.) that are *not based* on cost or expected cost differences and/or differences in productivity or expected productivity. This definition, of course, excludes statistical discrimination and other cost or productivity reasons for wage differences or differences in treatment.

Moreover, we need to differentiate between labor market and human capital discrimination—that is, between discrimination in employment and/or wage levels and discrimination in access to opportunities for skill development. Because of the close and interactive relationships between "flows" and "stocks," we can expect to observe human capital effects of labor market discrimination, and vice versa.

Labor Market Discrimination

Much of the serious work on labor market discrimination is of recent origin, has been limited largely to the United States, and has been concerned chiefly with race discrimination. Of late, attention has turned to sex discrimination. Nevertheless, the theoretical approach and the techniques of analysis are of general applicability.

In 1922 F. J. Edgeworth discussed sex discrimination in an early work entitled "Equal Pay to Men and Women for Equal Work."[3] He suggested that there are three categories of jobs: those in which women have a comparative advantage, those in which women have a comparative disadvantage, and those in which men and women are equally adept. He argued that wage differentials in his time resulted from the overcrowding of women into women's jobs (which therefore were less remunerative), not from differences in skills. However, Edgeworth did not model or describe the socioeconomic mechanisms that kept women out of the positions for which they were equally adept. Indeed, until the publication of Gary Becker's seminal work in 1957,[4] economists devoted little time or attention to the topic of discrimination.

The crux of Beckerian analysis is tastes and the way in which these tastes are observed in the market. For the purpose of a general exposition of the Beckerian approach, "As" will be identified as members of one group—a majority or more powerful group (in some sense); "Bs" will be considered members of a second, less powerful group. It is important to recognize at the outset that the tastes of all As and all Bs regarding the employment of members of the other group are not generally uniform. Those A (or B) employers who are profit maximizers (in accordance with the theory of derived demand) will employ As or Bs such that

$$(9\text{--}1) \qquad \frac{MP_A}{P_A} = \frac{MP_B}{P_B}$$

Discriminators, however, will follow the following rule:

$$(9\text{--}2) \qquad \frac{MP_A}{P_A(1 + d_A)} = \frac{MP_B}{P_B(1 + d_B)}$$

where the d_i's for each employer represent equalizing differentials for tastes, analytically equivalent to those introduced in Chapter 1 with respect to the tastes of communards.

Where an employer has "feelings" for As—perhaps his own group or tribe—and "feelings" against Bs, his d_A will be ≤ 0 and his $d_B > 0$. Thus, the discriminator will act *as if* the employment costs of As are less than the costs of an equivalent amount of Bs services even at equal compensation levels for the two. He will seek to hire As and will be induced to hire Bs only when the wage levels for Bs are low enough to compensate him for the nonpecuniary losses of hiring or associating with "one of them." Note that discriminating employers may have stronger tastes against Bs in nontraditional jobs than in traditional ones.

Indeed, A-type employers may discriminate against As with respect to employment in traditional "B jobs."

Aggregating across employers—most of whom are assumed to be in the predominant capital-owning "A" group—yields the two demand curves pictured in Fig. 9–1 and an average market discrimination coefficient (d). That coefficient reflects both demand and supply conditions. Employers with d_B's $< d = W_A - W_B$ (including those with d_B's $= 0$) will employ only Bs. Effective discriminators will employ only As. At market equilibrium, W_A will be $> W_B$, and employment for Bs will be reduced relative to what it would have been in the absence of discrimination, assuming upward sloping supply curves. Note that in this analysis, As and Bs are assumed to be substitutes in production.

Discrimination therefore leads to employment alterations and to wage differences that are unrelated to costs or skills. In addition, by introducing differential d's for various jobs, the discrimination model clearly predicts observable patterns of occupational segregation ("black jobs," sex-typed jobs, "Chinese" versus "Malay jobs," etc.). Moreover, by collectively raising the relative price of their preferred labor inputs, discriminators pay the wage cost of their own discrimination (up to d, not necessarily up to each one's respective d_B). Finally, it is useful to note that the discrimination always "comes through" the demand side of the model—whether the employer is reflecting his own tastes, the tastes or presumed tastes of his clients or customers, or the tastes of his existing workforce. (In the latter two cases, additional assumptions about substitutes or input limitations are required to complete the analysis). Finally, the model does not necessarily assume that discrimination

Figure 9–1 *Wage and Employment Discrimination in the Labor Market*

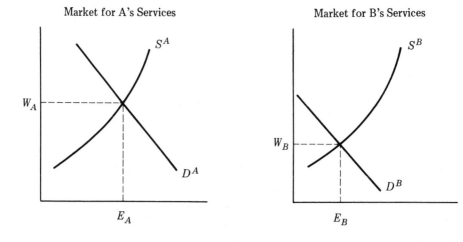

Market for A's Services   Market for B's Services

**LABORERS WANTED
NO IRISH NEED APPLY**

against *B*s (in particular jobs) comes only from *A*-type employers, or vice versa.

The market equilibrium pictured in Fig. 9–1, however, may be only a short-run phenomenon. To demonstrate why this is so, consider all *A* and *B* workers as equally competent (remember the definition of equality in Chapter 7). Under discriminatory conditions in the market, it will pay profit-maximizing employers to "buy" *B*, obtaining the same quality of labor at lower costs (or where wages are somehow fixed, obtaining a higher quality of work per dollar of compensation). Thus, production costs will be lower for the nondiscriminators unless discriminating firms have special compensating advantages in production costs. Generally, at full employment, profit maximizers will have cost advantages, and thus the market will contain incentives for the removal of discriminators (and therefore discrimination) from the market. In a twist on a familiar communist expression, one can say that "Discriminators plant the seeds of their own demise." (Note: Fixed employment costs will reduce the cost advantages of profit maximizers.)

The workings of the market, however, will be limited in several cases. Remember (from Chapter 7) that under certain less-than-full employment conditions, it will pay profit maximizers to discriminate statistically. Under such circumstances, information costs lead profit maximizers to act as if they were discriminators, and the market incentives for the elimination of discrimination will be blunted or eliminated. In addition, nonprofit, fraternal, charitable and similar organizations (government, clubs, unions, etc.) are not as directly exposed to market pressures as are commercial enterprises. Limited profit enterprises are similarly protected and may find little or no reason to buy in the cheapest market.[5] Nevertheless, the general case is that at full employment, the competitive market is the strong ally of those persons who are subject to discrimination.

> **At full employment, the competitive
> market is the strong ally
> of those persons who are subject to
> discrimination.**

The very market pressures that work against discriminators, however, will induce the discriminators *as a group* to take defensive action so as to reduce or eliminate the competitive advantages of the profit maximizers. This can be accomplished by shrinking the availability of low cost, equally skilled *(B)* labor (say by altering the stock of human capital among *B*s and/or legally restricting the use of *B*'s services in competing employments. It may also "pay" discriminators as a group to prevent the entry or establishment of nondiscriminating firms by legal or even extralegal means. The activities of the Ku Klux Klan for many years are consistent with this explanation, as are similar activities elsewhere, for example, *apartheid* in South Africa, separate and unequal opportunities for public schooling in various nations, and so forth.

Some economists, notably Anne Krueger,[6] have sought explanations for labor market discrimination based on profit-maximizing (monopoly or cartel) behavior rather than on utility maximization. In the view of Kenneth Arrow, all such models fail to capture the essence of discrimination, even though in some formulations, particularly those involving complementarities and externalities of *A*s and *B*s in production, it is possible for discrimination to yield monopoly rents for *A*s as a group.[7] Referring to American experience, Arrow notes:

I do not see how the process of [racial] *discrimination can begin in the economic sphere or out of purely economic motives. It always pays any group with enough power to discriminate against some other, but redheads and blue-eyed individuals do not seem to suffer much. Since color is seized on as the basis for discrimination, there must be an extra-economic origin, although it is not precluded that its economic profitability reinforces the discrimination once started.*[8]

One model, developed by Theodore Lianos,[9] is consistent with Arrow's dictum, but has some of the characteristics of monopoly or cartel behavior emphasized by Krueger. Lianos traces discrimination not to particular d_i's, but to the adherence of employers to some general principle, for example, "A woman's place is in the home" or "Our boys ought

Figure 9–2 *The Lianos Model of Labor Market Discrimination*

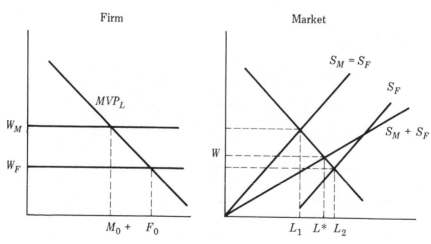

to be hired before those foreigners." Thus, each employer (or a majority of employers) will hire "*Bs*" only when "*As*" are scarce. Figure 9–2 shows that each firm will hire (say) males up to M_0 and only then will it hire females at lower wage rates up to F_0. As with the Beckerian case, both wages and employment are affected if relatively large numbers of employers adhere to the general *discrimination principle*. In contrast to Becker's model, however, total employment with discrimination in Lianos's model will be greater than without it ($L_2 > L^*$ in Fig. 9–2).

Like Becker's approach, the Lianos model has a short-run character. Discrimination costs are borne by employers, but are offset to some degree by the discriminatory rents and greater employment. Nevertheless, in classic cartel fashion, each employer has an incentive to buy (equally competent) "*Bs*" or females in this case, and there is an incentive for nonconforming prospective employers to enter the market and hire "*Bs*." Although Lianos does not elaborate on this point, some mechanisms— for example, strong social opprobrium, rigid customs, capital constraints, etc.—seem to be required to maintain this particular form of discrimination. In general, the longer run implications of Lianos's approach are similar to those of Becker's, and we are again left questioning the viability of labor market discrimination in the long run.

Human Capital Discrimination

Discrimination in access to opportunities for skill development must be differentiated from labor market discrimination even though "stocks" and "flows" are closely related and even though, as argued above, stock discrimination may have its origin partly or entirely in attempts to preserve flow discrimination. Making a sharp distinction between the two forms of discrimination helps one to address empirical problems and to formulate public policy with respect to discrimination.

Economists who believe strongly that modern economies can best be viewed as competitive market structures argue that the *only* way to maintain a segmented society is to discriminate in access to human capital. Human capital discrimination may be based on race or sex or national origin, or even "class." Certainly, one of the intentions of the English "red brick" universities is to eliminate class discrimination (as well as capital constraints). Similarly, the educational privileges afforded to children of high-ranking members of the Yugoslav Communist Party are cited by Milovan Djilas as evidence of a "New Class" emerging in that nation.[10] The key here is whether or not access to human capital is based on race, sex, class, and so on, rather than on productivity (or expected productivity) or differential costs.

As suggested by the examples above, discrimination in access to human capital may be easier to document than labor market discrimination. Easily observed examples from American experience include the establishment and maintenance of separate publicly supported schools according to race and sex (almost always involving different input proportions, expenditure rates, and human capital-generating processes), restricted entry by race and sex to labor union apprenticeship programs, and limited or no entry on the basis of race to other training programs ("farm clubs" for big league baseball, for example). Obviously, differences in access to human capital by race, sex, class, etc. have important implications for future incomes. Whether such entry restraints are based on productive characteristics or whether they are discriminatory is a very complex question. It is considered below in the section on empirical evidence.

Measuring Discrimination

Gross earnings differences are often cited in popular discussion as evidence of widespread and/or systemic labor market discrimination against persons of a particular race, sex, etc. Clearly, such evidence is not convincing unless the many other factors leading to earnings differences are accounted for. Among these are schooling and other measures of skill, job characteristics giving rise to equalizing differentials, search cost-compensation tradeoffs, union wage effects, locational and/or commuting cost differentials, differences in tenure, and so forth. Only when these factors are held constant can we isolate the influence of discrimination on earnings.

Although there are several ways of attempting to isolate the discrimination effect, most researchers in the United States have used an income- or earnings-generating function approach, including "race" and/or "sex" as a specific argument. Where race and/or sex still influence earnings or income, given the effects of all the other factors, the influence is ascribed to discrimination ("tastes"). The following equation provides a simplified example:

(9–3) $ln W = f(E, T, O, SM, CZ, \ldots, R, S)$ where

W = earnings or income (for each individual or the average for a group),

E = levels of schooling (for each individual or the group average),

T = the relevant tenure measure(s),

O = occupation [perhaps a set of qualitative (dummy) variables],

SM = search method,

CZ = city size,

U = union status or proportion,

R = race, and

S = sex.

This "residual method" is fraught with interpretation difficulties for the objective researcher. First, it is often difficult to obtain the necessary data or to standardize in other ways for the many factors that might cause "legitimate" (nontaste) differences in earnings or income. Moreover, in statistical analysis, the influence of any strong omitted variable may be "picked up" by a race, sex, or other demographic variable if the omitted variable and the particular demographic variable(s) are correlated, thereby producing a negative or positive bias. For example, one might ascribe to sex discrimination a wage effect that has actually resulted from the differential desire of women for part-time work or flexible hours (and the resulting wage adjustment). Of particular concern are measurements of schooling or skills that do not fully capture the qualitative aspects of those experiences. This problem (among others) was highlighted in the Coleman report,[11] which showed that achievement scores varied substantially across color and rural-urban groups (up to the equivalent of four grade levels) for the same number of school years completed. Thus, standardizing for years of schooling may not standardize for quality, and the omitted (quality) variable may be correlated with race, sex, class, etc. In addition, there is still the unresolved question of the correlation between "ability" (measured by various proxies) and race, sex, or some other demographic characteristic—a genetic effect.[12]

The possibility of "overcorrecting" (producing interpretation difficulties by including too many standardizers) also exists. For example, discrimination may result in the crowding of Bs into particular occupational categories. Wage differences within the category may not exist, but discrimination may take the form of occupational placement. Thus, one might find little (or a smaller amount of) discrimination when occupation is "controlled for," but more sizable effects when measures are made without occupational standardizers. It is difficult in such a case to determine, however, whether the results reflect occupational discrimination (the phenomenon first suggested by Edgeworth) or whether the occupation itself contains an equalizing differential.

Empirical Results on Labor Market Discrimination by Race

Despite these interpretation problems and perhaps because of them, American labor economists during the 1960s and 1970s employed detailed data and ingenious methods to gain greater insight into the existence and effects of labor market discrimination.[13] Consider first the research results obtained by the residual method. Most early studies[14] found black (or nonwhite) earnings to be 7–20 percent less than those for comparable whites after standardization for many other factors. James Gwartney found that the nonwhite-white income ratio was moving toward 1.0 during the 1937–67 period, but ascribed the improving ratio for nonwhites to the slow growth rate in incomes for white women.[15] More recently, rather comprehensive analyses have been conducted by James Smith and Finis Welch, jointly and separately, and published in a series of interconnected papers.[16] Using CPS as well as census 1/1,000 sample data, Smith and Welch found that black incomes rose relative to white incomes during the 1960s and 1970s (1960–70 and 1968–75 data) at rates much higher than previously experienced. They suggested and tested the following five explanations:

1. convergence of income producing characteristics (as conventionally measured),
2. a "cohort" or "vintage" improvement in the quality of these characteristics (e.g., a secularly changing quality of schooling),
3. migration from low-wage areas (out of the South until the late 1970s),
4. government affirmative action programs, and
5. business cycle variation.

They found some effects of business cycles (probably reflecting statistical discrimination), some effects of migration, and some convergence of income-producing characteristics. The principal explanatory factor, however, was the cohort or vintage changes in educational quality among blacks. Consistent with this, they found income convergence to be more rapid in the South than elsewhere, particularly among the younger cohorts. Moreover, their tests indicated that improvements in black/white earnings and income ratios occurred primarily in the (exclusively) private sector, not in the public sector or in that portion of the private sector affected by affirmative action requirements (defense contractors, etc.). Among females, Smith[17] found that black/white parity had been achieved by 1975. Much of the improvement among females—in contrast to males—resulted from increased direct and indirect government employment plus a considerable movement of black women from part-time to full-time work (often out of domestic service).

Table 9–1 shows a typical earnings or income function regression.[18]

Note that the effect of race (nonwhite) on labor incomes is negative, but not significantly different from zero, when the effects of schooling, tenure, city size, unionization, sex, etc., are held constant. The coefficient on females, however, is not only negative and large, but it is also statistically significant. Sex discrimination is further discussed below.

There are several alternative approaches for determining the existence and, to some degree, the extent of racial discrimination. The foundation for one approach is in the work of Dale Heistand,[19] who showed that employment and occupational advancement of blacks has depended closely on prior employment and prior occupational advancement of whites. Indeed, his data are consistent with the predictions of the standard statistical discrimination model, with downward sticky wages, search costs, and less-than-full employment. Heistand's historical results are also consistent with Lianos's model. Donald Osburn applied Heistand's approach to racial employment and occupational advancement patterns in the textile industries of North and South Carolina during the 1960s.[20] He found that as the labor market tightened, black employment and the search for black workers increased. Indeed, blacks previously considered unqualified became "employable" and were employed at several skill levels in most textile firms. Osburn's conclusions were supported by Phyllis Wallace and Maria Beckles,[21] who used separate EEO-1 data—reports on firm employment by race and sex required by the Civil Rights Act of 1964. In contrast, some firms did not adjust employment and search patterns in response to market opportunities and were thus pointed out as likely discriminators subject to legal action.

Another method for identifying discrimination is to investigate the presence of entry constraints as those constraints are reflected in earnings distributions by race. Most of these approaches have concentrated on a particular craft or activity, such as the study by Anthony Pascal and Leonard Rapping.[22] Their work looked at racial discrimination in organized baseball (after blacks were regularly "signed on" as team members). Pascal and Rapping found that entry constraints continued to restrict big league playing opportunities for blacks with the exception of those very well-paid blacks who were demonstrably superior to other (largely white) players. The observed salary patterns were clear evidence of either (1) discrimination in entry or (2) substantial differences by race in information about productivity or search costs. The latter explanation is not very likely in American baseball, replete as it is with performance statistics, big league scouts, and "farm clubs." Discrimination by trade unions is discussed in Chapter 10.

A final method for assessing the existence and extent of labor market discrimination is to compare rates of return to schooling, etc., across race, sex, class, or other dimensions. Where labor market discrimination exists and where such discrimination is greater for higher occupational or skill groups (as it is expected to be), marginal rates of return for

Table 9–1 *A Typical Income-Generating Function*
Log-Linear Regression Results[a]
(Dependent variable: log income)

Variables[b]		Coefficient[c]	t-Statistic
Intercept		8.31‡	76.43
Female	F	−0.39‡	−12.03
Nonwhite	N	−0.02	− 0.62
Nonmarried	S	−0.12‡	− 4.15
Union member	U	0.11‡	3.73
Schooling variables			
No schooling	ED0	−0.74†	− 2.07
Grades 1–7	ED1	−0.27‡	− 3.79
Grade 8	ED2	−0.12†	− 2.13
Grades 9–11	ED3	−0.12‡	− 3.02
Grades 13–15	ED5	0.05	1.34
Grade 16	ED6	0.28‡	5.05
Grade 16+	ED7	0.27‡	4.25
Tenure variables			
Less than 1 month	T1	−0.06	− 0.63
1–3 months	T2	−0.21‡	− 3.17
3–12 months	T3	−0.20‡	− 4.90
3–5 years	T5	−0.01	− 0.24
5–10 years	T6	0.11‡	2.63
10–20 years	T7	0.15‡	3.46
More than 20 years	T8	0.21‡	3.85
Occupation variables			
Managers and administration	OC2	−0.02	− 0.40
Sales	OC3	−0.17‡	− 2.50
Clerical	OC4	−0.08*	− 1.64
Craftworker	OC5	0.004	0.07
Operatives	OC6	−0.12†	− 2.05
Transport equipment operatives	OC7	−0.09	− 1.21
Nonfarm laborers	OC8	−0.29‡	− 3.18
Service workers	OC11	−0.26‡	− 4.45
Continuous variables			
Experience		0.0001	0.11
Hours per week		0.02‡	10.32
Population (coded in 000,000s)		0.0014‡	4.39
Density		0.000007	1.08
Rent		0.0016‡	2.55

$R^2 = 0.61$ F-statistic = 39.32
$N = 8.17$

Figure 9–3 *The Effect of Labor Market Discrimination on Human Capital Acquisition*

Income Streams for As

Income Streams for Bs

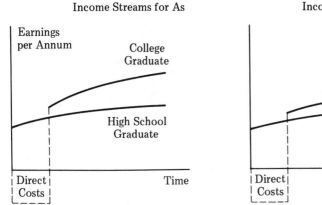
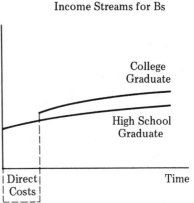

$$r_A > r_B$$

schooling or training by "*Bs*" are likely to be lower than for equivalent "*As*." Figure 9–3 shows this situation. The lower rate of return can be expected, *ceteris paribus,* to discourage *Bs* from skill acquisition relative to *As*, thereby lowering school enrollments, inducing less search for positions involving O-J-T, and so on.

Early research by Gary Becker and Giora Hanock[23] found lower rates of return to schooling for blacks than for whites. When adjusted for standard test scores, however, the differences in rates of return largely disappeared. Nevertheless, given the possibility that the tests contained meaningful cultural biases, the suspicion that $r_B < r_W$ remained. Thomas Johnson's work,[24] using other evidence, supported the proposition that

---

[a] Source: Hyman and Fearn.[18]

[b] All dummy variables take the value 1 if the respondent falls into that category, and zero otherwise. The base is a white, male, married worker who completed 12 years of schooling, was on the job from 1 to 3 years in a professional or technical occupation, and did not belong to a union.

[c] For a continuous variable, the coefficient is interpreted as a percent change in income resulting from a one unit change in the respective variable, *ceteris paribus.* For qualitative (or dummy) variables, exponentiation is required. For example, the effect on income of being female is $e^{-0.39} - 1 = -0.32$ or 32 percent below that of an equivalent male.

* Significant at the 0.10 level.

† Significant at the 0.05 level.

‡ Significant at the 0.01 level.

there was little difference between the r's for the two groups. Freeman[25] showed marginal rates of return to college training in 1960 of 0.09 for blacks and 0.10 for whites. By 1970, however, $r_B = 0.15$, while the rate for whites remained at 0.10. A similar pattern was found for the 1968–75 period by Smith and Welch.[26] The work also showed rates of return for black males to be higher than those for white males in 1975. In addition, their data indicated that returns to college training among whites fell during that period, while those for blacks remained steady or increased somewhat. If anything, these data reflect "reverse discrimination" by race during the mid-1970s.

Empirical Results on Human Capital Discrimination by Race

As suggested above, human capital discrimination is somewhat easier to document than is labor market discrimination. This is particularly true with respect to differences in schooling by race in the American South. As Freeman showed,[27] the expenditure rates for black and white students changed dramatically in various Southern states after black males were effectively disenfranchised in the 1890–1905 period. Other factors in the various areas influenced expenditure rates (changing property values, urbanization, proportion black, etc.), but the overwhelming effect came from disenfranchisement. Not only did white-to-black expenditure ratios change (often more than doubling), but a complex set of other changes worked against the acquisition of human capital by many, if not most Southern blacks. C. Vann Woodward's classic, *Origins of the New South*,[28] provides a detailed account of the segmentation of society—state by state—together with a discussion of the relationship of racial politics in education to other issues. In one of these areas, Wallace Huffman[29] has looked closely at the development of black and white land-grant colleges throughout the South. In his work, he outlines the sharp differences between the quality of the black and white agricultural extension services through which new and useful agricultural technology and practices were communicated to respective farm groups. Not only did Huffman find publicly sanctioned discrimination in the structuring of the universities, agricultural research services, and extension services, but he also found that information provided through the service was an important source of agricultural productivity. Thus, the lower quality of the black structure had an important influence on black versus white income levels in agriculture.

That there was a historical institutional bias in the acquisition of human capital for blacks, and that the bias weakened gradually and finally relaxed in the late 1950s and 1960s is consistent with the vintage phenomenon in the quality of education observed by Smith and Welch. It is also consistent with certain occupational position data developed by Freeman, who showed the index of black-to-white occupational positions roughly constant or declining from 1890 to 1940–50, with sharp increases after that period.[30]

Summarizing the evidence on black/white discrimination in the United States, it would appear that labor market discrimination existed historically, although the magnitude of its effect is undetermined. Whatever that magnitude(s), racial labor market discrimination may have been largely eliminated by the late 1970s. Indeed, the rate of return data among young persons suggest some reverse discrimination. The data on publicly supported discrimination in access to human capital is much more telling. The patterns of change in income, earnings, school enrollment—particularly the changes in educational quality—strongly suggest that much, if not most, of the observed earnings or income differences between blacks and whites had their origins in human capital discrimination enforced by the coercive power of the various states.

Sex Discrimination—Various Measures

Research on sex discrimination is less voluminous than that on discrimination by race. Nevertheless, there is enough to reach some tentative conclusions.

Sanborn, Fuchs, Cohen, B. G. Malkiel and J. A. Malkiel, and Oaxaca, employing earnings or income-generating functions, found that standardization alters the female-male earnings or income ratio, but that sizable differences remain. Adjusting for absenteeism, work experience, hours of work, and many other factors raised Sanborn's female-male earnings ratio in 1950 from 0.58 to 0.87–0.88, leaving a 12–13 percent gap.[31] Fuchs's adjustments, however, counted for only a 6-percentage point change, leaving a very large ($\approx$ 40 percent) gap.[32] Cohen's work reduced the observed difference of $5,000 to $2,550 in his sample, but this difference is still substantial.[33] A similar finding comes from Malkiel and Malkiel, who eliminated from 37 to 49 percent of the original earnings difference among professional workers by their statistical adjustments.[34] Nevertheless, the adjusted earnings of females were approximately 25 percent lower than those of comparable males. Oaxaca's work, based on 1967 Survey of Economic Opportunity data, found a 29 percent discrimination effect after adjustment for white females and a 25 percent effect for black females, also after adjustments.[35]

Most of the studies found some indication of occupational tracking or slotting. As Malkiel and Malkiel noted in their study of professional workers, one must answer "Yes" to the question: Do men and women with equal characteristics at the same job level get equal pay? However, the answer must be "No" to the question: Do men and women with equal characteristics get equal pay? Malkiel and Malkiel suggested that sexual pay differentials within occupations might be hard to justify and maintain in professional employment, and that occupational tracking is a readily available alternative. Fuchs notes, however, that the standardized earnings differential is larger for self-employed women than for private wage and salary workers, a situation which ought not to prevail where labor market discrimination exists. The pattern observed by Fuchs may suggest "role conditioning" (to use his term), discrimination by consumers, or some complex vintage phenomenon in skills and/or attitudes on both sides of the market.

Unfortunately, detailed evaluations of human capital discrimination or educational tracking simply have not been carried out. Casual evidence of such tracking abounds. The notion that "Girls are good in literature and English, but not in mathematics" may well be used to guide or influence curricular choices. In addition, some states (e.g., Virginia) historically segregated males and females into colleges with substantially different curricula (to prepare them for "male" or "female" jobs). Most important analytically is the possibility that the observed occupational patterns may have resulted from some amalgam of choice factors (see Chapter 3 for a discussion of what might be called voluntary tracking), publicly supported restriction, and discouragement or "guidance" for those females who seek "nontraditional" training. Such restrictive or guidance practices may be as unsubtle as the wearing of the chador in Iran or the veil in some Arab nations. Of course, either voluntary or involuntary tracking would produce overcrowding in traditional "female jobs."

At any rate, the jury is still out on human capital discrimination by sex. The available evidence, however, strongly suggests labor market discrimination against women either in earnings or job assignments. If labor market discrimination by sex abounds, however, we still have some perplexing questions to answer:

1. Why would profit-maximizing employers (the vast majority) not take the opportunity to "buy female" and enlarge their profits?

2. Are there particular sex-related costs, perhaps imposed by governments or custom, to which profit maximizers are responding?

3. To what degree are the patterns we observe the result of statistical, rather than overt, labor market discrimination?

4. Could it be that the observed occupation (and related income) patterns are largely voluntary?

Obviously, future researchers have much grist for their analytical mills.

Notes to Chapter 9

1. Robert Coughlan, *Elizabeth and Catherine: Empresses of All the Russias* (New York: New American Library, 1975), pp. 122–23.

2. *The Coming Decade: American Women and Human Resource Policies and Programs,* hearings before the Committee on Labor and Human Resources, U.S. Senate, 96th Congress, 1st Session, Part 1 (Washington, D.C.: U.S. Government Printing Office, January 31 and February 1, 1979), p. 469.

3. F. J. Edgeworth, "Equal Pay to Men and Women for Equal Work," *Economic Journal* 32, no. 128 (December 1922): 431–57.

4. Gary S. Becker, *The Economics of Discrimination* (Chicago: University of Chicago Press, 1957).

5. For a more general consideration of the role of market competition with respect to minorities, nonconformists, etc., see Almen A. Alchian and Reuben A. Kessel, "Competition, Monopoly, and the Pursuit of Money," Universities–National Bureau Committee for Economic Research, *Aspects of Labor Economics* (Princeton, N.J.: Princeton University Press for the National Bureau of Economic Research, 1962), pp. 157–75.

6. Anne O. Krueger, "The Economics of Discrimination," *Journal of Political Economy* 71, no. 5 (October 1963): 481–86.

7. See Finis R. Welch, "Labor Market Discrimination: An Interpretation of Income Differentials in the Rural South," *Journal of Political Economy* 75, no. 3 (June 1967): 225–40.

8. Kenneth J. Arrow, "Models of Job Discrimination," in *Racial Discrimination in Economic Life,* ed. A. H. Pascal (Lexington, Mass.: D. C. Heath and Co., 1972), p. 100. Also see Arrow, "Some Mathematical Models of Race in the Labor Market," pp. 187–204, in the same volume.

9. Theodore Lianos, "A Note on Discrimination in the Labor Market," *Southern Economic Journal* 43, no. 2 (October 1976): 1177–80.

10. Milovan Djilas, *The New Class: An Analysis of the Communist System* (New York: Frederick A. Praeger, 1957).

11. James Coleman, et al., *Equality of Educational Opportunity* (Washington, D.C.: U.S. Department of Health, Education and Welfare, 1966).

12. See Mary Corcoran, Christopher Jencks, and Michael Olneck, "The Effects of Family Background on Earnings," and Jere Behrman and Paul Taubman, "Intergenerational Transmission of Income and Wealth," *American Economic Review* 66, no. 2 (May 1976): 430–40, for a discussion of the possible biases produced by failing to account for ability differences and for a consideration of the possible effects of genetic versus environmental influences.

13. For excellent surveys of the literature, see Arrow, "Models" and "Some Mathematical Models"; Richard Freeman, "Labor Market Discrimination: Analysis, Findings and Problems," in *Frontiers of Quantitative Economics,* vol. 2, ed. M. D. Intriligator and D. A. Kendrick (Amsterdam: North Holland Publishing Co., 1974); Stanley H. Masters, *Black-White Income Differentials: Empirical Studies and Policy Implications* (New York: Academic Press, 1975); and A. H. Pascal, ed., *Racial Discrimination in American Life* (Lexington, Mass.: D. C. Heath and Co., 1972). Also see Orley Ashenfelter and Albert Rees, eds., *Discrimination in Labor Markets* (Princeton, N.J.: Princeton University Press, 1973), for several excellent summary articles.

14. W. Lee Hansen, Burton A. Weisbrod, and William J. Scanlon, "Schooling and the Earnings of Low Achievers," *American Economic Review* 60, no. 3 (June 1970): 409–18; Zvi Griliches and W. Mason, "Education, Income and Ability," *Journal of Political Economy* 80, no. 3, pt. 2 (May–June 1972): S74–S104.

15. James Gwartney, "Changes in the Nonwhite/White Income Ratio, 1937–1967," *American Economic Review* 60, no. 5 (December 1970): 872–933.

16. James P. Smith and Finis R. Welch, *Black/White Male Earnings and Employment: 1960–1970*, Rand Corporation report R-1666-DOL (Santa Monica, Calif. and Washington, D.C.: U.S. Department of Labor, June 1975); *Black/White Wage Ratios, 1960–1970*, Rand Corporation monograph P-5479 and P-5479-1 (Santa Monica, Calif.: The Rand Corporation, July 1975 and August 1976); *Inequality: Race Differences in the Distribution of Earnings*, Rand Corporation, monograph P-5481 (Santa Monica, Calif.: The Rand Corporation, October 1977); *Race Differences in Earnings: A Survey and New Evidence*, Rand Corporation report R-2295-NSF (Santa Monica, Calif. and Washington, D.C.: National Science Foundation, January 1978); and James P. Smith, *The Improving Economic Status of Black Americans*, Rand Corporation monograph P-6055 (Santa Monica, Calif.: The Rand Corporation, January 1978).

17. Smith, *Improving Economic Status of Black Americans*.

18. David Hyman and Robert M. Fearn, "The Influence of City Size on Labor Incomes," *Quarterly Journal of Economics and Business* 18, no. 1 (Spring 1978): 63–73.

19. Dale L. Heistand, *Economic Growth and Employment Opportunities for Minorities* (New York: Columbia University Press, 1964).

20. Donald P. Osburn, *Negro Employment in the Textile Industries of North and South Carolina*, EEOC research report 1966–10 (Washington, D.C.: Equal Employment Opportunity Commission, November 1966).

21. Phyllis Wallace and Maria Beckles, *Negro Employment Patterns in the Textile Industry*, EEOC research report 1966–11 (Washington, D.C.: Equal Employment Opportunity Commission, November 1966).

22. Anthony H. Pascal and Leonard A. Rapping, "The Economics of Racial Discrimination in Organized Baseball," in *Racial Discrimination in Economic Life*, ed. A. H. Pascal (Lexington, Mass.: D. C. Heath and Co., 1972).

23. Gary S. Becker, *The Economics of Discrimination*, 2d ed. (Chicago: University of Chicago Press, 1971); Giora Hanock, "An Economic Analysis of Earnings and Schooling," *Journal of Human Resources* 2, no. 3 (Summer 1967): 310–29.

24. Thomas Johnson, "Returns from Investments in Human Capital," *American Economic Review* 60, no. 4 (September 1970): 546–60.

25. Freeman, "Labor Market Discrimination," pp. 501–69.

26. Smith and Welch, *Race Differences in Earnings*.

27. Richard Freeman, "Black-White Economic Differences: Why Did They Last So Long?" (unpublished paper, Harvard University, 1976).

28. C. Vann Woodward, *Origins of the New South, 1877–1913* (Baton Rouge, La.: Louisiana State University Press, 1951).

29. Wallace E. Huffman, "Black-White Human Capital Differences: Impact on Agricultural Productivity in the U.S. South" (unpublished paper, Iowa State University, August 1978).

30. Freeman, "Labor Market Discrimination," pp. 502–6.

31. H. Sanborn, "Pay Differences between Men and Women," *Industrial and Labor Relations Review* 17, no. 4 (July 1964): 534–50.

32. Victor R. Fuchs, "Differences in Hourly Earnings between Men and Women," *Monthly Labor Review* 94, no. 5 (May 1971): 9–15.

33. Malcolm S. Cohen, "Sex Differences in Occupations," *Journal of Human Resources* 4, no. 4 (Fall 1971): 434–47.

34. B. G. Malkiel and J. A. Malkiel, "Male-Female Pay Differentials in Professional Employment," *American Economic Review* 63, no. 4 (September 1973): 693–705.

35. Ronald Oaxaca, "Male-Female Wage Differentials in Urban Labor Markets," *International Economic Review* 14, no. 3 (October 1973): 693–709, and "Sex Discrimination in Wages," in *Discrimination in Labor Markets,* ed. Orley Ashenfelter and Albert Rees (Princeton, N.J.: Princeton University Press, 1973), pp. 124–51.

10 | *The Economics of Unions*

The trade union movement represents the organized economic power of the workers. . . . It is in reality the most potent and the most direct social insurance the worker can establish.

Samuel Gompers, President,
American Federation of Labor[1]

Proletarians have nothing to lose but their chains. They have a world to win.

Marx and Engels,
The Communist Manifesto

Perhaps the best that can be hoped for is the prohibition of child labor under the age of twelve in the Southern mills.

U.S. Industrial Commission, 1901[2]

The quotations above suggest, but certainly do not exhaust, the variegated aspects of the American (and most other) labor union movements. Even a dozen or more citations, however, would not do justice to the nature, anomalies, objectives, emotions, defeats, victories, and personalities associated with this great movement—nor can a long chapter in this text.

As a consequence, emphasis will be given here (1) to the attitudinal and economic factors underlying the growth of unionism, and (2) to the effects of unions on employment and wage levels. The many historical, legal, ethnic, and other facets of unionism will be introduced whenever they are relevant to the major arguments. Much information of interest to a complete study of unions and unionization, however, will be ignored or merely touched upon. Nevertheless, if the examination of union behavior presented in this chapter does for the reader what is intended, his further study of labor union history, labor law, union structure and governance, techniques of collective bargaining, and related subjects will be richer and more productive. After a brief introduction to attitudes and

188 | *Labor Economics*

union objectives, unionism will be viewed from three interrelated points of view:

1. unionism as a consumer good,
2. unionism as a monopoly influence, and
3. unionism as a cheap screening device.

Using these approaches, the following questions will be addressed:

1. Why do people join unions?
2. What determinants of union membership are the most important and why?
3. What is the effect of unions on relative wages and on other terms and conditions of employment?
4. What determinants of union wage (or employment) effects are the most important and why?

In the process, a general model of unionism will be developed.

Attitudes and Union Objectives

Any historical survey of unionism and unions in the United States (or elsewhere) provides innumerable examples of different and sometimes conflicting union objectives. Table 10–1 provides some examples, ranging from the National Labor Union which sought to "free the worker from the control of the capitalists" to the "plain and simple unionism" (i.e., collective bargaining approaches) espoused by the American Federation of Labor. This table also includes the violent "Molly Maguire" offshoot of the Ancient and Honorable Order of Hiberians (AHOH); the Knights of Labor which sought for most of its history to provide relief for workers via political action; the radical and explosive International Workers of the World (IWW); and the orthodox communist-socialist unions which, in contrast to the IWW, understood "the need for party discipline in achieving the overthrow of capitalism." There is little wonder why early academic observers of the labor scene had difficulty in identifying the "true" objectives and the "true" nature of unionism. Indeed, multiple objectives appear to be the hallmark of any major socio-economic movement.[3]

One of the most expeditious ways to grasp the multifaceted nature of unionism is to hear or read "labor poems" and "labor songs."[4] These works encapsulize the hopes, fears, and desires that influenced the early unionists and still have an effect on the union movement. For example, "The Ballad of Joe Hill" proclaims a state of warfare between the workers

> 'The copper bosses killed you, Joe;
> They shot you Joe," says I.
> "Takes more than guns to kill a man,"
> Says Joe, "I didn't die."
>
> And standing there as big as life and
>   smiling with his eyes,
> Joe says, "What they forgot to kill
> Went on to organize."
>   From "The Ballad of Joe Hill"
>   by Earl Robinson and Albert Hayes

and their employers with Joe Hill's cry, "Don't mourn for me, but organize!" So do the tunes and words of "the little red songbook," the official hymnal of the IWW.[5] The majesty of Carl Sandburg's poetry also captures the moods of American workers from the late 1800s through the 1930s. Consider the poignant cry for industrial safety in "Anna Imroth," the class conflict in "The Mayor of Gary," and the cavalier dedication of "Dynamiter" to the cause of labor and the working class. Add to these insightful glimpses the insecurity of employment in cyclically sensitive industries, periodic business cycle fluctuations or financial crises, the ethnic solidarity and ignorance of immigrants in their new land, inter-ethnic competition and hatred, the social distance between "the boss" and "the working stiff," and the promise of a better life if only the "profits were returned to labor, the source of all wealth," and one has an emotional hold on some of the origins of unionism.

> Cross the hands over the breasts here—
>   so.
> Straighten the legs a little more—so.
> And call for the wagon to come and take
>   her home.
> Her mother will cry some and so will her
>   sisters and brothers.
> But all of the others got down and they
>   are safe and this is the only one of
>   the factory girls who wasn't lucky
>   in making the jump when the fire
>   broke.
> It is the hand of God and the lack of fire
>   escapes.
>   "Anna Imroth"
>   by Carl Sandburg

Table 10–1 *Examples of Post-Civil War Unionism in the U.S.A.*

Name and dates	*National Labor Union, 1866–1872*	*"Molly Maguires," AHOH 1870s*	*Knights of Labor, 1869–ca. 1900*
Form of Organization	Federation of city centrals	Secret society	Secret society, until 1881 included trade and mixed locals
Skill Composition	Skilled craftsmen	Unskilled workers largely of Irish descent and largely in the Pennsylvania coal mines	Chiefly skilled workers but initially organized and directed largely by intellectuals
Approach: Strategy, Tactics, and Objectives	To establish producers' coops in order to "free the workers from the control of the capitalists"; allied with Greenbackers in political action	To improve conditions via strikes and terror tactics against "the overlords"	To replace the competitive society with a cooperative one via education and political action, including the 8-hour workday, equal pay for equal work for women, etc.; during 1880s, under new "practical leadership," successfully struck the Gould Railway system and others for collective bargaining rights

How can one make some intellectual sense out of this welter of emotions and interests? In his early classic work on unionism, Robert Hoxie attempted to do so, identifying four functional union types: business unionism, uplift (or friendly) unionism, revolutionary unionism, and predatory unionism (including the hold-up and the guerrilla varieties).[6] He argued that another type, dependent or company unionism, should not be considered as legitimately representing the interests of union

International Workers of the World, ca. 1900–1920	American Federation of Labor, 1881—Federation of Organized Trades and Industrial Union; 1886—drew crafts out of the Knights of Labor	Orthodox Communist-Socialist Unions First Socialist International, 1864; Socialist Labor Party, 1874; Socialist Trade and Labor Alliance, labor wing of SLP, established 1895
"One big industrial union"	Craft unionism—those locals surviving the 1873 crash formed the AFL	Political union
Unskilled and migratory workers chiefly in the mines, lumber camps, and wheat fields of the West	Skilled workers	All workers welcome, but little organizing success
To promote "abolition of the wage system"; to prepare for the revolution; opposed WWI as an imperialist war; used terror tactics to close mines, war factories, etc.	To promote 8-hour workday, improved pay and working conditions via collective bargaining; nonpartisan, nonideological politics emphasizing regulation of employment of women and children, industrial accidents, etc., initially at the state level	To promote proletarian consciousness and prepare for the eventual revolution; joined AFL in 1901 to influence that organization toward more radical goals—a "popular front" tactic

members. Later researchers have usually considered Hoxie's predatory unions as criminal associations (rackets) rather than legitimate associations of employees or prospective employees representing the general desires of the membership. Moreover, these later researchers have identified political unions as a separate type. The following definitions will suffice for our purposes:

Uplift unions—associations of "workers" that seek to improve living levels and otherwise assist their members and "labor" in general by raising the skill and cultural levels of members and by otherwise ameliorating the vicissitudes of life (illness, family disformation, death, etc.). Leadership in these unions in the United States (and elsewhere) is often "external" (priests, rabbis, philanthropic volunteers) as distinguished from "rank and file."

Political unions—associations of "workers" that have the same objectives as uplift unions but seek to accomplish them primarily by political actions, often in an alliance with a political party or parties. Democratic socialist unions often fall in this category.

Revolutionary unions—associations that seek the same objectives by forcibly altering the property right system and/or the political structure of the society.

Business unions—associations that seek to alter living levels (and the terms and conditions of employment) primarily via collective bargaining. The political and economic *framework* of the society (including the system of property rights) is accepted by business unionists.

It is particularly important for American readers to recognize that business unionism, the dominant form in the United States, is not the most pervasive form in the world. The dominant form around the world is political (or political-uplift) in nature and is generally linked to some political party or movement. Under U.S. law, unions have exclusive jurisdiction in contrast to the nonexclusive unionism arrangements in much of Europe (one union in each jurisdiction), and it is tempting to say that legal differences are responsible for the differences in the respective union movements. Since the law in democracies reflects the popular will, however, some more fundamental forces must be at work creating these differences.[7]

Union objectives affect many things, including the nature of a strike.

> His name was in many newspapers as an enemy of the nation and few keepers of the churches or schools would open their doors to him.
> Over the steak and onions not a word was said of his deep days and nights as a dynamiter.
> Only I always remember him as a lover of life, a lover of all free, reckless laughter everywhere—lover of red hearts and red blood the world over.
>
> From "Dynamiter"
> by Carl Sandburg

I asked the Mayor of Gary about the 12-
hour day and the 7-day week.
And the Mayor of Gary answered more
workmen steal time on the job in
Gary than any other place in the
United States.
"Go into the plants and you will see men
sitting around doing nothing—Machinery does everything," said the
Mayor of Gary when I asked him
about the 12-hour day and the 7-day
week.
And he wore cool cream pants, the
Mayor of Gary, and white shoes, and
a barber had fixed him up with a
shampoo and a shave and he was
easy and imperturbable though the
government weather bureau thermometer said 96 and children were
soaking their heads in bubbling
fountains on the street corners.
And I said good-by to the Mayor of Gary
and I went out from City Hall and
turned the corner into Broadway.
And I saw workmen wearing leather
shoes scuffed with fire and cinders,
and pitted with little holes from running molten steel
And some had bunches of specialized
muscles around their shoulder
blades hard as pig iron, muscles of
their forearms were sheet steel and
they
Looked to me like men who had been
somewhere.
"The Mayor of Gary"
by Carl Sandburg

Uplift unions will hesitate to strike, while political unions are apt to call general strikes or slowdowns to indicate support for particular legislative initiatives or policies under consideration by government or to demand particular governmental actions. In contrast, the strike weapon is employed by business unionists to petition particular employers for redress of grievances or as a test of strength preparatory to a new collective bargaining contract. For "pure" revolutionary unions, a strike is none of these things. It represents, in its essence, a skirmish in the battle for class supremacy and/or practice for the eventual revolution.

Note, finally, that these union types are not mutually exclusive. American business unionists have from time to time formed very close alliances with particular political parties [e.g., the United Auto Workers (UAW) and the Democratic Party during the late 1940s]. In general, however, business unions leave their political options open so that they can act as independent pressure groups as "conditions dictate." As Sam Gompers suggested, they concentrate on collective bargaining (within a framework of law) and adhere to a policy of "rewarding labor's friends and punishing its enemies" in a politically nonpartisan way.[8]

One final taxonomic note on union structure is helpful. Unions that establish eligibility for membership on the basis of occupation, skill level, or craft are designated *craft unions*, e.g., the Carpenters, Plumbers, Laborers, Die Makers, and so on. Unions that include all or most occupation groups—without regard to craft or skill—within the same association (union) are termed *industrial unions*. Examples here include the United Mine Workers, the United Auto Workers, the United Steelworkers, etc. In a few national (or international) unions, some locals are organized on a craft basis and others on an industrial basis. For example, the United Brotherhood of Carpenters and Joiners (CJA) is organized by crafts in on-site construction, but as an industrial union in mobile home plants. Moreover, some unions have changed emphases over time. The International Association of Machinists and Aerospace Workers (IAM), for example, began as a craft union, but is now regarded largely as an industrial union.

Unionism as a Consumer Good[9]

In the first of our three interlocking approaches to the modeling of unionism, we treat unions as a consumer good. Consider each individual as choosing between unionism and wage levels per unit time. By this concept, we are implicitly asking for a measure of the tastes for unionism. Individual 1 has a distaste for unionism if $W_n = W_u$ and if

(10–1) $U_1(W_n) > U_1(W_u)$ where
           U represents utility
           W represents wages or compensation per unit time
           the numerical subscripts represent persons
           n and u represent nonunion and union, respectively.

Conversely, if for individual 2

(10–2) $U_2(W_n) < U_2(W_u)$
                                    given $W_n = W_u$,

individual 2 has a taste for unionization. In neither case does the utility level depend upon any real or supposed ability of unions to raise wages or income levels. It follows from Becker's theory of discrimination developed in Chapters 1 and 9 that we can find for each individual a value such that the respective utilities become equal. Say for individual 1, that we have a $W_n < W_u$ such that $U(W_n) = U(W_u)$ and that at that point $W_u/W_n = 1.1$. It follows that unless the actual relative wage difference $(W_u - W_n/W_n) \geq 0.1$, individual 1 will still prefer a nonunion situation, despite the higher union wage. Any wage premium above 0.1, however, would be sufficient to compensate for his distaste. Similarly, if individual 2 had an equalizing differential of 0.1, he might still prefer unionism even if the union wage were below that for nonunion employment, other things being constant.

With such equalizing differentials (taste or discrimination coefficients), one can plot a (hypothetical) distribution of union-nonunion wage rates, given $W_n = 1.00$, against the proportion of the population favoring unions at various relative prices (Fig. 10–1). Thus, if $W_n = W_u$, *ceteris paribus*, 40 percent of the population considered in Fig. 10–1 would freely prefer (and presumably choose) unionism.

Figure 10–1 *Hypothetical Distribution of the Tastes for Unionism (Frequency Polygon and Cumulative Distribution)*

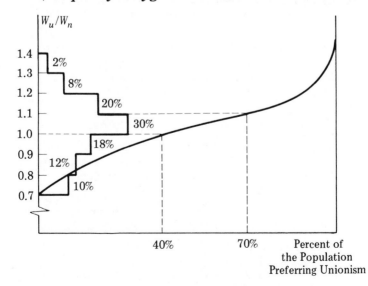

A little experimentation with the shape of the underlying taste distribution will convince the reader that the lower the tastes and distastes for and against unionism (or, more generally, for and against collective efforts among workers), the more peaked will be the frequency polygon and the longer will be the "flat" portion of the cumulative distribution (or union membership) curve.[10]

On what does this taste for collective labor market action depend? Although no detailed historical statistics are available, prounion sentiment in the United States appears to have been related, among other factors, to ethnic origin. Two general groupings of the American population appear to have had strong tastes for unions relative to the remainder of the population. The "underlying ethos" explained in Table 10–2 provides some examples. Historically, one of these groups has been characterized by strong distastes for or distrust of established authority and/or by strong "out-group" feelings. Among Irish-, Jewish-, and Afro-Americans, strong prounion feelings are probably the result of previous ethnic experiences with "foreign overlords" or "domestic masters" and of a deeply felt need to preserve ethnic or religious identity. A second population group appears to have been more class- and/or craft-conscious in their tastes, having strong feelings of allegiance to the "working class" and/or a strong sense of pride in their workmanship. Indeed, during the 1800s some craftsmen—"aristocrats of labor"—felt that they were particularly and perhaps uniquely responsible for the industrial progress of the United States. They "built" the skyscrapers, the machine tools, the steel mills, the railroad engines, and, more generally, the industrial "muscle" of America. It is clear that some of these prideful taste patterns "migrated" to the United States and that some were generated by the American experience in rapid industrialization. Similar differences in tastes can be traced to urban or rural origins, and so on. There is no attempt here to give these underlying taste factors more than a cursory examination, but—in the view of the author—their influence cannot be doubted by serious scholars of American history.

It follows from the discussion above and from the proposition that

Table 10–2 *Pro-union Tastes: Underlying Ethos*

Ethnic consciousness Mutual improvement and protection against "exploitation"	*Class or craft consciousness* The dignity of work and the importance of the working class
Irish-Americans Jewish-Americans	German-Americans Scandinavian-Americans Midlands (English)-Americans
(More recently) Afro-Americans Mex-Americans	

underlying tastes change slowly, that ethnic mix can and usually will be related to unionism. It is not surprising, therefore, that cities like Cincinnati, Minneapolis, Boston, Seattle, Pittsburgh, and San Francisco are "union towns" in contrast to Los Angeles, Dallas, Miami, Charlotte, and a number of midwestern cities.

It also follows that individuals with strong tastes for unions will willingly pay union dues as the price of "consuming" unionism, even if the union is unable to make $W_u > W_n$. Thus, most of the hypothetical 40 percent preferring unions (Fig. 10–2) would willingly pay "d" per unit time even if $W_n = W_u$. For them, $U(W_u - d) \geq U(W_n)$ even if $W_n > (W_u - d)$, i.e., position A in Fig. 10–2. In a substantial sense, this "taste" analysis of unionism is very similar to analyzing membership in the Masonic Order, the Knights of Columbus, the Lions, or other fraternal groups.

To formalize the argument to this point, we have

$$(10\text{--}3) \qquad U = f_1\left(\frac{W_u}{W_n}, d, E, \ldots\right)$$

where U is unionization, W_u/W_n is the relative compensation ratio, d represents dues or direct costs of unionism in the same time dimension, and E represents an appropriate set (vector) of ethnic variables. If, as H. Gregg Lewis has suggested, the underlying distribution of tastes for

Figure 10–2 *The Influence of Union Dues on Unionism*

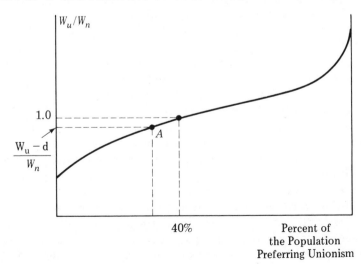

unionism is peaked (has a high degree of kurtosis), the proportion of unionism, *ceteris paribus,* should be sensitive to the union-nonunion wage relative.

Any careful reading of American union history suggests that we have failed to include in Eq. 10–3 one of the most likely and important variables—the indirect costs of unions and union membership. In the early 1800s, American unions were treated by the courts under English common law as criminal conspiracies, and the act of forming the conspiracy as well as the conspiracy itself (strike, slowdown, or whatever) was deemed illegal. After *Commonwealth* v. *Hunt* in 1842, unions per se were no longer illegal, but most of their economic actions were.[11] Strikes and other union activities were punishable by fine, imprisonment, or both. Moreover, after the Sherman Anti-Trust Act was applied to union activities, treble damage awards were a possibility. We incorporate the indirect costs into our analysis via the following equation:

$$(10\text{--}4) \qquad IC / UT = [E(F) + E(J) \cdot Y]P_A \cdot P_K + P_f \cdot P_A^* \cdot \overline{Y}$$

where IC / UT represents the indirect costs per unit time; $E(F)$ is the expectation of a fine times the value of the fine (expressed in \$s per unit time); $E(J)$ is the expectation of a jail sentence of a given length times Y, the value of foregone income while in jail; P_A is the probability of apprehension; P_K is the probability of conviction; P_f is the probability of being dismissed if engaged in union activity; P_A^* is the probability of being identified as a union "activist" or union member by management; and $\overline{Y}$ is the difference between current earnings and the next best alternative inclusive of expected income losses from unemployment. The cost of legal defense has been omitted for simplicity. The better the defense, of course, the lower is P_K and/or F or J. The defense itself, however, involves a direct cost. The equalizing value of utility losses resulting from social opprobrium might also be added here, but it also has been omitted to simplify the exposition. In general, it follows that the more rigorous the enforcement of the law and the more "sour" the political and judicial climate toward unions, the smaller will be the proportion of unionists in any given population. Where indirect costs are higher, however, the intensity of prounion feeling *among the membership* will be strong because only dedicated unionists will remain members. That dedication, of course, may be to either business, revolutionary, political, or uplift unions. Thus, even under such restrictive conditions, unions will not necessarily be homogeneous. Indeed, the patterns of unionism during the 1800s support this interpretation.

In addition to camaraderie, ethnic pride, and group solidarity, one is led by this taste analysis to ask "Is there anything else that union members are 'buying' when they support unionism?" Many studies testify to a strong demand for "fair treatment" or "equal treatment" and for a mechanism to assure such treatment in the everyday activities of the workplace. It would appear that some method is desired that allows an employee to complain about minor, but perhaps vexing, problems in the workplace without jeopardizing his job or incurring the permanent enmity of his superiors. The worker, of course, can always resign. In Freeman's terms, the choice may be between "exit voice" and "union voice."[12] Under business unionism, in particular, shop stewards, business agents, or other union leaders may intervene to help adjudicate or resolve problems via an established grievance procedure, subject to the union-management contract and "good sense." Individuals may also press their own grievances up to a specified point in the process. Given all the vagaries of the workplace, it is reasonable that such a mechanism might be highly valued by employees, particularly by those with seniority rights, firm-specific skills, and other economic rent-generating characteristics. Moreover, the larger the firm and/or plant, the greater will be the impersonality of the workplace and the greater the probability of communication difficulties and grievances. One might expect, therefore, that unionization would be positively related to plant size (or perhaps firm size), *ceteris paribus*. Thus, we add PZ (or FZ) to Eq. 10–3 above. Incidentally, management may also benefit from grievance procedures and other communication mechanisms. Many nonunionized (and unionized) firms maintain "open door policies," ombudsmen, and chaplain's offices to encourage such communication and to provide a regular check on the fairness and human relations activities of their supervisory staff. It follows from the discussion above that the greater the "social distance" between supervisors (particularly first-line supervisors) and workers, the greater may be the demand for unions, *ceteris paribus*. Note also that this factor may be inextricably related to the sense of class consciousness and class loyalty.[13]

Union literature, union history, and a raft of industrial relations studies suggest that unionization is related also to a strong demand for wage standardization. To many people, equal means equitable, and equality of treatment seems "fair." Despite any reservations one might have concerning the validity or limitations of this moral standard, unions have appeared to many to be a way of assuring such equal treatment. This is particularly true, one suspects, for those who believe or fear that management will use its "position" (more accurately, its information) to discriminate among workers. Certainly, the existence of shared rents (on O-J-T or other specificities) creates a climate conducive to such fears. Thus, union leaders who are truly representative of their memberships will reflect to a considerable degree the common ethical judgments, beliefs, and/or fears of their members. Some evidence of the relationship between union membership and various "equal treatment" variables is discussed in the empirical section of this chapter.

Union security arrangements (the union shop, the agency shop, maintenance of membership clauses, etc.) may also serve to increase membership or to maintain membership above what it might otherwise be. Union shop arrangements in particular may play this role. Closed shops, in which union membership is a prerequisite to (initial) employment, are a much stronger form of union security and have more far-reaching implications. They are discussed in greater detail below.[14]

> *Union shop*—a union security provision in which union membership is a prerequisite to *continued,* but not initial, employment. Membership is usually required after a 30–60-day trial period.

To summarize, we have a membership equation containing the following factors:

(10–5) $$U = f_1\left(\frac{W_u}{W_n}, d, IC, E, PZ, D, US\right) \text{ where}$$

$\dfrac{W_u}{W_n}$ = the relative wage effect of unions

d = dues or other direct costs

IC = indirect costs which are tied to the legal-political scene

E = an appropriate measure or measures of ethnicity and other taste variables

PZ = plant size (or firm size), a proxy for the demand for a grievance procedure

D = the strength of worker desires for "equitable" wage relationships in the plant

US = a vector of union security arrangements, excluding the closed shop.

To the degree that these factors determine union membership patterns, geographic and time series measures (in the United States and elsewhere) should reflect them. As noted above, the geographic distribution of U.S. unionism supports the idea that ethnicity has been and perhaps still is a powerful determinant. The pattern of union growth and decline over time supports the hypothesis that indirect costs *(IC)* have been an important determinant. The sharp increases in the rate of union growth in the early 1900s and the 1930s (see Figs. 10–3 and 10–4) coincide with changes in governmental or legal sanctions, and the decline in relative union strength after the passage of the Taft-Hartley Act in 1947 also fits this thesis. Union growth during the 1860–65 and

Figure 10-3 *Trade Union Membership, 1778-1974*

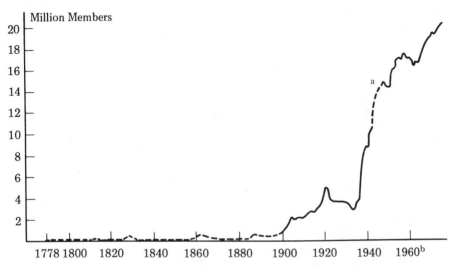

Source: Occasional data points, 1778-1897 from U.S. Department of Labor, *Brief History of the American Labor Movement*, BLS Bulletin 1000 (Washington, D.C.: Government Printing Office, 1976); data for 1897-1929 inclusive from Leo Troy, *Trade Union Membership, 1897-1962*, Occasional Paper 92 (New York: National Bureau of Economic Research, 1965) which includes Canadian members of U.S. based unions; 1930-1974 data from Bureau of Labor Statistics, *Handbook of Labor Statistics, 1978*, Bulletin 2000 (Washington, D.C.: Government Printing Office, 1979), Table 150, which data exclude Canadian members of U.S. based unions.
[a] Data somewhat questionable
[b] Alaska and Hawaii included after 1960

the 1941-45 periods is a more complex phenomenon. These and other complexities are considered in the following discussion of unions as monopolies and in the closing section of this chapter on empirical evidence.

Unionism as a Monopoly Influence

We suggested above that union membership, given tastes, may depend on relative union wage levels. The question therefore arises, "What determines the ability of unions to raise wages over what they would otherwise be?" Elementary economic theory indicates that the power of any group to raise relative prices (wages, interest rates, etc.) and earn monopoly rents for the group depends on the elasticity of demand. In this case, λ will be used as a symbol for the elasticity of demand for labor services. Thus, under competitive conditions,

Figure 10–4 *Unionism as a Percent of Labor Force and Employment*

Source: Bureau of Labor Statistics, *Handbook of Labor Statistics, 1978,*
Bulletin 2000, Government Printing Office, Washington, D.C., Table
150 (Excludes Canadian members of U.S. based unions).
[a] Data somewhat questionable
[b] Alaska and Hawaii included after 1960

$$(10\text{–}6) \qquad \frac{W_u}{W_n} = f_2(\lambda, \ldots)$$

with low elasticities of demand for union labor implying high relative
wage effects, and vice versa (remember Chapter 5).

What then determines the magnitude of λ? It is clear, for example,
that the elasticity of demand decreases during boom, wartime, and inflationary periods. The net effect of such vibrant market conditions on
W_u/W_n, however, is not clear, because λ declines for both unionized and
nonunionized workers. Unionism in the United States has usually grown
during such periods, particularly during wartime. A portion of this
growth may be traceable to lower λs, especially for unionized skilled
craftsmen. The demand for workers on the railroads and in metal trades
certainly increases during all wars, and the effect of that change in
the northern United States seemed particularly strong during the Civil
War. Some, even much, of the growth of unionism during wartimes,
however, may be traceable to the establishment of new government-union
relationships via a War Labor Board (WW I), a National War Labor
Board (WW II), a Wage Stabilization Board (Korean War), and so on.

Through these organizations, the national government in each case has formally recognized unions as legitimate organizations and solicited from them no-strike pledges and other accommodations in support of various war efforts. Thus, the indirect costs of unionism fell during these wartime periods, and λ may also have fallen. If so, the two changes would have induced increases in membership and in the union wage effects.

Alfred Marshall and, later, John Hicks[15] demonstrated that during "normal periods," the size of λ (at the industry or national level) depends upon several influences:

1. the ease with which consumers can substitute other products for the products of union labor—the elasticity of product demand (η),
2. the ease with which employers can substitute other inputs for union labor—the elasticity of input substitution (σ, the capital-labor elasticity of substitution in a two input world), and
3. the ease with which supplies of other factor inputs will be forthcoming in response to their own prices—the elasticity of supply of cooperating factors *(e)*.

In each case, the greater the ease, the greater is λ and the lower is union power to raise wages without major reductions in employment within respective jurisdictions (remember the minimum wage case in Chapter 5). Hicks also found that the proportion of labor cost in total cost *(k)* could have either a positive or a negative influence on λ.

Thus, unions representing workers who (1) produce "essential" products (those with few substitutes) in (2) production processes wherein the workers are themselves "essential" (very difficult or costly to replace by other inputs) and (3) for whom substitute inputs are either expensive or difficult to obtain will have more power than unions whose members lack these attributes. Compare, for example, an airline pilot with a sweeper in a textile plant. From the Marshallian-Hicksian conditions above, it follows that craft unions generally should face less elastic demand curves (and have more power to raise relative wages) than industrial unions. Even the form of union organization, however, appears to be related to the influences considered by Marshall and Hicks. In general, where k represents the proportion of labor costs in total costs, Hicks showed that:

(10–7) $\left.\dfrac{\Delta \lambda}{\Delta k}\right|_{\text{Given all other influences}} = (\eta - \sigma)$ times a positive number

Thus, craft unions will tend to be formed and maintained whenever $\sigma < \eta$. Under those conditions, $\Delta\lambda/\Delta k > 0$, so that "It's important (to union power) to be unimportant (as a proportion of total costs)." Where substitution in production is relatively easier than substitution in consumption ($\sigma > \eta$), $\Delta\lambda/\Delta k$ will be < 0, and an industrial form of organization will be relatively more powerful. Union structure and organizing success across time appear to fit these presumptions.

In order to identify some other potential determinants of union monopoly power, it is useful to consider the ways in which unions can raise relative wages:

1. Fixing a wage (or schedule of wages) above W_n and enforcing that standard by a concerted refusal of employees to work below that wage (or compensation level) or at any level other than a negotiated one. This method includes the "economic strike," but variations—the slowdown, the sick-out, etc.—can also be used.
2. Reducing the schedule of labor time or labor services offered per unit time—that is, shifting the effective labor supply backward. This method includes, but is not restricted to closed shops, licensing arrangements, certification procedures (under union control), and, in a more complex way, various apprenticeship programs.[16]

Figure 10–5 illustrates the two methods and assumes some positive elasticity of labor supply. In Fig. 10–5, I, where the wage-fixing method is shown, CF represents a rationing problem for the union. Without devising some politically and socially approved way of allocating "F" time supplied among "C" opportunities, the union will find it difficult to maintain $W_u/W_n > 1.0$. The selection or rationing method may be seniority, a lottery, a complex bidding system, or some other method. Seniority systems are widely used for this purpose. They are often justified on the basis of equity and under certain conditions elaborated in Chapter 7 may not be opposed by management.

Figure 10–5 *Two Methods to Obtain Union Wage Increases*

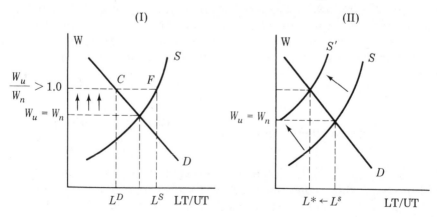

Obviously, the rationing problem will be larger (*CF* will be greater), the larger the elasticity of supply and/or the elasticity of demand. For short periods, before the stock of human and nonhuman capital can be changed to reflect new relative price relationships, the elasticities may be small, giving rise to little disemployment from high union wages, a small rationing problem, and even a sizable monopoly rent from $W_u > W_n$. Over time, however, both supply and demand elasticities increase as substitutes become available. Thus, disemployment and rationing problems grow unless entry to the (now more lucrative) occupation or activity is restricted. Indeed, if employers faced an infinitely elastic supply of labor to the firm in the shortest of runs, one would expect $W_u = W_n$. Thus, short-run supply elasticities are also an important determinant of union monopoly power. Therefore,

$$(10\text{--}8) \qquad \frac{W_u}{W_n} = f_2(\lambda, S, \ldots) \text{ where } S \text{ is elasticity of labor supply.}$$

It follows that from the supply side as well as the demand side of the market that craft unions with their relatively less elastic labor supply can be expected to be more powerful than unions of semiskilled workers. Although industrial unions may establish $W_u/W_n > 1$ by threat of strike, the maintenance of that monopoly position over time would appear to be more difficult than for craft unions. Over time, however, supply and demand elasticities can be expected to increase for *all* workers.

This supply-demand scenario has led Milton Friedman, among other commentators on union power, to argue that the second approach—control over supply—is essential to the maintenance of *any* long-run monopoly wage effect.[17] Entry controls or restrictions may be of many types, but they can be divided into two general catergories: (1) nonpriced entry restrictions (or controls) and (2) priced entry restrictions. A particular union may use either or both methods.

The chief nonpriced system of entry control employed by the American labor movement has been *the closed shop*. As noted above, it requires membership in a union (or union permission) as a *prerequisite* to employment. The closed shop needs to be distinguished analytically from the union shop and other weaker forms of union security. From the standpoint of a person with strong antiunion tastes (uncompensated by wage differences), it may be equally abhorrent to be required to join a union as a condition of employment whether that requirement applies before being employed or after (say) 30 days. The distaste or "individual rights" issue is similar or identical in the two cases. From a market point of view, however, the closed shop is quite different from the union shop and most other forms of union security. It allows the union to select the persons and the numbers over whom supply curves will be summed. Under the closed shop, by varying membership requirements for the union, the rate of apprenticeship training, and/or the number of temporary work permits, the supply curve can be positioned or "fine tuned" by the union. In this case, rationing comes about in the process of admitting union members rather than in allocating employment opportunities among workers. As the supply curve moves back, W_u/W_n will rise. As long as η (at the competitive wage) is less than 1.0, it pays all existing union members to reduce the supply of labor inputs. Thus, $CS =$ closed shop is included in the relative wage equation.

Among the nonpriced entry criteria are the following:

Nepotism—where selection of those to be admitted to the union, to apprenticeship programs, and/or to be employed depends upon one having relatives in the union (a research director of a large international union once equated this with "being born to the purple").

Race, sex, color or ethnic origin—where selection is limited to persons of particular racial, ethnic, or sex groups without any necessary relation to competence or productivity.

Licensure—where selection depends upon some objective or nonobjective test or training program. Such licensing arrangements may or may not be discriminatory and may include "bar exams," "medical exams," the CPA exam, teachers' exams, master plumbers' or journeymen's exams, and so on.

In all cases of licensure, whether a union is or is not involved, the exam may serve to limit entry and raise compensation levels over those which would otherwise exist. Indeed, "fine tuning" of the labor supply may exist in a number of nonunion circumstances. It is commonplace, for example, for plumbing inspectors, who control entry to particular labor markets, to be less lenient in issuing "one-job" or "two-job" permits to outside journeymen or outside master plumbers when local business is slack than when local business is brisk.

The power to control entry may not be initially or even primarily intended as a monopoly device. It may be, for example, an attempt on the part of the public to avoid negative externalities or compensate for information costs by standardizing the quality of practitioners of the trade. For example, in plumbing, electrical, medical, and other areas, the public may find it very difficult to judge competency, and mistakes in judgment in these areas can be very costly.[18] Regardless of intent, control of entry implies the ability to raise compensation levels above what they might otherwise be.

From the standpoint of the union or the group that seeks to control entry, each nonpriced method requires some more or less costly mechanism for deciding "who," "why," and "how many" will be admitted to the union, to practice, etc. The cost of the control mechanisms may be shifted to the public in some cases, but in general the entry control system will not be self-enforcing.

A priced entry control system is largely self-enforcing because it relies on the market to limit entry. Given the existence of some monopoly power, an income stream greater than alternative income streams will be generated. That income stream can be a gratuity delivered to third parties ("being born to the purple"?) or it can be sold in the open market. The purchase price may be expressed as a large initiation fee, as a kick-back to a corrupt union official (indeed, the monopoly rent creates an incentive for corruption), or as a legal purchase price for a license. (Ask any New York City cab driver about the price of a medallion—the legal right to drive cabs in the City—and then ask yourself why it is so high.) If the "price of entry" is determined in the open market, it will automatically restrict entry by "pricing out" the monopoly rent implicit in the restricted numbers of persons in the activity. Thus, unless a particular buyer can somehow "get a good deal" on the right to enter, he will earn only a competitive rate of return on his new "asset." At equilibrium, the market value of this right to enter will be the discounted value of the expected monopoly returns, as in the following equation:

(10–9) $$PV_I \cong \sum_{t=1}^{N} \frac{I_t}{(1 + r)^t} \text{ where}$$

PV_I = the present market value of the monopoly rents

I_t = the income stream per unit time, the difference between expected earnings via the monopoly less the next best alternative, $(W_u - W_n)_t$

r = the market interest rate

t = a time index in years

N = the maximum number of annual time periods.[19]

When r and I_t are fixed for all time periods, Eq. 10–9 collapses to the familiar capitalization formula:

(10–10) $$PV_I \cong \frac{I}{r} \text{ when } N \text{ is large.}$$

If a union can establish some entry fee approximately equal to the present value of the monopoly rent or if there is an active market price for the right to enter, the market will select out the limited number of those who "qualify" for entry; specifically, those who will pay the price. Obviously, this arrangement works to the relative disadvantage of the poor, minorities, and others with limited cash reserves. Note that the Labor-Management Relations Act of 1947 (the Taft-Hartley Act), which banned the closed shop in much of the American labor market, also sharply limited the magnitude of union initiation and entry fees.

To this point, we have discussed W_n as if it were the result of competitive wage determination. It could, however, be a monopsony wage. Under such conditions, the union can countervail against the monopsony, raising W_u with little or no decrease in employment and, perhaps, with an increase. The analysis here is identical to that for minimum wages (see Chapter 5) and need not be repeated. With the appropriate additions, our union wage equation becomes:

$$(10\text{--}11) \qquad \frac{W_u}{W_n} = f_2(\overset{-}{\lambda}, [\overset{-}{S}, \overset{+}{CS}] \text{ or } [\overset{+}{M}], \ldots)$$

with the signs above Eq. 10–11 indicating the direction of the expected effects and where M stands for the presence (1) or absence (0) of monopsony prior to unionization.

Where union membership is high relative to total employment (say) in a firm or industry, the union boycott tactic (I, above) is more credible. Thus, unions that do not represent a substantial portion of the workers in the relevant firm (or market) will be weaker than those who do. As a consequence, U is an argument in the relative wage function, just as W_u/W_n is an argument in the membership function, making the model fully simultaneous.

One caveat on U is necessary here. Where the membership is related to union shop or other "forced" unionization provisions, the effect of membership in the relative wage equation may be slight. Members who join unions involuntarily and/or with little adherence to union objectives can hardly be counted on to "hit the bricks" and are even less likely to be willing to sustain a long or bitter strike or other tests of union strength.

Finally, it is important to remember that the different demand and supply elasticities will alter W_u/W_n across skills, geographic regions, industries, and time in fairly predictable ways. The empirical findings discussed below illustrate some of these ways.

Unionism as a Cheap Screening Device

As noted above, the closed shop and associated hiring hall practices have been illegal in most employments since the passage of the Labor-Management Relations Act of 1947.[20] Hiring halls and closed shops, however, continue to exist. Because the cost of enforcing any such law is borne by the public rather than by the litigant, the continued existence of the closed shop, hiring halls, and so on, forces us to ask the following question: Why don't employers faced with closed shops (and presumably higher W_u/W_n's) simply complain to the authorities?

One answer could be that the employers or the authorities are afraid of the unions or are wary of the violence-producing potential of these organized groups. This answer implies that private enforcement power (or muscle) is greater than public power or that public officials have been "bought off." Such a scenario might be reasonable in limited cases, but it is difficult to imagine this mobster-type explanation applying generally throughout the nation.

An alternative explanation is suggested by the kinds of employment in which the de facto closed shop continues to exist. These include on-site construction, entertainment, brewing, and longshoring. One characteristic these activities have in common is intermittent, but not seasonal or regular, fluctuations in employment. Moreover, particular but different sets of industry-specific skills are required in each industry.

Consider the available alternative employment arrangements for an employer in these or similar industries. He could employ his workers year round at an annual salary approximately equal to what an equally skilled individual could earn elsewhere. Thus, he could assure himself of an adequate labor supply if he could correctly anticipate his changing demand, paying more than the MVP of his workers in the off-season and less during the season. Now, although estimating fluctuating demand is relatively easy for seasonally sensitive employment, it is difficult and risky for intermittent employment. Alternatively, the firm could search for skilled workers when and if it wanted them, bearing the costs of search and skill ascertainment each time demand fluctuated. Third, the firm could contract out the search process to a manpower specialist, again at some cost, but perhaps a cost that would be shared by the prospective employees (or those hired).

Consider now the functions of a closed shop. Generally, the union guarantees some acceptable level of skill. A journeyman (a term of respect in union circles) is expected to be able to perform up to journeymen's standards. Moreover, the union supplies such journeymen on demand to be employed at union wages until the time when they are no longer "needed" and are returned to the hiring hall. The compensation to union members for their services *and* for the services of the hiring hall is contained, of course, in W_u. The union as an institution will receive dW_u per period. It follows that the closed shop can serve as a cheap screening device for employers in areas of intermittent employment. To the degree that the union is an efficient broker, both sides may gain. Moreover, to the degree that $W_u - W_n$ does not exceed the cost per employee per unit time of using the cheapest alternative screening device, *ceteris paribus*, the union wage differential does *not* represent a monopoly return, but merely a search cost differential. Equation (10–12) describes the existence or nonexistence of the closed shop as a function of irregularity of employment, industry-specific skills, and alternative costs of search for employers:

(10–12) $CS = f_3(Ir, Sk, SC, \ldots)$ where

$CS = \{^1_0\}$ depending upon the existence or nonexistence of a closed shop

$Ir = \{^1_0\}$ depending upon the presence or absence of irregular employment

$Sk = \{^1_0\}$ denoting the presence or absence of industry (but not firm) related skills

$SC =$ the level of alternative search costs per employee per period expected by employers.

The final determinant of CS is institutional in nature, i.e., a Davis-Bacon Act or similar "prevailing wage" acts. Originally passed in 1931, this act requires that construction projects financed in whole or in part by federal funds pay wages equal to "the prevailing wage level" in the locality. It has been alleged that the U.S. Department of Labor has often used the "union scale" as "the prevailing wage level." Now, if the contractors are required to pay "union scale," it makes little sense for them not to use the construction unions as cheap screening devices.

Thus, with respect to the construction industry, the Davis-Bacon Act may be an important determinant of the closed shop and W_u/W_n. Empirical evidence on this issue is discussed later in this chapter.

The Simultaneous Model

As indicated above, union membership and trade union power may be closely interrelated and mutually determined. Moreover, a wide variety of (exogenous) institutional and economic factors impinge upon that joint determination, creating a large number of potential "outcomes." Among these are numerically large unions which are economically weak, small unions which are very powerful (as measured by W_u/W_n), and unions whose power to fix $W_u > W_n$ falls rapidly over time. Moreover, swings in the business cycle can have disparate effects, as can (1) government wage regulation and control in particular periods and (2) labor legislation. The simultaneous model presented here is intended to represent most of these important influences, but it does not and cannot exhaust all possible determinants. The reader should, however, have the model clearly in mind during the next portion of this chapter—a review of empirical evidence. For that reason, the full model is presented below:

(10–13) $U = f_1\left(\dfrac{W_u}{W_n}, d, IC, E, PZ, D, US, \ldots\right)$

$$\frac{W_u}{W_n} = f_2\,(\lambda,\,[S,\,CS]\;\text{or}\;[M\,];\;U,) \left| \begin{array}{l}\text{skills and other human}\\ \text{capital measures}\end{array}\right.$$

$$CS = f_3\,(Ir,\,Sk,\,SC;\,DB,\,\ldots\,)$$

$\lambda = f_4\,(\psi,\,\eta,\,\sigma,\,e,\,k,\,\ldots\,)$ where ψ represents the stages of the business cycle.

Empirical Determinants of Union Membership and of Union Wage Effects

Given the complexity of the general model developed above and the unique circumstances surrounding union organizing campaigns, it is not surprising that the general simultaneous model has not been fully "solved." Indeed, mathematically and econometrically sophisticated readers will see that the general model is "overdetermined," that is, amenable to more than one simultaneous solution for U and for W_u/W_n. Faced with the difficulties of fitting the full system as simultaneous equations and of collecting all the appropriate data, labor economists have sought simpler approaches. First, they have estimated U and W_u/W_n as separate equations without taking explicit account of any interrelationships between the respective equations. Second, a few researchers have tried to fit simplified simultaneous systems. These approaches are considered in turn.

Estimates of the Membership Equation

Orley Ashenfelter's and John Pencavel's early attempt to explain econometrically the growth of American labor unions took place against the backdrop of a long-term controversy among institutionalists and industrial relations specialists.[21] John R. Commons in the 1930s and Selig Perlman in the 1960s along with other "saturationists" argued that unionization was closely related to business cycles with those patterns interrupted by periodic spurts and declines induced by major institutional changes—hence, the expectation that in the absence of major institutional changes, the stages of the business cycle would move the saturation level up or down. John Dunlop, Joseph Shister, I. Bernstein, Phillip Taft, and other members of the "historical school" contended throughout the 1940s and 1950s that unionism was too complex and variegated a phenomenon to be explained so simply.[22] Rather than basing predictions on what they believed to be the "unproven" psychological assumptions of the saturationists, these scholars saw union growth resulting from a number of factors, including a gradual growth of union acceptability among American workers. For the most part, the controversy was noneconometric in nature, and tests of the various explanatory notions were very limited.

Ashenfelter's and Pencavel's econometric study and a subsequent study by R. B. Mancke provided some support for each side of the controversy.[23] The A & P time series analysis indicated that American union growth had been related to changes in the price level, with union membership rising by 0.6 percentage points per period for each 1 percent change in the price level, *ceteris paribus*. It also indicated that the growth rate of unionization is negatively affected by the proportion of the "unionizable sector" of the economy already unionized, a finding supporting the saturationist position. Moreover, the A & P study found union growth to be positively related to the proportion of Democrats in the national House of Representatives, presumably reflecting a higher level of "popular favor," or, in our terms, lower indirect costs of unionism. Mancke argued for more specificity in the estimating equation and used "dummy variables" to capture the effect of major labor legislation, particularly the National Labor Relations Act of 1935 (the Wagner Act). He found strong support for the proposition that favorable legislation was a major determinant of union growth. Moreover, his results suggested that business cycles had little effect until after the Wagner Act was passed and tested in the federal courts (1937).

Using cross-sectional (state) data for 1967, Alan Blinder's study, "Who Joins Unions," found support for the proposition that unionism was particularly attractive to males, blacks, operatives, persons of lower educational attainment, and urbanites who were born on farms.[24] In addition, his work found that southern and western workers were less likely to be union members than were workers in the eastern and north-central portions of the United States, *ceteris paribus*. These general findings are not inconsistent with the taste analysis developed above. Similar cross-sectional findings by William Moore and Robert Newman, using data for 1950, 1960, and 1970, emphasized the positive relationship between union membership and nonwhites, and between union membership and urbanization, as well as the negative relationship between union membership and the South.[25] Moore and Newman also found union membership and state right-to-work laws to be negatively related. Their two-stage estimating technique, which involves an element of simultaneity between right-to-work laws and union membership suggests that right-to-work laws lower union membership by about 4 percentage points, a small but statistically meaningful impact. Because state right-to-work laws outlaw the union shop and usually some weaker forms of union security, the Moore and Newman findings are consistent with the expectation in the general model that union shop arrangements can be expected to have some, apparently small, impact on union membership.

Finally, in a separate work, John Pencavel "fit" a demand equation for unionism to British data for 1928–66.[26] He argued that the demand for union membership—as an asset—should respond to "permanent" wealth positions, the relative price of union membership (dues), and the prices of substitute assets among other factors. As he expected, Pencavel found unionism to be positively related to real income per capita and negatively related to union dues and interest rates on alternative assets, with some lags for each effect. Moreover, he found unionism in Britain to be negatively related to wartime conditions. Pencavel saw this effect as the result of negative transitory incomes during wartime periods in England. As suggested by the simultaneous model developed above, it is not clear whether union membership in Pencavel's approach is "produced" by wealth levels (or real income), or whether the causation is reversed. In the latter case, a more complex simultaneous model is required.

Finally, a unique study of voting behavior in union representation elections by Henry Farber and Daniel Saks[27] provides both supportive and unique evidence in a number of areas. Farber and Saks found that blacks were likely to "vote union" and oldsters less likely, *ceteris paribus*. No difference between the sexes in adherence to unionism was found in their data (full-time workers in manufacturing). The study, however, indicated that unions were more likely to win if unionism was seen *prior to the election* as promoting fairness and less likely if it was seen as producing a deterioration in worker-management relations. Those workers who believed that it would be difficult to replace their current jobs were less likely to "vote union," but that diffidence could be overcome if unions were perceived as enhancing job security among the same workers. Moreover, if unions were seen as reducing promotion possibilities *among those workers who expected promotion in the future,* the probability of a positive union vote was reduced. While none of these findings are particularly surprising, the fact that they emerge from the statistical tests supports some of the ideas developed in the membership equation above.

Farber and Saks also found that workers expect unions to raise wages *and* that workers vote *as if* they believe union wages would be more standardized than nonunion wages. Workers in the lower portion of the intrafirm wage distribution were found to be more likely to vote union than were workers in the higher segments, all other factors held constant. This finding, suggest Farber and Saks, should be distinguished from the interfirm wage effect—what we have been calling the relative union wage effect. One interpretation of this Farber-Saks result is that it reflects the desire for "equal treatment" via unionization.

To summarize, although none of the empirical studies discussed here are definitive, the findings are generally consistent with the model of union membership developed in the first part of this chapter. Particular ethnic and regional groups show marked preferences for unions (blacks, urbanites, males). Labor laws and, more generally, particular political climates appear to have sizable effects. Moreover, the small, but positive effect of union shop provisions on union membership appears quite reasonable. The Farber-Saks study, in particular, breaks new ground, finding the demand for unionism as reflecting a desire for the reduction of intrafirm wage dispersion. Finally, upswings in the business cycle appear to be positively related to union membership, apparently because employer retaliation is less effective in boom periods and labor demand elasticities are smaller. The latter point, of course, reintroduces simultaneity. Only one study looked at the explicit influence of dues and wartime conditions, and that was for Britain. Dues had the expected negative influence on membership as did wartime conditions. As argued above in the general model, wartime conditions in the United States appear to have been positively related to union membership.

Although the findings of these (largely) single-equation approaches are generally supportive of the hypotheses suggested by theory and historical observation, one must approach them with caution. If union membership, union wage effects, and perhaps labor laws are simultaneously determined, empirical results from single equation approaches may be subject to serious (simultaneous equation) biases.

Estimates of the Union Wage Effect

Many of the early case studies and single equation estimates of union wage effects are summarized in H. Gregg Lewis's classic work, *Unionism and Relative Wages in the United States.*[28] This highly technical work, which includes reinterpretations of Ph.D. dissertations by Lewis's students and of other studies, concentrates on the standardization of wage levels for skills, locations, and other wage determinants so that W_u/W_n can be correctly estimated. In general, Lewis found sizable differences in W_u/W_n across unions and time periods.

The available data showed union wage effects ranging from 100% in 1921–22 for bituminous coal mining to an insignificant effect in 1945 in the same industry. Only a few studies, however, indicated relative wage effects ≥ 25 percent. Lewis estimated that at or near full employment, the average union wage effect shown by these studies was approximately 10–15 percent. Many apparently strong unions, however, had little or no effect on wages. This phenomenon (where unionism is solely a consumer good?) appears most often in industrial sectors in which respective employers are faced with substantial nonunion and/or foreign competition. Using the accumulated findings of the various studies, Lewis estimated relative wage impacts of 20 percent or more covering less than 6 percent of the labor force. In particular, he cited bituminous coal (for some time periods), the building trades, and barbering. In each case, the relevant industrial sector was characterized by relatively high degrees of unionism and low elasticities of demand. In some cases, strong licensing and other restrictions on competition prevailed. Even high proportions of unionism, however, did not yield sizable union wage effects among the Amalgamated Clothing Workers. Similarly, small or zero union wage effects were found after World War II for the Amalgamated Street Railway and Motor Coach Operators. The reduction of their previously positive wage effect to zero is quite consistent with the increasing elasticity of labor demand in this (then) declining industry. Finally, although the research is not definitive, the declining wage effects for printers and typographers in recent years appear to have been related to the technological revolution which has swept the industry, a revolution which substitutes machinery, computers, and other forms of labor for the (previously) essential printers and typographers (i.e., larger σs and therefore larger λs).

In addition, union wage effects are cyclically sensitive. Albert Rees's work suggests that union wage levels tend to fall behind nonunion rates during rapid inflations.[29] This phenomenon appears to result both from the periodicity of contract negotiations and from the hesitancy of (at least) some employers to agree to the same wage increases for workers under union contract as for nonunion workers. Union workers are, of course, protected from subsequent internal labor market adjustments by seniority and other constraints. Thus, Rees argues that union wage effects tend to decline in rapid inflations. Conversely, during severe economic downturns, union wage levels are more downward rigid than nonunion levels. In that event, employment tradeoffs, of course, may be substantial and union membership may decline. Mild inflation, however, appears to be "good" for union membership, with tightening labor markets allowing unions to take credit for money wage (and any real wage) increases that might have occurred anyway.

Marvin Kosters[30] presents evidence that during the inflation(s) of the 1970s, unions sought to reduce their wage lags by including more cost-of-living (COL) wage adjustment provisions in their contracts, introducing more wage reopening provisions, and shortening contract periods. This analysis reinforces the original contentions by Rees, while also indicating that union leaders learn from experience and alter their approaches during sustained rapid inflations. These attempts to minimize real wage reductions (and maintain W_u/W_n) may also be to some degree in the interests of management during rapid inflations. If real and relative wage levels for unionized firms fall "too far" during such periods, firms can expect higher turnover and higher recruitment and training costs. Thus, managers who expect sustained inflation will be less hesitant to institutionalize COL arrangements than those who expect, for example, a slowdown in the rate of inflation. Nevertheless, the degree to which union workers employing such tactics have kept up with recent rapid inflations and the degree to which inflation produces a warping of the interindustry wage structure remain fertile areas for research.

Recent single-equation, econometric models generally support earlier findings, although there is a considerable spread in the estimated wage effects. The estimated effects depend upon the time period, industrial sector or sectors, geographic location, and sex-race dimensions examined in the respective studies. The median wage effect for the 1960s and 1970s shown by these studies seems to be approximately 11 percent, with some effects as low as 6 and some as high as 25–30 percent.[31] My own single-equation estimate for 1972–73 suggests an average effect of 11–12 percent.[32] Despite some continuing differences in estimates of average effects, the evidence in general appears to conform to the expectations of our wage effect equation, becoming larger or smaller as demand and supply elasticities vary, as membership varies, and as union security provisions vary.

As noted above, the general consistency of the empirical results over a long time period can be questioned and has been questioned as neglecting the simultaneous determination of union membership, union wage effects, and even skill levels. Failure to account for simultaneity may result in biased estimates. For example, most single-equation approaches standardize for differences in human capital—education or skill levels, etc.—in order that wage differences from these influences not confound the estimates of the union wage effect. If, however, employers respond to positive union wage effects by raising skill levels or otherwise changing the mix of skilled labor, low-skilled labor, and capital, a single equation estimate may understate the union wage effect. The available simultaneous equation estimates will be further discussed below.

The problem of estimating the "true" union wage effect is also complicated by "threat" or "spillover" effects. The usual scenario suggests that nonunion employers may systematically raise wage levels in order to discourage unionization, matching or partially matching union wage levels. Hence, union wage effects will spill over into the nonunion sector. Such behavior has allegedly been observed from time to time, but economic theory argues against long-run effects of this type for a given distribution of skills among the work force. Union wages that involve monopoly rents necessarily will reduce employment opportunities in the union sector and will raise labor availability (and lower the equilibrium nonunion wage, *ceteris paribus*) in the nonunion sector of the market unless, of course, all displaced workers from the union sector drop out of the labor force or remain unemployed. Nevertheless, if the probability of becoming unionized depends positively on the union-nonunion wage differential, some nonunion firms may "hedge their bets" by paying more than "market rates." In the long run, however, entry into the industry and interproduct competition ought to constrain this threat effect.

As the reader might imagine, there are few systematic tests of these complex tradeoffs. Sherwin Rosen's study,[33] using interindustry data, looked not only at the spillover or threat effect, but also at the effect of increased union organization of an industry on the union wage effect (coverage), and at the relationship between coverage and threat effects. Rosen found, as we surmised above with respect to control of labor supply, that wage effects and coverage were positively related, *ceteris paribus*. The threat effect of further unionization on wages, however, appears to fall at relatively high levels of unionization. In addition, Rosen suggests that business managers and union leaders are involved in playing a strategic game. On the one hand, nonunion managers can presumably decrease the probability of organization by raising nonunion wages relative to union wages. On the other hand, it pays union leaders to raise W_u/W_n in order to maximize coverage and further enhance union power. Nevertheless, given the elasticity of demand for union workers, increases in union wages imply a wage-employment tradeoff for union workers. In the long run and with free entry, we would expect this elasticity to be very large, effectively restraining both the union wage and the threat effect. As Rosen recognizes, the full long-run explanation depends upon how the subjective probability of unionization is formed and how the elasticity of demand for union labor changes over time. Those two dimensions have not yet been adequately examined, so that the threat effect question remains in an analytical limbo, at least in longer time periods. Rosen's work, however, points the way toward the resolution of this issue.

Estimates of the Closed Shop Equation

The closed shop equation has received relatively less empirical attention, although the higher trade union wage effects for building and some other trades may be regarded as implicit verification. The lack of attention probably results from the fact that the closed shop has been illegal in most American establishments since the passage of the Labor-Management Relations Act of 1947. As noted above, however, union hiring halls and limited apprenticeship programs—the hallmarks of the closed shop—continue to exist as effective institutions wherever employment is irregular and search costs are high. The usual wording of the closed shop clause in collective bargaining contracts, however, no longer requires employers to use the hiring halls and/or union apprentices exclusively [except for contracts under the Railway Labor Act (1926)]. Union control over labor supply is therefore no longer de jure. Casual observation suggests, however, that many unionized employers in intermittent employment areas have de facto closed shop arrangements. We argued above that the closed shop may be in the interests of management in such cases. Indeed, it is hard to believe that an illegal institution could continue to exist for over 30 years if employers in these economic areas were unalterably opposed to it and/or if monopoly rents were large. It follows that to the degree that the closed shop is a screening device, some portion of the union wage effect (say, in construction) represents a wage-search cost tradeoff rather than a monopoly rent.

One area of the CS equation has been studied in considerable detail—the Davis-Bacon Act. This federal act, originally passed in 1931 and intended to provide a floor to downward bidding on government contracts during the Great Depression, was subsequently extended over the years by attachment to at least 77 other acts that provide federal assistance to numerous activities. Under the act, the Department of Labor is required to determine the prevailing wage levels for each building trade or specialty in each geographic area prior to bid submission. In all, about $37.8 billion dollars of construction and 22 percent of the nation's 3.8 million construction workers were covered in 1977 by such wage determinations.[34]

Research by Damodar Gujarati, John Gould, Arnold Thieblot, and others[35] indicates that the Employment Standards Administration of the Department of Labor and its predecessors have usually used negotiated union rates as the basis for the determination of prevailing wages, even adopting the union rates for noncontiguous areas in some cases. Considering the workload of the Employment Standards Administration, their use of available cheap screening devices rather than conducting continuous, detailed wage surveys or using other costly methods is understandable.

These procedures, however, have several effects, including:

1. A higher cost for government and governmentally assisted projects than might otherwise be experienced.

2. Increased demand for union members, created because employers who are required to pay the higher union rates (or higher rates generally) are more likely to use union services. A special variant of this screening effect finds unionized contractors bidding for Davis-Bacon Act jobs at some distance from their home offices with local open shop contractors eschewing such projects.

3. Increased support for union organization, which is a reflection of the above effect.[36]

4. A spillover effect on nonunion wages. Some evidence indicates that the Davis-Bacon Act induces open shop employers on non-Davis-Bacon Act jobs in nearby areas to raise wage levels in order to hold their workers. Both because of this spillover and because the Davis-Bacon Act generally applies a union wage or an average wage as *the* minimum for government projects, average wages around each Davis-Bacon Act site are increased, contradicting the intent of the initial legislation.

The "emergency" suspension of the Davis-Bacon Act by President Richard Nixon on February 23, 1971 has provided some additional, but limited evidence on the influence of the act on wage levels. President Nixon suspended the act as part of his anti-inflation program and, during the period from February 23 to March 29, bids were resubmitted, resulting in some lower average construction costs. Given other possible explanations of the lower wages, however, these data cannot be interpreted as definitive support for a Davis-Bacon Act wage effect. The Building Trades Department of the AFL-CIO, however, interpreted President Nixon's suspension as a strong attack on the constituent unions. Rather than "fighting it out" with open shop contractors in the market, however, they negotiated an agreement with the president to hold future wage increases to his target level of 6 percent per annum. Upon receiving that assurance of "cooperation," President Nixon revoked the suspension.[37]

Simultaneous Equation Approaches

Following some suggestions by Melvin Reder and H. Gregg Lewis,[38] Ashenfelter and Johnson[39] proposed that causation of the W_u/W_n in the usual single-equation models could flow both ways, with relative wage levels depending upon unionization and unionization depending upon wage levels. If this were true, they argued, a simultaneous approach would be required "to capture" the true union wage effect. They developed such a model. Several other analysts followed Ashenfelter's and Johnson's lead, some with data on individual wage levels and union membership, and some with aggregate or "interindustry data" from several sources.[40] In a few cases, the analysts also attempted to capture the simultaneous effects of unions and wage rates on skill levels.

In general, the estimates of the union impact on wage levels obtained from these simultaneous models are relatively small, ranging from zero to about 7 percent. Ashenfelter and Johnson, for example, found an interindustry wage effect that was not significantly different from zero, as did John Pencavel.[41] Peter Schmidt and Robert Strauss,[42] who used individual data, found about a 7 percent union wage effect, but the statistical significance of that effect was questionable—that is, the true effect could have been zero. In all these cases, however, the effects of wage levels on unionism were larger and usually more statistically significant than the union wage effect.

In a further development, Lawrence Kahn sought to isolate direct union wage effects from the indirect effects of union wage levels on production techniques.[43] Using interindustry data for U.S. manufacturing, Kahn found small direct, but larger indirect effects. Moreover, he suggested that the indirect effects contribute to (more?) labor market segmentation by moving unionized manufacturing toward more capital- and skill-intensive production techniques.

The results from simultaneous models, however, do not universally support a small or zero direct union wage effect. Using a three-equation model involving a union wage, a nonunion wage, and a membership equation, Lung-fei Lee found a union wage effect for operatives of 15–16 percent when observed across a wide spectrum of economic activities.[44] The measured effect was even larger for nonwhite males ($\cong 28$ percent), but females were paid more in the nonunion sector (except for older females). In addition, Lee found the union wage effect to be the strongest single influence on union membership ("union status," in his words). His numbers indicate that a 10 percent union wage difference could increase union membership by over 20 percentage points. Although the magnitude of this effect seems high, the direction is consistent with other simultaneous studies and with the presumption, discussed above, that the cumulative frequency curve for union membership may be relatively flat near $W_u/W_n = 0$ or slightly above that level. With a relatively flat curve, small differences in relative wages will induce large differences in membership. Lee found that city size, region, and industrial concentration (firm size) are also significant determinants of union membership. The effect of union shops (or the converse, right-to-work laws), however, was not examined in Lee's study. In addition, his study suggests that unionized firms contain the most productive workers (as measured by education and labor market experience), but his analysis did not explicitly "model" skill selectivity as a response to union wage effects. Duane Leigh also found causation running in both directions, a positive effect of unions on relative wages and a positive effect of relative wages on union membership.[45]

It is difficult to summarize and assess the net contribution of these simultaneous equation models. The available models use different data sets and different statistical procedures (chiefly second- and third-stage least-squares and/or mixed logit approaches), and indicate considerable sensitivity to the particular variables used in the estimation procedures. Moreover, the simultaneous models usually do not standardize for institutional or legal factors, which may impinge strongly on the membership equation (e.g., right-to-work laws), although firm size or other proxies for instutitional factors are sometimes included. The results from these attempts would be more convincing if the various legal and institutional influences (indirect cost factors) which seem to have been important in the growth of unions were also tested in the models. Nevertheless, simultaneous approaches are in the mainstream of "the new industrial relations" (mentioned in the Introduction), and simultaneous models will continue to be elaborated and perfected. A number of the simultaneous model results indicate that single-equation estimates of union wage effects may be too high, particularly in manufacturing. In my judgment, however, the evidence from simultaneous models is not yet sufficient or sufficiently uniform to overturn "the conventional wisdom," although the body of evidence from these models is growing.

Notes to Chapter 10

1. David Kin, ed., *Dictionary of American Maxims* (New York: Philosophical Library, 1955), p. 539.

2. For this quotation, I am indebted to an excellent, brief history of American labor and the American labor movement by Henry Pelling, *American Labor* (Chicago: University of Chicago Press, 1960). Readers seeking an additional brief historical treatment should see U.S. Department of Labor, *Brief History of the American Labor Movement*, BLS bulletin 1000, bicentennial edition (Washington, D.C.: U.S. Government Printing Office, 1976).

3. For an elaboration of this point, see the interesting description of the several intellectual-attitudinal-social movements that have swept across the American scene since the late 1700s by Stewart H. Holbrook, *Dreamers of the American Dream* (Garden City, N.Y.: Doubleday & Co., 1957). The labor movement was among these. Others include the utopianist, prohibitionist, populist, women's suffrage, and humanitarian movements. Unfortunately, the book—written in the late 1950s—does not include the civil rights movement and the women's liberation movement (Women's Lib II?).

4. See Archie Green, "Recorded Labor Songs: An Overview," *Western Folklore* 27 (1968): 68–76. Also found as Reprint no. 188, Institute of Labor and Industrial Relations, *University of Illinois Bulletin* 66, no. 23 (September 27, 1968).

5. *Songs of the Workers to Fan the Flames of Discontent*, 13th ed. (Chicago: Industrial Workers of the World, 1962).

6. Robert F. Hoxie, *Trade Unionism in the United States* (New York: D. Appleton and Co., 1920)

7. Elsewhere, I have speculated that these differences in union movements are related to differences in class consciousness and in the breadth of popular support for egalitarian principles. See Robert M. Fearn, "Unionism and Income Distribution," in "Freedom and Equality in the American Economy," Winston–Salem, N.C.: Center for the Study of Human Values, March 9–11, 1978, pp. 63–70. (Mimeographed conference proceedings.)

8. See Pelling, *American Labor*, pp. 137–43 for a description of Gompers's approach to political activities.

9. This segment of the chapter has been strongly influenced by H. Gregg Lewis, "Competitive and Monopoly Unionism," in *The Public Stake on Union Power*, ed. Phillip D. Bradley (Charlottesville, Va.: University of Virginia Press, 1959).

10. A bimodal distribution with a mode below and one above 1.0 may indicate strong class consciousness. Examination of the cumulative distribution of union tastes for such a society yields some interesting insights. Also see note 13.

11. See Sanford Cohen, *Labor in the United States*, 5th ed. (Columbus,

Ohio: Charles E. Merrill Publishing Co., 1979), or any other good industrial relations text for details on the "criminal conspiracy doctrine."

12. Richard Freeman, "Individual Mobility and Union Voice in the Labor Market," *American Economic Review* 66, no. 2 (May 1976): 361–68.

13. The Vichy government in France during the early 1940s provides an interesting example of the role of class feelings in defining loyalties and motivating different behaviors. When the wartime struggle was treated by individual Frenchmen as if it were a choice solely between communism and fascism, it appears that individuals often relied on class identifications to determine their personal political roles. When the issue was cast as a struggle between nations or cultures as it was by General Charles DeGaulle, class identification was a more remote consideration.

14. Other forms of union security, spelled out in the specific collective bargaining contract provisions, are less stringent than union shops or closed shops. These include (1) maintenance of membership provisions whereby all union members must *remain* members of the union until the expiration of the contract, and (2) agency shop provisions that require membership in the union or the payment of a fee in lieu of dues to compensate the union for its services as the bargaining agent. Agency shops are often sought by unions in states having "right-to-work" laws which outlaw union shops. Check-off procedures may also be contractually required whereby union dues are automatically deducted from payroll checks and paid to the union. Under the Labor-Management Relations Act (the Taft-Hartley Act) amendments to the National Labor Relations Act (the Wagner Act), the closed shop has been illegal in most American enterprises since 1947.

15. Alfred Marshall, *Principles of Economics,* 8th ed. (New York: Macmillan Co., 1949), bk. v, chap. 4, and J. R. Hicks, *The Theory of Wages,* 2d ed. (London: Macmillan & Co., 1964), pp. 241–46.

16. Unions might also seek to induce potential customers to "buy union," decreasing the elasticity of demand for union labor. Unless the elasticity of supply of union labor is low and unless nonunion labor supplies are limited by tactic I and/or II above, it is likely that "buy union" or union label actions will have only small effects on relative wages.

17. Milton Friedman, "Some Comments on the Significance of Labor Unions for Economic Policy," in *The Impact of the Union,* ed. David McCord Wright (New York: Harcourt Brace, 1951).

18. Alternatively stated, it may be cheaper socially for the public to substitute some licensing arrangement than for each person to bear the costs of search necessary to reduce the level of risk for each demander to some "acceptable" level. It may also be deemed essential to control the quality of (say) doctors in order to reduce the large possibilities of externalities, e.g., failure of a "quack" to recognize the symptoms of a highly communicable disease.

19. Equation (10–9) can also be written in continuous form:

$$\sum_{t=1}^{N} \frac{I_t}{(1 + r)^t} \cong \int_{t=0}^{N} I_t e^{-rt}\, dt = PV_I.$$

20. The Railway Labor Act (1926), however, permits closed shop arrangements in the jurisdictions covered by the act.

21. Orley Ashenfelter and John Pencavel, "American Trade Union Growth,

1900–1960," *Quarterly Journal of Economics* 81, no. 3 (August 1969): 434–48. These authors' results were anticipated in a less technical article by Horace B. Davis, "A Theory of Trade Union Growth," *Quarterly Journal of Economics* 55, no. 4 (August 1941): 611–37.

22. The terms "saturationists" and "historical school" are taken from I. Bernstein, "The Growth of American Unions," *American Economic Review* 44, no. 3 (June 1954): 301–18.

23. R. B. Mancke, "American Trade Union Growth: A Comment," *Quarterly Journal of Economics* 85, no. 1 (February 1971): 187–93. Also see John Pencavel, "The Demand for Union Services: An Exercise," *Industrial and Labor Relations Review* 24, no. 2 (January 1971): 180–90.

24. Alan S. Blinder, "Who Joins Unions" (unpublished working paper no. 36, Princeton University: Industrial Relations Section, February 1972).

25. William J. Moore and Robert J. Newman, "On the Prospects for American Trade Union Growth: A Cross-Section Analysis," *Review of Economics and Statistics* 62, no. 4 (November 1975): 435–45.

26. John Pencavel, "Relative Wages and Trade Unions in the United Kingdom," *Econometrica* 41, no. 162 (May 1974): 194–210.

27. Henry S. Farber and Daniel H. Saks, "Why Workers Want Unions: The Role of Relative Wages and Job Characteristics," *Journal of Political Economy* 88, no. 2 (April 1980): 349–69.

28. H. Gregg Lewis, *Unionism and Relative Wages in the United States* (Chicago: University of Chicago Press, 1963).

29. Albert Rees, *The Economics of Trade Unions*, 2d ed., rev. (Chicago: University of Chicago Press, 1977).

30. Marvin Kosters, "Wage and Price Behavior: Prospects and Policies," in *Contemporary Economic Problems, 1977*, ed. William Fellner (Washington, D.C.: American Enterprise Institute for Public Policy Research, 1977), pp. 159–201, and "Wage Behavior and Inflation in the 1970's," in *Contemporary Economic Problems, 1978*, ed. William Fellner (Washington, D.C.: American Enterprise Institute for Public Policy Research, 1978), pp. 137–66.

31. See, for example, George Johnson and K. Youmas, "Union Relative Wage Effects," *Industrial and Labor Relations Review* 24, no. 2 (January 1971): 171–79; Orley Ashenfelter, G. Johnson, and J. H. Pencavel, "Trade Unions and the Rate of Change in Money Wages in the U.S. Manufacturing Industry," *Review of Economic Studies* 39, no. 1 (January 1972): 27–54; Leonard Weiss, "Concentration and Labor Earnings," *American Economic Review* 56, no. 1 (March 1966): 96–117; A. W. Throop, "The Union-Nonunion Wage Differential and Cost Push Inflation," *American Economic Review* 58, no. 1 (March 1968): 79–99; Sherwin Rosen, "On the Interindustry Wage and Hours Structure," *Journal of Political Economy* 77, no. 2 (March/April 1969): 249–73, and "Unionism and the Occupational Wage Structure in the U.S.," *International Economic Review* 11, no. 2 (June 1970): 269–86.

32. David Hyman and Robert Fearn, "The Effect of City Size on Labor Incomes," *Quarterly Review of Economics and Business* 18, no. 1 (Spring 1978): 63–73, showed a union wage effect of $e^{+.11} - 1 = 0.116$ or 11.6 percent. Introducing an interaction term for unionized construction workers in the Hyman-Fearn equation yields a statistically significant union wage effect for them of approximately 25 percent and lowers the wage effect for other unionized workers to

about 8 percent. A similar attempt to isolate the union wage effect for unionized transport operatives was statistically unsuccessful, although the estimated union wage effect of about 20 percent appears reasonable.

33. Sherwin Rosen, "Trade Union Power, Threat Effects and the Extent of Organization," *Review of Economic Studies* 36, no. 2 (April 1969): 185–96.

34. Comptroller General of the United States, *The Davis-Bacon Act Should be Repealed*, HRD 7–18 (Washington, D.C.: General Accounting Office, April 27, 1979).

35. Damodar N. Gujarati, "The Economics of the Davis-Bacon Act," *Journal of Business* 40, no. 3 (July 1967): 303–16; John P. Gould, *Davis-Bacon Act: The Economics of Prevailing Wage Laws* (Washington, D.C.: American Enterprise Institute for Public Policy Research, November 1971); Armand J. Thieblot, Jr., *The Davis-Bacon Act* (report no. 10, Industrial Relations Unit, The Wharton School, University of Pennsylvania, 1975); Ronald G. Ehrenberg (with the aid of Marvin Kosters and Michael Moskow), "The Economic Impact of Davis-Bacon Type Legislation: An Econometric Study" (unpublished preliminary paper, March 1971); Robert Goldfarb and John Morrall, "An Analysis of Certain Aspects of the Administration of the Davis-Bacon Act" (Washington, D.C.: Council on Wage and Price Stability, May 1976).

36. Garth Mangum, *The Operating Engineers: The Economic History of a Trade Union* (Cambridge, Mass.: Harvard University Press, 1964).

37. For particulars, see Gould, *Davis-Bacon Act.*

38. Melvin Reder, "Unions and Wages: The Problems of Measurement," *Journal of Political Economy* 73, no. 2 (April 1965): 188–96, and Lewis, "Competitive and Monopoly Unionism."

39. Orley Ashenfelter and George E. Johnson, "Unionism, Relative Wages and Labor Quality in U.S. Manufacturing Industries," *International Economic Review* 13, no. 3 (October 1972): 488–508.

40. Peter Schmidt and Robert Strauss, "The Effect of Unions on Earnings and Earnings on Unions: A Mixed Logit Approach," *International Economic Review* 17, no. 1 (February 1976): 204–12; Lung-fei Lee, "Unionism and Wage Rates: A Simultaneous Equations Model with Qualitative and Limited Dependent Variables," *International Economic Review* 19, no. 2 (June 1978): 415–33; Duane E. Leigh, *An Analysis of the Interrelation between Unions, Race and Wage and Nonwage Compensation* (Washington, D.C.: Employment and Training Administration, U.S. Department of Labor, 1978); Lawrence M. Kahn, "Union Impact: A Reduced Form Approach," *Review of Economics and Statistics* 59, no. 4 (November 1977): 503–7; Lawrence M. Kahn, "Unionism and Relative Wages: Direct and Indirect Effects," *Industrial and Labor Relations Review* 32, no. 4 (July 1979): 520–32.

41. John Pencavel, *An Analysis of the Quit Rate in American Manufacturing Industry* (Princeton, N.J.: Industrial Relations Section, Princeton University, 1970).

42. Schmidt and Strauss, "The Effect of Unions on Earnings."

43. Kahn, "Unionism and Relative Wages."

44. Lee, "Unionism and Wage Rates."

45. Leigh, *An Analysis of the Interrelation.*

11 | *The Economics of Geographic Migration*

The immigrant, with his low rate of wages, drives out of his trade
men formerly employed therein, who are either forced down in the
scale of wages or else obliged to compete for work in higher
occupations, where they again reduce wages. Thus the effect of the
competition of immigrants is felt not only in the unskilled, but
also in the semi-skilled and skilled trades, and even in the
professions. The immigration of great bodies of unskilled workmen,
moreover, of various races tends to promote and perpetuate racial
antagonisms, and these racial jealousies are played upon by
employers in the attempt to reduce wages, to prevent the formation
of trade unions, and to keep the workmen apart.

John Mitchell, President,
United Mine Workers of America, 1903[1]

The study of migration is probably the area in which economics and sociology have the closest interrelationship. Indeed, sociologists have been responsible for collecting detailed migration data and for formulating the concepts of gross migration, net migration, and others which make sense out of these data. The intellectual debt owed to them by economists and others is considerable.[2] Although we cannot summarize in this chapter all the fine sociological and economic research on migration, we can develop a framework for thinking about migration and provide an introduction to the evidence on patterns and determinants of migration. Specifically, we will concentrate on the following questions:

1. What are the determinants of migration? Why do some people migrate to other geographic areas while others "stay put"?
2. How does migration influence the economy as a whole? In particular, does migration lead to higher or lower aggregate economic efficiency? Under what conditions?

Most studies of migration have concentrated on the first set of questions above, and that topic, therefore, will absorb most of our attention. The second set, however, is crucial to some important questions of public policy. Those questions will be considered briefly, probably too briefly, and the policy pitfalls will be highlighted.

Migration Models

As early as 1932, J. R. Hicks stated that "differences in net economic advantages, chiefly differences in wages, are the main causes of migration."[3] In short, Hicks argued that the same mechanism that serves to allocate labor resources within (external) labor markets also allocates them among such markets. Hicks's argument raises two fundamental questions:

1. If the same mechanism is at work, how can we differentiate between job changing and migration? Alternatively stated, how can we delineate local labor markets?
2. Can the Hicksian argument (or hypothesis) be tested or is it fundamentally tautological?

Recall, with reference to the first question, that labor supply curves in a given (local) labor market were obtained by summing the supply curves of the relevant, resident population. Implicit in Hicks's position, therefore, is the question of which population is relevant and what one means by resident—that is, resident in what time dimension.

To approach these issues, let us establish by fiat two labor market areas on the basis of some given criterion—political jurisdiction, a particular radius around a (the) central city (cities), average commuting time, or whatever. Call the two areas "a" and "b." Now if the cross-elasticity of supply to area "a" from persons residing in area "b" is sizable, obtaining a supply curve for "a" by summing only over those residents in "a" will understate the labor time forthcoming to employers in "a" in response to an increase in w_a, ceteris paribus. The closer that cross-elasticity (shown in Eq. 11–1) is to 0, the smaller is the error in considering the two areas as separate labor market areas given the time dimension for the elasticity.

(11-1) $$\frac{\Delta L_{b \cdot a}}{\Delta \left(\frac{w_a}{w_b}\right)} \cdot \frac{\left(\frac{w_a}{w_b}\right)}{L_{b \cdot a}} = \eta_{b \cdot a \cdot w_a} \Bigg|$$ w_b and all other determinants

Thus for short-run estimation, analysis, or prediction, delineating labor markets by commuting time, distance from the central city, contiguous areas around the city, etc., may involve very little error. For longer time spans, such ad hoc formulations may lead to substantial errors. In longer-run dimensions, such formulations fail to account for labor force relocation over time, if Hicks's hypothesis about wage effects is valid. Moreover, in longer-run analyses, there is no guarantee that the net flows to "a" from contiguous areas will be larger than those from faraway or other noncontiguous areas. The actual magnitude of the flow—if Hicks is right—depends upon both the elasticity and the wage differences, provided that the wage differences themselves do not respond quickly to the migration flow. Thus, our conclusion concerning the delimitation of local labor markets will hold only if local area wage levels are determined largely by factors *within* each local labor market in that time dimension. Chicago, therefore, may obtain many of its migrants from the central South or from the high plains, as it did in the 1950s and 1960s, rather than from the adjacent corn lands of the central Midwest. Thus, if Hicks's wage position is valid, the cross-wage elasticity between any two areas should be larger, the longer the length of run, as depicted in Fig. 11-1.

Figure 11-1 shows an exogenous shift in demand (say, resulting

Figure 11-1 *Short and Long Run Supply Effects by Geographic Areas*

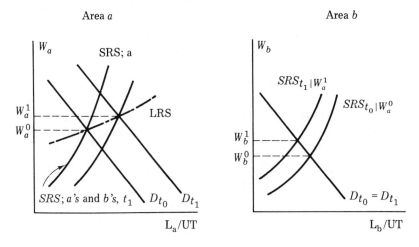

from government policies) that widens area wage differentials in the short run and induces migration from area "b" to area "a." Subsequently, the migration, *ceteris paribus,* reduces the differential and raises earning levels in both areas. The dotted line in area "a" represents the observed long-run supply. Note that the long-run supply curve may be upward sloping even if in the short run the area "a"-specific supply curve is backward bending. Note also that the initial and final (money) wage difference between "a" and "b" just equalizes for transport costs, living costs, and the amenities of the respective locations. Note finally that it is this expected response to wage differences over time that has led economists to argue that area supply curves are infinitely elastic in the longest of runs. This also amounts to saying that in the longest of runs and without constraints on movements, there are no separate labor markets.

When, however, the Hicksian argument is expressed in terms of net advantages, rather than in terms of net wages, there is a danger that the argument is totally tautological and therefore irrefutable. The Hicksian-style conclusion on net advantages follows as a necessary consequence of the assumptions that individuals seek to maximize their utility and that they are rational and informed. Unless one specifies the *particular* determinants of net advantage—for example, wages, climatic conditions, pollution rates, ethnic characteristics, etc.—no tests are possible. As a consequence, most analyses of migration have concentrated on responses to specific determinants, particularly to earnings or wage levels.

Larry Sjaastad widened and deepened our view of migration, viewing it as an investment in human capital in a lifetime context.[4] In a manner similar to the human capital view of education, Sjaastad saw migration as involving resource expenditures and foregone income *now* in exchange for *future* returns. Migration will occur, according to Sjaastad, if the discounted expected benefits of the move exceed the costs of migration, with both pecuniary and nonpecuniary benefits and costs entering into the economic calculus. Viewed this way, migration simply represents a particular application of the utility maximization process over time. Figure 11-2 illustrates Sjaastad's migration model. In principle, then, one could calculate an expected internal rate of return and/ or an expected benefit-cost ratio for migration, and movement would be predicted to occur when such measures are favorable.[5]

Because researchers have been most interested in the determinants of migration, they usually do not calculate B/C ratios or internal rates of return. Instead, they seek to estimate equations like Eq. (11–2) which permit them to test the significance of various (suspected) determinants and to measure relative responses (the expected signs are above the equation):

$$(-) \qquad (+) \qquad (?)$$

$$(11\text{–}2) \qquad M = \sum_{i=1}^{n} \alpha_i C_i + \sum_{j=1}^{m} \beta_j B_j + \sum_{k=1}^{p} \gamma_k D_k \text{ where}$$

M represents migration for an individual (1 or 0) or for a group (a rate of flow)

C_i's represent cost factors (including proxies for nonpecuniary or psychic costs)

B_j's represent benefits or net benefits

D_k's represent demographic variables intended to capture taste or nonpriced behavioral (customary) differences

αs, βs, and γs represent behavioral response rates.

Whether one looks at migration in a response equation form or whether one calculates B/C ratios, one is implicitly assuming that knowledge is complete or at least adequate. In these forms, therefore, migration does not involve elements of imperfect information such as those seen in the search models developed in Chapter 6. The impact of imperfect information and search behavior on migration is discussed below.

On an aggregate rather than an individual level, theory suggests that migration flows should check and then narrow the initial earnings (or net advantage) differential that led to the flow of migrants. That at least would be the case if labor demand in the various areas remained constant or was only slightly influenced by migration. Some researchers, however, argue that the labor demand in the "sending" areas will be affected by the migration itself. If migration is selective of the young, the well educated, and so on, income in the sending areas may well fall. If the demand curve for labor shifts down because of this migration

Figure 11–2 *Migration as an Investment in Human Capital*

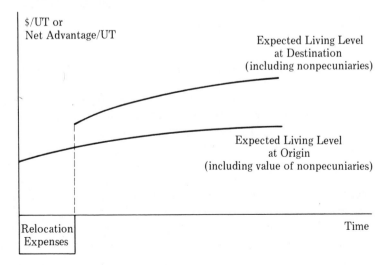

selectivity, the observed earnings gap between sending and receiving areas may widen substantially before it narrows, if narrowing occurs at all.[6] Such a possibility has led some researchers to doubt the self-correcting mechanism implicit in the migration flows. In the view of this author, the demand shift is not the crux of the problem. Indeed, if skills remain in the sending area and become relatively cheaper, an inducement exists for the importation of physical capital into that locale. What may happen, however, as a result of the migration is a diminution of the ability of the "depressed area" to finance the maintenance and acquisition of skills. Thus, average educational and skill levels may fall for extended periods of time unless alternative means of generating sufficient human capital are obtained. If this argument is correct, the problem of depressed areas is related to public finance, capital constraints, and the generation of human capital rather than simply to changes in the demand for skills in the "sending" areas. Even so, if wage rates for given skills can and do fall in the sending area, one would expect nonhuman (physical) capital flows toward the low-wage area, at least for capital that is complementary to the existing, low-priced stock of labor. Although researchers are seeking to understand this complex interactive process via simultaneous equation techniques, no aggregate model has been developed to date that fully incorporates the human capital and public finance aspects of the adjustment.

> . . . the main trouble with this area is that anybody with any get-up-and-go has long since gotten up and gone.
>
> Folk saying in
> Southeastern Ohio,
> ca 1952.

Empirical Evidence on Migration

For many years, casual evidence has supported Hicksian net wage (and perhaps the net advantage) hypothesis. It is the high-wage nations and regions to which migrants flow, some of which welcome "the wretched refuse," "the poor," "the homeless," and "the tempest-tost." It is also the relatively wealthy areas that seek from time to time to limit or condition migration. Note the flows from Mexico and the Caribbean Islands to the United States, the flows from southern and eastern Europe to northern Europe, etc. Note also that backward bending supply curves create incentives for employers individually and as a group to recruit immigrant labor. Finally, note that it is almost always the low-income and low-potential areas within a nation that experience out-migration. The flow from the U.S. dust bowl in the great plains to the far-western states in the 1920s and 1930s, the south-to-north and south-to-west movement from the 1940s through the early 1960s in the United States, and the worldwide movement during the 19th and 20th centuries from rural to urban areas all provide casual support for Hicks's net wage hypothesis. There are, however, more precise tests in which other possible determinants are held constant.

Informational Deficiencies and the Determinants of Migration

Employing a number of standardizing techniques (including multiple regression), economists and sociologists have examined the various determinants of migration in considerable detail. Some of their work has also taken account of informational imperfections and search costs. To show how these elements can be incorporated into the analysis of migration, consider the possibility that migration decisions may be based on limited information. Indeed, the full dimensions of the pecuniary and nonpecuniary costs and benefits of migration might not be apparent to the migrant until he has experienced the move. Under such conditions, it would be reasonable that areas experiencing heavy (gross) inmigration would also experience heavy (gross) outmigration. This is indeed indicated by the data on gross and net migration rates. Some, if not much, of the outmigration is return migration.

Return migration may be related in other ways to incomplete information or misinformation. Migration research clearly indicates that recent migrants fare worse in earnings and/or income than do permanent or long-term residents with the same characteristics. That research finding may, of course, result from mismeasurement of the characteristics of migrants versus those of permanent residents. For example, the same number of years of schooling may represent different qualities of education in sending and receiving areas. It is more likely, however, that the observed earnings difference reflects a locational (or old-boy) rent—a return to information acquired by long residence in a particular community. If that rent were particularly large and if the migrant actually expected prior to his move to be able to earn what long-term residents earn, his expectations would not be satisfied and return migration might easily result.[7] The work of Barry Chiswick on the effect of Americanization on the earnings of foreign-born men is instructive in this regard.[8] His data show that male immigrants to the United States (as a group) initially earn less than comparable native-born men, but that the wage differential narrows to zero after 10–15 years. After that, the wages of foreign-born males either equal or exceed those of apparently comparable native-born Americans. The nature of Chiswick's data, however, makes it difficult to hold ability and motivational factors constant. These special factors may account for the fact that after a time the foreign-born outstrip the apparently comparable long-term residents.

In addition to providing insights into the effects of limited information, the migration literature reflects what we already know about the search process. Evidence from a number of studies shows a greater flow or a higher propensity to migrate into areas in which friends and relatives are located. The presence of close contacts provides particularly trusted information about wages in the new area plus information on job availability and relative prices. Moreover, friends and relatives may provide temporary quarters and/or direct financial assistance for the migrants. Certainly, the psychic costs of migration are lowered when friends and relatives are nearby (provided, of course, that "friends" are truly friendly and that the migrant is friendly with his relatives). This strong informational support mechanism helps to explain the phenomenon of migration streams as compared with more diverse migration patterns, and it also probably explains some of the crowding phenomena in the slum or low-income districts of burgeoning urban areas. To some degree, therefore, crowding in "transient areas" reflects the economically efficient techniques employed by migrants.[9] Some possible external effects of these techniques are discussed below.

Most analyses show that income or earnings differences are strong inducements to migration, although the resulting migration patterns are affected by information and friendship relationships. In short, Hicks's net wage hypothesis is strongly supported by the data. Among the nonpecuniary determinants of migration are distance, age, education, and (in some cases) unemployment patterns. On the cost side, distance is the most important and persistent variable, *ceteris paribus*. In the various studies, however, the effect of distance on migration seems too large to be reflecting simply the cost of transportation and/or relocation expenses. Thus, most researchers have interpreted "distance" as a proxy for psychic costs and information differences in addition to transport or relocation costs. Throughout the various studies, migration is negatively related to age (among adults), *ceteris paribus*. This is exactly what one would expect from a Sjaastad life cycle model because the younger the individual, the greater the expected present value of a given difference in earnings between areas and, therefore, the greater the inducement to migrate. Moreover, psychic costs and locational rents at "home" probably increase with age.

Although psychic costs may increase with age, they should not change systematically with education. Yet, some researchers have found that education significantly reduces the effect of distance on migration.[10] Moreover, as noted above, the absence (presence) of friends and relatives in the destination areas appears to be a strong deterrent (stimulant) to migration. In the studies involving education, distance, and close associations, however, it is generally not possible to disentangle psychic costs from differences in information. Further research may be able to clarify how education, distance, and personal associations interact to alter migration flows.

Finally, many persons expect unemployment levels at origin and destination to affect migration. It seems reasonable that the relevant earnings streams (or levels) at origin and destination should be adjusted for the respective probabilities of unemployment, as in the equation:

(11–3)   Expected   Annual earnings of the
            annual   full-time employee at
            earnings   = a given skill level $\times$ (1 – Expected un-
            (origin or   (origin or   employment
            destination)   destination)   rate)

To date, however, the empirical findings on this unemployment variable are mixed or inconclusive. It is conceivable that unemployment levels are not important determinants of migration either because migrants fail to take the unemployment levels into account or that unemployment insurance or welfare benefits effectively compensate for any expected income shortfalls. There are, however, more likely explanations. Perhaps, as suggested by some analysts,[11] migration and unemployment are simultaneously determined, biasing the effect of the unemployment rate downward in single-equation models and giving inconclusive results. Alternatively, it may be that the unemployment levels expected by the migrants differ from the actual (or measured) rates used in the various prediction equations. For example, Eq. (11–3) implicitly assumes that the unemployment rates for the respective local areas, the U_A's, represent involuntary unemployment. If measured unemployment rates contain both voluntary (search) and involuntary components in different proportions among areas, the unemployment variable generally included in the prediction equation is, in principle, the wrong one. Under these circumstances, even though unemployment may have an effect, inconclusive or mixed results would be expected in empirical work. Chapter 12 discusses voluntary and involuntary unemployment.

Aggregate Migration Research

Research on the aggregate effects of migration is sparse relative to research on the determinants of migration. Indeed, as of 1975, American researchers were inclined to doubt the predictions of the simple demand constant model presented above and also the suggestion that physical capital would flow into areas in which skills were apparently becoming relatively cheaper. In short, they doubted that migration would effectively or eventually narrow economic differences among areas experiencing migration flows. Referring to U.S. migration at the time, Michael Greenwood stated:

> . . . The persistence of sizeable regional earnings and unemployment rate differentials suggests that the predicted consequences of migration have not been borne out, even in the presence of relatively heavy interregional migration.[12]

By the 1970s, however, using data standardized for skills and cost-of-living differences, Don Bellante showed that the traditional North-South earnings differential in the United States had virtually disappeared.[13] This finding is consistent with the gradual reduction in outmigration from the South and the migration reversal experienced in the late 1960s and 1970s for whites and then for blacks (see Table 11–1). Bellante's results are also consistent with the substantial flow of new physical capital into that historically low-wage and low-skilled region of the nation.

Although the North-South turnaround in migration and the flow of physical capital into the South appears to support the predictions of economic theory, the relative roles of market and nonmarket forces in this process are not clear. As noted above, the maintenance and enhancement of the stock of human capital may be the key to the recovery of a depressed or "sending" area. Clearly, considerable amounts of public funds for social overhead capital and education were expended in the South (and Southwest) during the period of heavy outmigration. We know that during the mid-1960s, southern states regularly spent about the same proportion of personal income per capita on publicly supported schooling as did other states, although in absolute magnitudes, expenditure rates per student were relatively low.[14] Further research is needed

Table 11–1 *Total Net Migration Flows from the South,*[a] *1940–77 (Thousands)*

	Total	Native White	Negro
1940–50	−2810	−1117	−1699
1950–60	−2783	−1184	−1620
1960–70	−791	567	−1447
1970–77	1809	n.a.[b]	n.a.[b]

[a] The South includes Virginia, North Carolina, South Carolina, Georgia, Kentucky, Tennessee, Alabama, Mississippi, Arkansas, Louisiana, Oklahoma, and Texas, but excludes Florida, Maryland, and the District of Columbia. Sources: U.S. Bureau of the Census, *Historical Statistics of the United States: Colonial Times to 1970*, series C 27–75, and *Statistical Abstract of the United States, 1978*, p. 14. Each of the twelve states evidenced positive inmigration in the 1970–77 period.

[b] Breakdown by race unavailable for 1970–77, but U.S. Bureau of the Census, *Current Population Report*, series P-20, no. 331, concludes that by 1977, "the South does, in fact, have a small net inmigration of blacks."

regarding the way in which state and federally supported training interacted with (or was coordinated with) the inmigration of physical capital. Included in federal expenditures were funds to encourage public school integration. Research is also needed on the extent and effectiveness of O-J-T. A full explanation of the Southern revival probably also reflects the influence of federally supported social overhead capital (e.g., the Tennessee Valley Authority, river, dam, and highway projects and so forth), a slowing down in the relative rate of agricultural mechanization, the strong impact of World War II, and the immense creativity unleashed by the desegmentation of southern society through the American civil rights movement.[15] Thus, although recent experience in the American South supports the proposition that heavy interregional migration will plant the seeds for its own demise, the degree to which this would or would not have occurred solely through market forces remains debatable.

Some Special Analytical and Policy Problems

In this segment of the chapter, several special problems are introduced and discussed briefly:

1. push-and-pull factors in migration,
2. family migration,
3. the brain drain, and
4. externalities and the efficiency of migration.

Push-and-Pull Factors in Migration

Some migration researchers have divided the determinants of migration into push-and-pull factors. As they see it, push factors reduce income (income prospects and/or expected utility) in the origin areas with little or no change in alternative prospects. Pull factors increase income or net advantages in the destination areas (or lower relocation costs) with income and other advantages in the origin areas remaining constant. This subdivision into pushes and pulls creates a tendency to view push migration as if it were "forced" and pull migration as if it were a matter of choice.

However appealing this subdivision of causes may seem, it is of little analytical use. For the purpose of analyzing and predicting migration flows, it matters little why the net gain or net advantage calculus has changed. Whether the impetus is labeled as a push or a pull, the rate of return has changed or benefits have changed relative to costs.

One potential and initially appealing analytical justification for the push-pull framework is to help us distinguish empirically between factors which affect sizable population groups versus those which are more specific to individuals. For example, the dust bowl conditions of the 1920s and 1930s in the American plains—push factors—influenced sizable numbers of people to move en masse. Pull factors are usually considered to be less group-related, with response rates differing substantially among individuals and being more heavily dependent upon information flows and psychic costs. Even that analytical justification, however, is of questionable validity. Witness the pulling power of the Statue of Liberty (and the benefits it represented) on vast groups of individuals from eastern and southern Europe. It would appear, therefore, that the push-pull distinction does not have its origin in analysis, but rather in the feeling that human dignity is offended by the choices with which some persons are faced. The distinction, therefore, is a moral or ethical one, and adds nothing substantial to positive economic analysis.

These seemingly negative comments about the push-pull distinction, however, do not imply that public actions should not have been taken or should not be taken to assist migrants faced with particularly agonizing choices and/or personal degradation or death. Attempts to assist, support, or relocate destitute peoples—like the migratory tribesmen of the southern Sahara during droughts or the Vietnamese "boat people"—depend largely upon love or compassion for fellow humans rather than on any analytical category or designation of migration into push-and-pull categories.

Family Migration

Until the late 1970s, little attention was paid to the family as a unit of analysis in migration. In part, this was a reflection of the way migration data are collected—by particular demographic groups such as age, sex, race, education, marital status, etc. More importantly, it seems to have reflected (1) implicit assumptions that only the income or earnings opportunities of heads of households are relevant to migration decisions, and (2) our preoccupation with market income in contrast to household productivity. Viewed from a modern perspective, it seems obvious that migration choices, like most others, are simultaneous decisions of all family members attempting to maximize family utility, with the gains and losses of all members of the family entering into the decision. Where the value of household services is not locationally specific and where returns to labor force activities are largely dependent upon male earnings, the old adage of "Whither thou goest, I will go" makes considerable economic sense. Under such conditions, a migration model that explains or predicts migration flows by looking toward the net benefits of heads of households may do so reasonably well. Such individual or head-of-household-oriented models are flawed, however, where these conditions do not hold. Julie DaVanzo in 1976 and Jacob Mincer in 1978 called attention to this problem,[16] with Mincer emphasizing the way in which differential net advantages from migration among family members, particularly for the husband and the wife, can lead to marital instability.

Although focusing on "the new household economics" led economists to consider these questions in the late 1970s, history has provided many examples of migration phenomena that can probably be examined best in a family context. Throughout history, there are instances in which married males migrated separately from their families and remained separated from them for long periods of time without the dissolution of the family as a consuming or utility-maximizing unit. Indeed, in many of these instances, males appear to have acquired a "stake" and considerable market information in the new area before "sending" for the rest of the family. This pattern of male-dominated migration may, of course, easily lead to return migration.

A brief view of migration patterns around the world indicates that the reconceptualization called for by DaVanzo and Mincer is past due. The huge flows of male-dominated migration throughout much of Asia makes this approach very relevant.[17] For example, where rice farming is not sex-specific, but urban employment is, the male-dominated pattern makes considerable sense. The increased labor force participation of women in developed economies also makes this approach a relevant one. For example, if the value of household activities varies less across geographic areas than female earnings, one might expect either less migration in two-career families due to migration (or more family dissolution), *ceteris paribus,* than in those families with one "breadwinner." Using U.S. data, DaVanzo finds that two-career families are no less likely to migrate than single-career families.[18] No doubt, other researchers will question her findings and/or the reasons behind her statistical results. What is true is that migration research using the family as the unit of observation is still in its infancy, and we can expect much more emphasis on this approach and these family-related questions.

The Brain Drain

The brain drain—the selective migration of highly skilled individuals or professionals—is a topic of considerable public policy interest around the world. To the degree that migration drains a nation (or region) of its pool of "brain power" and to the degree that skill acquisition is or has been publicly supported, such emigration is considered as a high-priority public problem. Public administrators are heavily pressured to "do something" about selective emigration, support for training, and related problems.

One concern is that the exporting nation will no longer be able to tax the income flow of the emigrants, increasing domestic fiscal and expenditure problems and "failing to recover" the nation's or region's investment in the emigrants. From a broader viewpoint, the availability of skilled persons trained by "others" encourages each nation to skimp on educational expenditures, preferring to "free ride." Quite obviously, if all nations followed such a "free riding" practice (and they all have the incentive to do so), if capital constraints exist, and if returns to schooling or education are large and positive, opportunities for worldwide income enhancement could be foregone as a result of brain drains.

Despite the scenario developed here, usually echoed in one or another form in popular and public discussion about the "brain drain problem," there are more subtle aspects to this question. First, to the degree that the emigrants maintain families in the home country and/or send income back home, there may be little fiscal "loss" to the nation. Second, in considering the brain drain or any other migration process, one should always ask why the income-producing or net advantage-producing potential of a particular set of skills is so much higher in another land than at home. Interestingly, that question is seldom asked when nations attempt to prevent brain drains by restricting emigration, limiting travel, etc. The difference in income-producing potential may, of course, be a function of different availabilities of complementary capital, complementary labor, higher technology, and, in short, comparative advantage. It may, however, reflect particular domestic constraints on the income-generating potential of these skilled individuals—e.g., limits on complementary capital imports, wage regulations, high income taxes, or labor market strictures imposed by the "home" government. To the degree that such restrictions limit maximum income or utility generation at home, the brain drain is but a symptom of an underlying domestic problem or set of social choices. The migration of physicians from countries with socialized medicine is a case in point. In all such cases, the issue revolves around the trade-off the society and the affected individuals are willing to accept between the income transfer objectives of the domestic programs and the potential output losses (and/or gains) from migration. Similar comments might be made about the migration of scientists, scholars, and artists seeking academic or artistic freedom. To the degree that the home area prevents by custom, law, regulation, or social opprobrium the maximum development of scholarly and research pursuits or artistic expression, the brain drain is a symptom of an important social problem— one that probably transcends the economic losses or gains from the brain drain. As noted above, public discussion of the brain drain is not usually couched in these terms.

Third, when the brain drain does not reflect underlying socioeconomic barriers, the problems of indentured servitude and capital constraints discussed in Chapter 4 are revisited on the scale of a nation rather than of a firm. Where there is a widespread belief that skill acquired (in part, remember) at public expense will be exported, where capital constraints exist, and where political or other pressures induce governments not to subsidize the export of such skills, it may be sensible for the respective "home" government to investigate alternative arrangements for the financing of human capital acquisition. Variants on indentured servitude arrangements, expense sharing, and/or more careful estimation of the income-generating potential of various professions may help to alleviate the problem.

Finally, it is useful to note that much of the public policy concern comes from erroneous economics. In addressing the brain drain question, spokesmen for some nations speak as if their nations were profit-maximizing firms, concerned solely with the benefit/cost ratio of the educational system *to the state*. See the comments in Chapter 4 on the uselessness of public benefit/cost ratios as tools for evaluating economic efficiency or predicting individual or group behavior.

Externalities and the Efficiency of Migration

Throughout the migration literature, there are expressed concerns about the efficiency of migration and the possibility that migration may be privately beneficial but socially nonoptimal or costly. Thus, arguments are regularly advanced for public control over the rate of inmigration or for the discouragement of outmigration. Economic theory argues that if there are no negative externalities in production from migration, if individuals or families respond to net advantages by migration, and if their information concerning these advantages is adequate, the migration that occurs for private advantage will also be socially efficient (Pareto optimal). Where the act of migration produces net external technical disadvantages, with costs borne by third parties, however, a large private rate of return may represent a smaller or even a negative social rate of return.

The identification of negative technical externalities is therefore the crux of the matter. It might be and it is argued, for example, that outmigration imposes costs on the merchants, the employers, and the public treasury in sending areas, and that these costs are externalities. Such effects—often called pecuniary externalities—are seen as losses because the investigations usually fail to note that demand and tax revenues in the new area are (at least potentially) larger than in the old area if the migration is privately productive for the migrant. National myopia in the brain drain problem is a case in point. Similarly, one might argue and some have argued that inmigration requires additional welfare, schooling, and other public costs, and that the inclusion of these very heavy public expenditures in response to migration may make private and unfettered migration socially wasteful. One can hardly question the likelihood that migration will raise social or public expenditures in the receiving areas, but that effect is clearly not an externality in production. Instead, it is an alteration in the way in which income transfer programs work in the presence of migration. This distinction is very important. Note that the northern European nations who willingly accept (even recruit) foreign workers from Greece, Turkey, southern Italy, Yugoslavia, etc., sometimes exempt these guest workers from welfare and other social programs, clearly separating "temporary" migration from income transfer programs.[19] Indeed, such workers may be "sent home" in economic downturns.

The general point to be remembered is that one must distinguish between externalities in production on the one hand, and the external pecuniary effects of migration through markets or via the structure of income transfer programs on the other. Indeed, it is difficult to identify negative externalities in production resulting from migration. Perhaps that is the hidden reason why the Statue of Liberty proclaims the open door and why immigration into America has been privately and socially optimal. Nothing in this argument, however, denies John Mitchell's contention at the outset of this chapter that migration can result in market readjustments.

Without being able to identify negative externalities in production, the presumption is that private optimizing decisions will also be socially optimal, provided, of course, that the migration flow is not induced solely or predominantly by differences in income transfer arrangements in the various locales. The reader will find it useful to work through the output and the income distribution effects of a migration flow induced *solely* by differences in welfare (or support) levels and to identify whether the result can best be described as a negative externality of migration or an inefficiency induced by the operations of the welfare system.

Notes to Chapter 11

1. John Mitchell, *Organized Labor* (Philadelphia: American Book and Bible House, 1903), p. 183.

2. See Michael J. Greenwood, "Research on Internal Migration in the United States: A Survey," *Journal of Economic Literature* 13, no. 2 (June 1975): 397–433, for a fine review of sociological and economic migration literature up to that date and for an extensive bibliography.

3. J. R. Hicks, *The Theory of Wages* (London: Macmillan & Co., 1932), p. 76.

4. Larry A. Sjaastad, "The Costs and Returns of Human Migration," *Journal of Political Economy*, supplement, 70, no. 5 (October 1962): 80–93.

5. It will be useful for readers to consider what the word "favorable" means in this context, and how the rate of interest and limited sources of loanable funds might have a differential impact on the propensity to migrate.

6. Gunnar Myrdal, *Rich Lands and Poor* (New York: Harper and Row, 1957); B. Oken and R. W. Richardson, "Regional Income Inequality and Internal Population Change," *Economic Development and Cultural Change* 9, no. 2 (January 1961): 128–43; James R. Rook, *Labor Skill Composition, Elasticities of Substitution and Industrial Migration: The Case of Cotton Textiles* (Ph.D. diss., North Carolina State University, 1979).

7. Leon B. Perkinson, "Rural In-migration: Are Migrants Universally Disadvantaged?," *Growth and Change* 11, no. 3 (July 1980): 17–25.

8. Barry R. Chiswick, "The Effect of Americanization on the Earnings of Foreign-born Men," *Journal of Political Economy* 86, no. 5 (October 1978): 897–922.

9. Two days before the USSR invasion of Czechoslovakia in August 1968, the author, camping in Innsbruck, Austria, met a fellow camper—a middle-aged mechanical engineer who was defecting with his family from Czechoslovakia. The engineer intended to look for employment in Innsbruck. Recognizing Innsbruck as an internationally renowned center for winter sports, the author found the relocation choice puzzling. The engineer explained that as a young man during World War II, he had been forced to live and work in the Reich, specifically in Innsbruck. He then told the author what every labor economist should know, "When one leaves one's country, one must go where one has friends."

10. J. K. Folger and C. B. Nam, *Education of the American Population* (Washington, D.C.: U.S. Government Printing Office, 1967), a 1960 census monograph prepared in cooperation with the Social Science Research Council; Elizabeth M. Suval and C. Horace Hamilton, "Some New Evidence on Educational Selectivity in Migration to and from the South," *Social Forces* 43, no. 4 (May 1965): 536–47.

11. See Greenwood, "Research on Internal Migration," pp. 408–11, for a detailed discussion of attempts to capture the influence of unemployment on migration.

12. Greenwood, "Research on Internal Migration," p. 414.

13. Don Bellante, "The North-South Differential and the Migration of Heterogeneous Labor," *American Economic Review* 69, no. 1 (March 1979): 166–75. Also see P. R. P. Coelho and M. A. Ghali, "The End of the North-South Wage Differential," *American Economic Review* 61, no. 5 (December 1971): 932–37.

14. James G. Maddox, *The Advancing South: Manpower Problems and Prospects* (New York: The Twentieth Century Fund, 1967), pp. 98–111.

15. See William N. Parker, "The South in the National Economy," *Southern Economic Journal* 46, no. 4 (April 1980): 1019–48.

16. Jacob Mincer, "Family Migration Decisions," *Journal of Political Economy* 86, no. 5 (October 1978): 749–74; J. DaVanzo, *Why Families Move: A Model of the Geographic Mobility of Married Couples*, Rand Corporation report R-1972-DOL (Palo Alto, Calif.: The Rand Corporation, 1976).

17. UNESCO, *Population and Education in Asia: A Source Book* (Bangkok: UNESCO Regional Office for Education in Asia, 1975).

18. DaVanzo, *Why Families Move*.

19. For historical background, see Charles P. Kindleberger, *Europe's Postwar Growth* (Cambridge: Harvard University Press, 1967), particularly ch. 5, and Margaret S. Gordon, "Retraining and Labor Market Adjustment in Western Europe," mimeographed (Berkeley, Calif.: Institute for Industrial Relations, July 1964). Also see International Labor Office, *Some Growing Employment Problems in Europe*, report II (Geneva: International Labour Office, 1973), ch. 4, and Bernard Kayser, *Manpower Movements and Labour Markets* (Paris: Organization for Economic Cooperation and Development, 1971). Guest workers are given particular attention by Ursula Mehrlander, "Federal Republic of Germany," and Theodore P. Lianos, "Greece," in *The Politics of Migration Policies*, ed. Daniel Kubat (New York: Center for Migration Studies, 1979).

12 | *Unemployment and Underemployment*

*Unemployment is like a headache or a high temperature—
unpleasant and exhausting but not carrying in itself any
explanation of its cause. A high temperature may be got by catching
malaria or by breaking one's leg or by eating too much. . . . Until
one finds out which of these and many other possible causes is at
work, one will not have gone far in finding a cure simply by knowing
how many degrees of fever one has. The clinical thermometer is
an indispensable but limited instrument.*

Sir William H. Beveridge,
Causes and Cures of Unemployment[1]

This chapter deals with several of the most controversial
and most important questions in labor economics. In line with the approach in previous chapters, a full treatment of the many theoretical,
empirical, and policy problems will not be offered. Attention will be concentrated on two key questions:

1. To what degree is measured unemployment involuntary and to what
degree is it voluntary?
2. Is the term "underemployment," as it is commonly used, consistent
or inconsistent with economic theory?

Economic literature and a number of political and policy commen-
taries offer several answers to each of these questions. Moreover, each
answer is apt to have its own theoretical frame of reference, more or
less disjoint from the others. In a sense, we have here the modern equivalent of the Tower of Babel. Our objective in this chapter is to tie together
the various approaches wherever possible and to point up some remaining
incongruities in this important area of analysis and policy. The more
ambitious objective of fully synthesizing the various approaches is left
to others.

Unemployment—Voluntary or Involuntary?

As indicated in Chapter 1, the measurement of labor force and unemployment in the United States and elsewhere was induced by the apparent need for a "thermometer," to use Sir Beveridge's very apt term. The lack of a usable thermometer in the United States and in a number of other countries was dramatized by the worldwide depression of the 1930s. Indeed, the primary purpose for collecting unemployment data was to assess the degree of involuntary unemployment resulting from cyclical downturns (1) as a measure of economic privation and (2) as an index of the degree to which *all* productive factors were underutilized.

Thus, upward movements in the deseasonalized level of measured unemployment were and are usually interpreted as signals of declining national economic health as well as measures of personal deprivation. This interpretation implies that the unemployment is involuntary and is consistent with national (or international) monetary and/or fiscal actions to eliminate the underutilization of resources. Moreover, the interpretation of measured unemployment as involuntary ties in well with much Keynesian and neo-Keynesian analysis.

Few economists and policy makers questioned the involuntary unemployment interpretation during the 1940s and 1950s, with the exception of those few concerned with structural unemployment problems. What was at issue in the late 1950s and 1960s was the accuracy of the statistics themselves, not the underlying interpretation. As noted in the Introduction, that issue motivated both the President's Committee to Appraise Employment and Unemployment Statistics ("the Gordon Committee") and the many researchers involved in the added worker-discouraged worker controversy of the 1950s and 1960s. In the latter case, the question was whether census-CPS measurement techniques systematically overestimated or underestimated the extent of cyclical unemployment. Predictably, concern with measurement error has given rise to numerous measures of unemployment, some of which are summarized in Table 12–1. Each of these is derived from CPS data, and each is intended to measure or include some particular aspect of underutilization of resources or the economic hardship accompanying that underutilization. The National Commission on Employment and Unemployment Statistics (the Levitan Commission), submitting its report in late 1979, also interpreted changes in deseasonalized unemployment levels as largely cyclical and involuntary.[2]

Some researchers, while accepting generally the involuntariness of unemployment, have been more chary of the cyclical explanation, expressing concern that structural changes and restraints can and often do affect the observed statistical magnitudes. The general dimensions

Table 12–1   **Various Measures of Unemployment**[a]

		May 1975 (Seasonally Adjusted)
U-1	Persons unemployed 15 weeks or longer as a percent of total civilian labor force	2.7
U-2	Job losers as a percent of civilian labor force	5.1
U-3	Unemployed household heads as a percent of the household head labor force	6.1
U-4	Unemployed full-time job seekers as a percent of the full-time labor force (including those employed part-time for economic reasons)	8.5
U-5	*Total unemployed as a percent of civilian labor force (the official unemployment measure)*	*8.9*
U-6	Total full-time job seekers plus half of the part-time for economic reasons as a percent of the civilian labor force less half of the part-time labor force	10.9
U-7	Total full-time job seekers plus half of the part-time job seekers plus half of those on part-time for economic reasons plus discouraged workers as a percent of the civilian labor force plus discouraged workers less half of the part-time labor force	12.0

[a] Source: Julius Shiskin, "Employment and Unemployment: The Doughnut or the Hole?," *Monthly Labor Review* 99, no. 2 (February 1976): 3–10.

of the 1950–60 concern with structural unemployment were noted in the Introduction and will not be repeated here. Obviously, the policy implications of structural unemployment differ substantially from cyclical unemployment although both forms of unemployment are usually treated as involuntary. Persons concerned with structural unemployment, for example, often call for locally oriented manpower or industrial stimulation programs as opposed to monetary-fiscal policy changes. Readers will find a detailed investigation of Titles I, II, and IV of the initial Comprehensive Employment and Training Act (CETA) very instructive in this regard.[3] That act reflects an interesting amalgam of manpower programs intended to deal with human capital generation, structural factors, and cyclical influences on unemployment.

The subdivision of unemployment into frictional (voluntary search), seasonal, cyclical, and structural components has a long and respected academic history. Perhaps the clearest and one of the earliest uses of this taxonomy is by Sir William Beveridge,[4] who used the expression "disorganization of the labour market" to denote what we now call structural unemployment.

A very lucid explanation of the macro causes of cyclical unemployment has been provided by Robert Barro and Herschel Grossman.[5] Briefly expressed, Barro and Grossman have a derived demand for labor that

Figure 12-1 *Macro Disequilibrium in the Labor Market*

Labor Market   Product Market

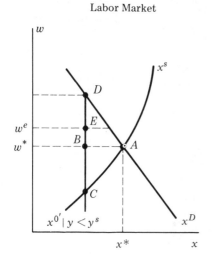 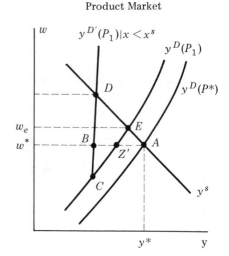

Key: P^* = full-employment price level x^* = full-employment labor input
         P_1 = higher-than-full-employment price level x^D = labor demand
         y^D = output demand in real terms x^s = labor supply
         y^s = output supply in real terms w = real wages
         y^* = full-employment output in real terms x = labor input = $f(w, y)$

Source: Robert J. Barro and Herschel I. Grossman, "A General Disequilibrium Model of
Income and Employment, "*American Economic Review*, 61, No. 1 (March 1971),
pp. 82-93.

depends upon both real wage levels and sales expectations. They reason
that when the general price level (related to the stock of money and
institutional factors) in any short-run period is above the full-employment
price index, there will be excess supply in the product market. Labor
demand then shifts down from DX^D in Fig. 12-1 to DC, creating either
short-run unemployment *(AB)* where wage levels are downward rigid
or a reduction in employment from the full employment level *(X*)*. Thus,
disequilibrium in money and product markets creates disequilibrium
in the labor market, which further reduces the output supplied to the
economy as a whole *($Y^D|x < x^s$)*. Moreover, reductions in the real wage
will not remove that underutilization. Real wages may go down to C
in Fig. 12-1, but x will not rise to x^* or y to y^*. Thus, the underutilization
will show up either as unemployment or as underemployment (in one
sense of that term). In neither the rigid wage nor the flexible wage case
can the lower utilization of labor time be considered voluntary.

Quasi-voluntary Unemployment and the Natural Rate

A different interpretation of measured unemployment gradually emerged during the early 1960s from an amalgam of job search theory, Phillips curve analysis, and other macroeconomic investigations. In general, these approaches are termed "the new microeconomics" or "the microeconomic foundations" of income and employment theory.[6]

In one way or another, the new approaches to the interpretation of unemployment argue that workers cannot and do not differentiate easily between (1) shifts in the offer distribution of wages and (2) "poor" or "good" draws or samples from that offer distribution (remember Chapter 6). Thus, workers searching sequentially will tend to reject job and wage offers during cyclical downturns which they would have accepted had they recognized the true position of the offer distribution. Alternatively stated, they will fix their critical wages too high, reducing the probability of offer acceptance. Conversely, in periods of business buoyancy, workers can be expected to accept jobs which they would have rejected save for an underestimation of the position of the wage offer distribution. The scenario also suggests that it takes time before workers in general, and unemployed workers in particular, recognize via their samplings from the offer distribution that a shift has occurred and alter their respective critical wages.

As a consequence of this *differential ignorance* (author's term) between the demand-and-supply sides of the labor market, a Phillips curve pattern (*PP* in Fig. 12–2) might be expected in the short run.[7] *PP*, of course, implies a tradeoff between the rate of change in prices ($\Delta P/\Delta$Time) or in wages ($\Delta W/\Delta$Time) and the level of unemployment. The other relationship in Fig. 12–2 (*NN*) argues that the Phillips curve tradeoff in the longer run is nonexistent—that there is a natural (frictional and/or frictional-structural) rate of unemployment which will reassert itself once worker ignorance concerning real wage levels is dispelled.[8]

A number of sophisticated econometric tests provide support for the proposition that the short-run tradeoff declines to zero with the passage of time.[9] Moreover, the fact that unemployment appears to "settle down" to some historical rate in nations experiencing sustained (and largely anticipated) inflation and/or in which wages are indexed has been interpreted as empirical support for this analysis.[10]

For the purposes of this discussion, the point is that cyclical unemployment is seen as the result of the equating of the apparent marginal costs of search with the apparent marginal benefits. The results of these voluntary decisions, however, are conditioned by the unanticipated monetary and fiscal shocks to which the economy is subjected. Hence, the term we have adopted here—quasi-voluntary unemployment.[11]

The policy implications of this neoclassical or microeconomic inter-

Figure 12-2 *The Phillips Curve and the Natural Rate of Unemployment*

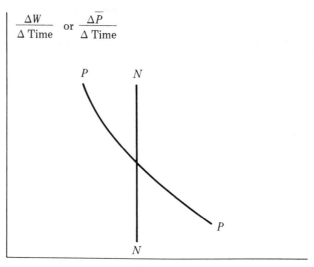

pretation of cyclical unemployment differ substantially from the disequilibrium or Keynesian interpretation. The latter calls for stimulatory monetary and fiscal programs, always with an eye to the inflationary consequences of those policy actions. The quasi-voluntary or natural rate interpretation implies "steady-as-you-go" monetary and fiscal policies in the short run. In the long run, the quasi-voluntary explanation leads one toward a policy of "improving" labor markets, providing mechanisms for better job matching so that the natural (or frictional) rate will be lower. Similarly, one might treat structural problems within the quasi-voluntary rubric, seeking to dispell the ignorance of the true offer distributions which presumably "produces" the high unemployment levels accompanying a structural change.

The short-run "steady-as-you-go" policy option was clearly enunciated and to some degree exercised by the Nixon administration. Unfortunately, a full test of the effectiveness of such a policy cannot be made unless special monetary and fiscal shocks are largely avoided, a condition that did not prevail under President Nixon.[12]

Albert Rees has wisely cautioned against using a search or quasi-voluntary scenario as the only or even the predominant explanation for cyclical unemployment. While not discounting the usefulness of the quasi-voluntary explanation to our general understanding, he asks:

How long does it take workers to revise their expectations of normal wages in light of the facts? Unemployment was never below 14 percent of the labor force

between 1931 and 1939 and was still about 17 percent of the labor force in 1939,
a decade after the depression began. It is hard to imagine the long-term unemployed
holding out for jobs comparable to their old jobs, at their old real compensation,
over periods up to ten years.[13]

Rees's argument is, of course, that long-term unemployment is apt to
be largely involuntary. Like Barro and Grossman, Rees envisions that
the economy or substantial portions of it could be below the production
possibility frontier as a result of monetary disequilibriums and the failure
of markets to clear. If Rees, Barro and Grossman, and many other economists are substantially correct, and if employers use cheap screening
devices (race, sex, education, certification, etc.) to select "qualified" workers under less-than-full employment conditions, the impact of involuntary unemployment will be upon particular ethnic and/or lower (mean)
skilled groups in the population as well as upon those persons who have
few firm-specific skills.

Institutionally Induced Unemployment

Some measured unemployment may involve little or no job seeking. According to Martin Feldstein, many individuals who are laid off simply
expect to be rehired, often in line with seniority.[14] Indeed, they expect
to be rehired in their old or similar positions at earnings substantially
above their next best alternative in the open market. Whether that difference results from trade union wage effects, specific O-J-T, the rigidity
of a nonunion firm's wage structure, or the search costs of firms (remember Chapter 7) is of little moment in this argument. The point is that
such workers on "temporary layoff" do not search in the manner presumed by the search theorists, and thus the short-run–long-run Phillips
curve scenario is not germane. Feldstein-type unemployment obviously
reflects the operations of segmented and rigid labor markets, and has
been dubbed "wait unemployment."

In addition to wait unemployment, higher levels of unemployment
may result from the availability and/or the monetary amounts of unemployment compensation. One can easily see the potential for such an
effect via search theory. Unemployment compensation, particularly if
it represents a substantial portion of expected earnings, can raise the
critical wage and induce the unemployed to search less intensively.

A substantial body of literature finds that unemployment compensation has significant effects on the level and/or duration of unemployment
in the United States. Although the effects, summarized by Daniel Hamermesh,[15] differ in magnitude depending upon the timing of the studies,
the source of the data, the econometric procedures, etc., they are considerable. The availability of unemployment compensation may lower the
weekly probability that a person will leave unemployment by as much
as 25–50 percent. It also follows from this evidence that the availability

of supplementary unemployment benefits from labor unions can be expected to reduce search. In this case, Feldstein and the search theorists may be looking at related phenomena. Daniel Benjamin and Lewis Kochin argue that the influence of unemployment compensation on unemployment is not limited to the United States. In particular, they find that unemployment compensation levels in Great Britain had a significant effect on the high unemployment levels experienced in that nation during the 1930s.[16] Similar effects have been found in other nations.[17]

A considerable body of recent evidence suggests, therefore, that measured levels of unemployment are strongly influenced by the institutional structure itself—by segmented markets and job rights and by unemployment compensation. The evidence is so strong that the U.S. General Accounting Office recommended in 1979 that unemployment compensation payments be subject to the income tax.[18] That change among others was designed to narrow the gap between taxed earnings and untaxed unemployment compensation payments, thus lowering measured unemployment.

A Possible Synthesis?

Some studies attempt to synthesize these approaches to the unemployment question. Recognizing that the probability of leaving unemployment depends upon the intensity of search and the willingness of prospective employers to make job offers to particular individuals, as well as upon the willingness of prospective employees to accept those offers, both Stephen McCafferty and John Warner et al. looked at the influence of voluntary (i.e., supply) and involuntary (i.e., demand) factors on unemployment in unified or synthesized models.[19] Given an offer distribution of wages and either utility- or wealth-maximizing assumptions, both studies simultaneously examine:

1. job search by workers or prospective workers,
2. the intensity of search by job seekers, and
3. the screening approaches of employers.

In doing so, the models provide for the interaction between the probability, per unit time, of generating and accepting wage offers as those probabilities are influenced by unemployment compensation, the offer distribution and critical wages, race, sex, and other factors. The study by Warner et al. involves direct empirical tests and concludes:

Our analysis of the weekly probability of leaving unemployment provides evidence that this probability is affected by both "voluntary" and "involuntary" factors. The empirical results support the main search theory hypothesis that higher ac-

ceptance [critical] *wages are negatively related to the weekly probability of leaving unemployment. The analysis also indicates that the receipt of unemployment compensation strongly affects the weekly probability of leaving unemployment, with recipients being nearly 55 percent less likely to leave unemployment each week than nonrecipients. Most of this effect apparently is due . . . to the impact of unemployment compensation on search intensity rather than its effect on (higher) acceptance wages. Moreover, sizeable differences in the effect of race on the weekly probability of leaving unemployment were found across city areas. These differences suggest that racial effects are highly dependent upon the state of the local labor market. That finding is supportive of* [the] . . . *screening models* . . . *incorporated into our general model.*[20]

Thus, research has begun on a synthesis of the various, seemingly disjointed approaches. Further efforts should help to bracket the degree to which measured unemployment levels reflect the various diseases affecting the body economic. As anyone familiar with medicine might have expected, the task of the diagnostician has been complicated by our increasing knowledge of the determinants of unemployment, including the effects on our economic thermometer of our medications.[21]

Underemployment

To use Ethel Jones's phrase, underemployment is among the most elusive concepts in all of economics.[22] Despite or perhaps because of that elusiveness, a number of underemployment concepts are in common use, each of which has its particular emphasis.

John Keynes, for example, used the term to denote the underutilization of resources during cyclical downturns. That malallocation is precisely what one is attempting to measure (or at least to index) by the various measures of cyclical *unemployment* discussed above. Other scholars have identified underemployment as part-time or part-year work (say, in agriculture) and have suggested alterations in physical capital availabilities to soak up this "underemployment"—e.g., canning factories to operate in the off-season. Alternatively, underemployment is considered to be the failure of some group of workers (say, in agriculture) to earn what some "comparable" group of workers earn in other employments. Another definition involves the identification explicitly or implicitly of individuals with low or zero marginal products and is often described as the "labor-released definition." More commonly, the term "underemployment" is used to identify a situation in which individuals are currently employed at jobs that do not utilize their full capabilities or skills. That particular definition, involving the comparison of "abilities versus utilization," is the one used by the Levitan Commission.[23]

The complexities involved in this last and most common definition of underemployment can be illustrated by recognizing that the valuation of human capital, as well as of labor time, is market-related. Formally stated, the capital value of any asset rises or falls with the market rental rate for the services of that asset. Consider, for example, a person trained as a nuclear engineer who can find no employment or only low-wage employment in that specialized area after the government or the electric utilities or both have decided to scale back nuclear power generation. Although the nuclear engineer may have serious adjustment and income flow problems, it hardly seems reasonable to designate him as underemployed. What has happened is that the market value of a portion of his skill portfolio has declined. The capital loss is real, as are the adjustment problems, but given the market valuation of skills, there is no social underutilization involved. Instead, the market is redirecting labor time in other directions by revaluing labor time and, therefore, revaluing a portion of his skill portfolio. Nuclear engineers in this instance are in the same situation as were the buggy whip and harness makers of an earlier era. It makes little economic sense to protect buggy whip or harness makers or nuclear engineers from such "underemployment." Indeed, in a technologically changing economy, it cannot be in the general public interest to guarantee or seek to guarantee protection from that kind of "underemployment." We do not need to designate this state of affairs as "underemployment" in order to address the labor market adjustment and human capital or retraining problems endemic to a technologically changing economy. The principles which underlie such considerations are contained in the chapters on job search and human capital generation.

"Underemployment" defined in this way, however, could represent a substantial social loss if the earnings rates to which individuals respond are not scarcity values. Of course, underemployment of skills resulting from such market imperfections *does imply* social losses.

Up to this point in our discussion and in much of the literature, underemployment is considered to be a flow concept, reflecting some less than optimal flow of labor time. Moreover, it is explicitly or implicitly assumed to be involuntary in nature. Alternatively, one might view underemployment as a stock concept, defining it as a failure of the human capital-generating system to develop human potential up to the point where the rate of return to human capital acquisition is equal to the rate of return on nonhuman assets. Under such conditions, the social investment potential is underutilized, the employment mix is less productive than it could be, and the society's human *assets* are underemployed. Anyone who has viewed the underutilization of human potential in traditional, class-oriented, and/or totalitarian societies recognizes the personal and social opportunity losses from this condition. John Gardner argues not only that it is possible "to keep a good man down," but that most societies have been structured historically to do just that.[24]

Given the confusion and the analytical difficulties surrounding the flow definitions of underemployment, the author would prefer to limit the term to stock underemployment. Such a limitation clarifies the thought processes, clearly separates unemployment from underemployment, and sharpens the relevant policy questions. Enough has been said, however, to alert the reader to the terminological traps into which one can easily fall from careless or imprecise uses of the term "underemployment." Indeed, it would be useful *and amusing* for private citizens to insist that the term be precisely defined by any politician or public official with chutzpah enough to use it in public utterances. Certainly, recognition of the imprecision of this concept is an important step toward understanding and formulating efficient social policy.

Notes to Chapter 12

1. Sir William H. Beveridge, K. C. B., *Causes and Cures of Unemployment* (Westport, Conn.: Greenwood Press, 1976). Reprint of *Unemployment: A Problem of Industry*, rev. ed. (London: Longmans, Green and Company, 1931), p. 1.

2. National Commission on Employment and Unemployment Statistics, *Counting the Labor Force* (Washington, D.C.: U.S. Government Printing Office, September 3, 1979).

3. William Mirengoff and Lester Rindler, *CETA: Manpower Programs under Local Control* (Washington, D.C.: National Academy of Sciences, 1978); *The Comprehensive Employment and Training Act: An Interim Report* (Washington, D.C.: National Academy of Sciences, 1976); William Mirengoff, ed., *Transition to Decentralized Manpower Programs: Eight Case Studies* (Washington, D.C.: National Academy of Sciences, 1976).

4. Beveridge, *Causes and Cures of Unemployment*, pp. 8–9.

5. Robert J. Barro and Herschel I. Grossman, "A General Disequilibrium Model of Income and Employment," *American Economic Review* 61, no. 1 (March 1971): 82–93 and "Suppressed Inflation and the Supply Multiplier," *Review of Economic Studies* 61, no. 2 (January 1974): 87–104. David H. Howard's work confirmed the implications of the Barro-Grossman suppressed inflation model using Soviet data. See David H. Howard, "Disequilibrium in a Controlled Economy: An Empirical Test of the Barro-Grossman Model," *American Economic Review* 66, no. 5 (December 1976): 871–79. Robert Barro subsequently backed away from his "non-market clearing paradigm" because of the failure of the disequilibrium models (including his own) to specify adequately the mechanisms perpetuating excess supply and because of some additional concerns with macroeconomic policy. See Robert Barro, "Second Thoughts on Keynesian Economics," *American Economic Review* 69, no. 2 (May 1979): 54–59.

6. See A. A. Alchain, "Information Costs, Pricing, and Resource Unemployment," and C. C. Holt, "Job Search, Phillips Curve Relations and Union Influence: Theory and Evidence," in E. S. Phelps, ed., *Microeconomic Foundations of Employment and Inflation Theory* (New York: W. W. Norton and Company, 1970), pp. 27–52 and pp. 53–123, respectively. Also see D. T. Mortensen, "Job Search, the

Duration of Unemployment and the Phillips Curve," *American Economic Review* 60, no. 5 (December 1970): 847–62; P. Gayer and R. S. Goldfarb, "Job Search, the Duration of Unemployment and the Phillips Curve—Comment," *American Economic Review* 62, no. 4 (September 1972): 714–17; and Edmund S. Phelps, "The New Microeconomics in Inflation and Economic Theory," *American Economic Review* 59, no. 2 (May 1969): 147–67.

7. A. W. Phillips, "The Relations between Unemployment and the Rate of Change in Money Wage Rates in the United Kingdom, 1862–1957," *Economica* 25 (November 1958): 283–99; Richard G. Lipsey, "The Relation between Unemployment and the Rate of Change in Money Wage Rates in the United Kingdom, 1962–1957: A Further Analysis," *Economica* 27 (February 1960): 1–31. Also see P. A. Samuelson and Robert M. Solow, "Analytical Aspects of Inflation Policy," *American Economic Review* 50, no. 2 (May 1960): 147–67.

8. Milton Friedman, "The Role of Monetary Policy," *American Economic Review* 58, no. 1 (March 1968): 1–17; R. E. Lucas, Jr., "Expectations and the Neutrality of Money," *Journal of Economic Theory* 4, no. 2 (April 1972): 103–24; J. A. Trevitick and C. Mulvey, *The Economics of Inflation* (New York: John Wiley & Sons, 1975); C. Mulvey and J. Trevitick, "The Expectations Hypothesis and the Theory of Inflation: An Appraisal," *Economic and Social Review* 3, no. 2 (January 1972): 227–50.

9. Robert E. Lucas, Jr. and Leonard A. Rapping, "Real Wages, Employment and Inflation," *Journal of Political Economy* 77, no. 5 (September–October 1969): 721–54, and "Price Expectations and the Phillips Curve," *American Economic Review* 59, no. 3 (June 1969): 352–50.

10. R. E. Lucas, Jr., "Some International Evidence on Output-Inflation Tradeoffs," *American Economic Review* 63, no. 3 (June 1973): 326–50; M. Arak, "Some International Evidence on Output-Inflation Tradeoffs: Comment," *American Economic Review* 67, no. 4 (September 1977): 728–30; Edward Foster, "The Variability of Inflation," *Review of Economics and Statistics* 60, no. 3 (August 1978): 346–50.

11. Note that downward wage rigidity during recessions and depressions in this model can also be "explained" by search, with critical wages being established at "artificially" high levels in the short run.

12. Albert Rees, "On Equilibrium in Labor Markets," *Journal of Political Economy* 78, no. 2 (March/April 1970): 306–10, and "Real Wages and Inflation: Rejoinder," *Journal of Political Economy* 80, no. 1 (January–February 1972): 192.

13. Rees, "On Equilibrium in Labor Markets," p. 308.

14. Martin Feldstein, "The Economics of the New Unemployment," *The Public Interest* (Fall 1973): 3–42, and "The Importance of Temporary Layoffs," *Brookings Papers on Economic Activities* 4, no. 3 (1975): 725–44.

15. Daniel Hamermesh, *Jobless Pay and the Economy* (Baltimore and London: Johns Hopkins University Press, 1977). Also see A. Katz, ed., "The Economics of Unemployment Insurance: A Symposium," *Industrial and Labor Relations Review* 30, no. 4 (July 1977): 431–526 and Herbert G. Grubel and Denis R. Maki, "The Effects of Unemployment Benefits on U.S. Unemployment Rates," *Weltwirtschaftliches Archiv* 112, no. 2 (1976): 274–99.

16. Daniel K. Benjamin and Lewis A. Kochin, "Searching for an Explana-

tion of Unemployment in Interwar Britain," *Journal of Political Economy* 87, no. 3 (June 1979): 441–78.

17. See Herbert G. Grubel and Michael A. Walker, *Unemployment Insurance: Global Evidence of its Effects on Unemployment* (Vancouver, Canada: The Fraser Institute, 1978).

18. General Accounting Office, *Unemployment Insurance—Inequities and Work Disincentives in the Current System,* report to the Congress of the United States by the Comptroller General, HRD 79-79, Washington, D.C., August 28, 1979.

19. Stephen A. McCafferty, "A Theory of Semi-Permanent Job Search," *Southern Economic Journal* 45, no. 1 (July 1978): 46–52; John T. Warner, J. Carl Poindexter, Jr., and Robert M. Fearn, "Employer-Employee Interaction and the Duration of Unemployment," *Quarterly Journal of Economics* 93, no. 2 (March 1980): 211–34.

20. John T. Warner et al., "Employer-Employee Interaction."

21. Some researchers have also attempted to disentangle cyclical from seasonal and structural influences. See Robert M. Fearn, "Cyclical, Seasonal and Structural Factors in Area Unemployment Rates," *Industrial and Labor Relations Review* 28, no. 3 (April 1975): 424–31, for one method and for a bibliography of other articles and efforts.

22. The structure of this discussion is shamelessly borrowed from Ethel Jones, "The Elusive Concept of Underemployment," *Journal of Human Resources* 6, no. 4 (Fall 1971): 519–24. Professor Jones, however, does not necessarily agree with my interpretations or predilections concerning the concept of underemployment.

23. National Commission on Employment and Unemployment Statistics, *Counting the Labor Force,* p. 150.

24. John W. Gardner, *Excellence* (New York: Harper and Row, 1961), chap. 1.

13 | *The Distribution of Income*

The modern laborer . . . instead of rising with the progress of industry, sinks deeper and deeper below the conditions of existence of his own class. He becomes a pauper, and pauperism develops more rapidly than population and wealth.

Marx and Engels,
The Communist Manifesto

This chapter might be regarded as redundant, for we have already discussed the stock and flow determinants of earnings levels, the role of income transfers, and so on. In particular, we have argued throughout the first twelve chapters that earnings levels (and income levels) depend upon:

1. the amount and distribution of the stock of human capital as well as the institutions and relative prices influencing human capital acquisition,
2. the demand and supply of labor time per unit time given skill levels, as demand and supply are influenced by technological changes, marginal products, alterations in household time allocations, search costs and benefits, migration, et al.,
3. the structure of labor markets—competition, monopsony, unionization, duality, and internal markets,
4. the levels and types of income transfers—those for skill acquisition, income maintenance, etc., together with such "unobservables" as shame coefficients, and
5. monetary disequilibriums yielding both voluntary and involuntary unemployment in addition to other transitory shocks that may result in the revaluation of existing stocks of human capital.

Moreover, because payment for labor services constitutes the majority of all income flows in any economy, one might argue that we have already covered much of the income distribution question in different portions of this text.

We have not, however, examined in any detail payments for the services of nonhuman assets and/or the way in which those payments are determined. We have not investigated, for example, the legal structures that validate income claims from nonhuman assets under capitalism, socialism, or other systems. Nor have we examined in any detail the markets through which incomes from nonhuman assets are generated. Although we leave most of these questions to texts dealing with comparative economic systems, investment, capital theory, finance, macroeconomics, and so forth, income from nonhuman assets does enter into observed distributions of income. Indeed, that is the nubbin of the distinction between the *functional* and the *personal* distribution of income. The first looks to the flow of income resulting from various legally supported categories of assets (types of economic activity). The second looks to much the same income flow as it accrues to individuals or families, given their ownership and use of both human and nonhuman assets.

This chapter concentrates on two related questions:

1. How do the levels and the distributions of income—the aggregate results of the productive process—differ across various economies, and how do we measure such differences?
2. Can we predict what the effect(s) of income redistribution will be on the level of income (output) attained or attainable by that economy?

The first question, of course, is directed toward problems of both conception and measurement. The second, in a sense, returns to the set of issues discussed in Chapters 1 and 2 concerning the viability of a commune and the effects of income transfers. In contrast to the communal viability question discussed in Chapter 1, the size of the economy with which we are concerned now is much larger. Rather than examining the viability of an isolated commune, we are asking about the possible tradeoffs (and/or complimentarities) between output levels and the distribution of output in very complex economies. Moreover, such an inquiry into the "communality question" applies to economies with all forms of property rights (socialist, capitalist, etc.).

Despite the analytical difficulty of the second question when it is applied to complex economies, the issue is so important that it ought not to be ignored in any text on labor economics. Since the 1800s and particularly since the 1930s, there have been persistent attempts to alter income distributions in many Western and Eastern nations, usually toward more equal distributions of income. Given these apparently strong egalitarian desires and efforts, and given the many existing and proposed income transfer programs around the world—subsidized schooling, categorical welfare programs, socialized or subsidized health care, negative income taxes, etc.—the second question must be confronted even if our examination falls short of obtaining a fully satisfying answer.

Levels and Distributions of Income

As suggested above, economists generally distinguish between the distribution of the total flow of income (output) per year *by type of economic activity* and the distribution of income *by persons or families*—the functional versus the personal distribution of income. Generally, in considering the second of these, attention is given to the spread of income claims among persons or families—*the size distribution of income*. Personal and size distributions, of course, reflect not only income claims derived from wages and salaries, but also from interest, dividends, rents, etc.—that is, returns to the various nonhuman factors of production. Moreover, certain measures of the size distribution show the effects of income transfers on the degree of income equality or inequality.

Before considering the functional and the size distributions of income in more detail, it is helpful to look briefly at income (output) levels per capita in various countries and/or economies. Table 13–1 lists the gross national product per capita of most nations in 1978. Obviously, there are many analytical problems in arriving at these estimates and in assuring comparability across nations. The figures in Table 13–1 should therefore not be taken as gospel, but viewed solely as reasonable measures of approximate orders of magnitude. Even with this caveat, these data provide the base for several useful insights. In examining the data, note first, the GNP/capita is gross of capital consumption allowances—the value of physical capital "used up" in the process of income generation. GNP/capita is, therefore, an *overstatement* of the sustainable income levels of these nations (without additional capital inputs). Second, note that in vast portions of the world, GNP/capita in 1978 was lower than $1,000 (1978 U.S. dollars), including the People's Republic of China, India, and Indonesia—the first, second, and fifth most populous nations. Indeed, GNP/capita in those three nations was below $600 per annum in contrast to $7,000 or more in the advanced Western and some non-Western, oil-rich nations. For much of the world, therefore, relatively small reductions in the level of output and/or productivity can raise the specter of increased human misery, malnutrition, and starvation, and the loss of hope for more satisfying lives. Hence, our concern in this text is with economic efficiency and the possible effects of communal redistribution on levels of output (income). Before leaving these comparisons, it is also useful to note that average (or mean) income levels per capita reveal little about the distribution of income flows among the resident population. Indeed, much of the interest in income distribution is generated

Table 13-1 *Gross National Product per Capita, 1978 (In 1978 U.S. Dollars. Nations listed alphabetically within categories)*

	More than $7,000	
Australia	Iceland	Qatar
Austria	Japan	Saudi Arabia
Belgium	Kuwait	Sweden
Bermuda	Liechtenstein	Switzerland
Canada	Luxembourg	United Arab
Denmark	Nauru	Emirates
France	Netherlands	U.S.A.
Greenland	Norway	West Germany
	$5,001 to $7,000	
Bahrain	Libya	New Zealand
Finland	Monaco	United Kingdom
	$3,001 to $5,000	
Bahamas	Hong Kong	Romania
Brunei	Iceland	San Marino
Czechoslovakia	Israel	Singapore
East Germany	Italy	Spain
Faroe Islands	Martinique	U.S.S.R.
Gabon	Oman	Venezuela
Greece	Poland	
	$1,001 to $3,000	
Algeria	Hungary	Nicaragua
Andorra	Iran	Panama
Argentina	Iraq	Portugal
Barbados	Ivory Coast	Puerto Rico
Brazil	Jamaica	South Africa
Bulgaria	Lebanon	South Korea
Costa Rica	Malaysia	Surinam
Cyprus	Malta	Taiwan
Falkland Islands	Mexico	Trinidad and
Fiji Islands	Namibia	Tobago
French Poly-	Netherlands	Turkey
nesia	Antilles	Uruguay
Guadeloupe	New Caledonia	Yugoslavia
	$801 to $1,000	
Chile	Equador	Peru
Cuba	French Guiana	Syria
Dominican	Guatemala	Tunisia
Republic	Mauritius	

$601 to $800

Antigua	Gibraltar	Morocco
Belize	Gilbert Islands	Paraguay
Bolivia	Jordan	Seychelles
Columbia	Mongolia	Swaziland
El Salvador		

$401 to $600

Albania	Guyana	Senegal
Botswana	Honduras	St. Lucia
Cameroun	Liberia	Thailand
Congo	Nigeria	Tonga
Cook Islands	North Korea	Western Samoa
Dominica	North Yemen	Zambia
Egypt	People's Repub-	Zimbabwe-
Ghana	lic of China	Rhodesia
Grenada	Philippines	

$201 to $400

Angola	Lesotho	Sri Lanka
Benin	Macao	St. Christopher-
Central African	Madagascar	Nevis-Anguilla
Empire	Mauritania	St. Vincent
Djibouti	Pakistan	Sudan
Equatorial	Papua-New	Tanzania
Guinea	Guinea	Tonga
Guinea	São Tomé/	Uganda
Haiti	Príncipe	West Sahara
Indonesia	Sierra Leone	Zaire
Kenya	South Yemen	

Less than $201

Afghanistan	Ethiopia	Mali
Bangladesh	Gambia	Mozambique
Bhutan	Guinea-Bissau	Nepal
Burma	India	Niger
Burundi	Kampuchea	Rwanda
Cape Verde	Laos	Somalia
Islands	Malawi	Upper Volta
Chad	Maldive Islands	Vietnam

Source: National Foreign Assessment Center, *Handbook of Economic Statistics*, ER 79–10274 (Washington, D.C.: Central Intelligence Agency, August 1979), pp. i–ii. Most of these estimates were derived from official sources of the respective nations.

by the concern that higher mean levels of income may result in (or from) more unequal distribution of that income ("the rich get richer and the poor get poorer"). To assess that concern, we need to examine more precisely the various measures of income and of income inequality.

The Functional and Personal Distribution of Income

Using the United States as an example, we now turn to the functional distribution of income. As indicated by the U.S. Department of Commerce, the United States generated a national income of $1,724.3 billion in 1978. Table 13–2 shows the total distribution by functional shares. About 75 percent or $1,304.5 billion of the total was payment for labor services, including wages and salaries, supplements to wages and salaries, employer contributions to social insurance, and so on. The remaining shares were divided between proprietors' income, rental income, corporate profits, and net interest. Note the relationship of these categories to the classical economists' definition of the "basic factors of production"—land, labor, capital (and management?).

Table 13–3 shows the distribution of personal income in 1978 by functional shares, including some transfer payments. The transfers, total-

Table 13–2 *Functional Distribution of U.S. National Income, 1978 (All data before taxes)*

	Billions of Dollars	Percent*
National income	1,724.3	100.0
Compensation of employees,	1,304.5	75.7
including employers' contribution to social insurance	94.6	
Proprietors' income	116.8	6.8
with inventory valuation and capital consumption allowances, including: Farm	27.7	
Nonfarm	89.1	
Rental income	25.9	1.5
with capital consumption allowances		
Corporate profits	167.7	9.7
with inventory valuation and capital consumption allowances, including: Dividends	47.2	
Undistributed profits	74.3	
Net interest	109.5	6.4

Source: Bureau of Economic Affairs, *Survey of Current Business,* 59, no.9 (Washington, D.C.: U.S. Department of Commerce, September 1979), Tables 7 and 10.
* Subtotals may not add up to 100.0 percent due to rounding.

Table 13–3 *Functional Distribution of U.S. Personal Income, 1978*

	Billions of Dollars	*Percent**
Personal income	1,717.4	100.00
Wage and salary disbursements	1,103.3	64.2
Other labor income	106.5	6.2
Proprietors' income	116.8	6.8
Rental income	25.9	1.5
Dividends	47.2	2.8
Personal interest income	167.3	9.7
Transfer payments, including:	224.1	13.0
Old age and survivors, disability, and health insurance benefits	116.3	
Government unemployment compensation benefits	9.2	
Veterans' benefits	13.9	
Government employee retirement benefits	32.9	
AFDC	10.7	
Other	41.1	
Less:		
Personal contributions for social insurance	61.3	3.6
and personal tax and nontax payments	259.0	15.1
Equals:		
Disposable personal income	1,458.4	84.9
Personal outlays	1,386.4	80.7
Personal savings	72.0	4.2

Source: Same as Table 13-2.
* Subtotals may not add up to 100.0 percent due to rounding.

ing $224.1 billion, constituted 13 percent of the total and were larger than any other source of income except wage and salary disbursements. Table 13–3, however, includes as transfers only categorical programs (such as AFDC, veterans' benefits, etc.). Public allocations for education and training and other noncategorical allocations are not included in the value of transfers.

The Size Distribution of Personal or Family Income

The size distribution of personal or family income measures the equality or inequality of an income distribution(s) in various ways, indicating the proportions or amounts of income distributed to various proportions or numbers of the population. Naturally, it is to the size distribution of income that most people concerned with income inequality direct their attention. By such measures, we may observe, as an example, that 16 percent of the total income is distributed to the upper 5 percent of families and/or that the lower 30 percent of families receive 19 percent of the income flows (Mexico, 1956, by one estimate).[1] Table 13–4 shows the personal distribution of money income in the United States in 1969 by income class. Such data are easily converted into a cumulative frequency distribution indicating the proportions of income received by the successive income classes. Incidentally, performing the actual calculation is a useful exercise. The resulting relationship is shown generally in a Lorenz diagram (the bowed line in Fig. 13–1). The hypothetical distribution illustrated here indicates that the lowest 70 percent of income recipients receive 40 percent of the total income. Obviously, the upper 30 percent receive 60 percent of the total income flow in our hypothetical example. Total income equality in a Lorenz diagram is represented by the diagonal (the dashed line in Fig. 13–1).

Generally, economists studying the size distribution of income(s) calculate from the available personal income data certain summary measures of inequality—quintile measures, the coefficient of variation $(\sigma/\overline{X})$, and others, and use these for comparison and analysis. Among the many possible measures, *Gini coefficients* have been the most popular. "Ginis" are calculated by dividing the area between the Lorenz curve

Table 13–4 *Distribution of 1969 Money Income among Recipients, 14 Years of Age and Older, by Income Class, U.S.A.*

Income Class (Thousands of Dollars)	Number (Percent of Total)*	Income (Percent of Total)*
Less than 0.5	10.4	0.4
0.5 to 0.99	8.6	1.2
1.0 to 1.49	7.5	1.7
1.5 to 1.99	5.6	1.9
2.0 to 2.49	5.4	2.3
2.5 to 2.99	3.9	2.1
3.0 to 3.99	8.5	5.5
4.0 to 4.99	7.5	6.2
5.0 to 5.99	7.0	7.1
6.0 to 6.99	6.4	7.8
7.0 to 7.99	6.0	8.5
8.0 to 9.99	8.7	14.5
10.0 to 14.99	9.9	22.3
15.0 to 24.99	3.6	12.8
25.0 and over	1.0	5.6
Total (Millions of Persons and Billions of $'s)	114.1	608.0

Source: U.S. Bureau of the Census, *Current Population Reports, Income in 1969 of Families and Persons in the United States*, Series P-60, no. 75 (Washington, D.C.: Government Printing Office, 1970), Table 17.
* Percentages may not add up to 100.0 percent due to rounding.

Figure 13–1 *A Lorenz Diagram*

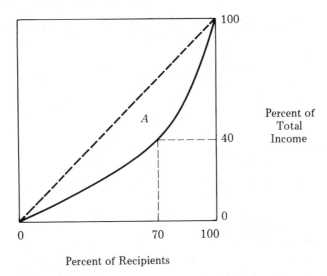

Percent of Recipients

and the equal income line (area A in Fig. 13–1) by the triangular area below the equal income (dashed) line. Thus, the more bowed the Lorenz curve, the greater the Gini and the greater the measured inequality. The Gini calculated from the data in Table 13–3, for example, is 0.489. If nonrecipients of income (including housewives, househusbands, etc.) are included (added to the less-than-0.5 category), the Gini is 0.601.

Unfortunately for those interested in questions of inequality and the relationship of growth to inequality or income transfers, the usefulness of the various summary measures themselves is a subject of great debate which extends beyond the usual problem of "getting good income data." First, the summary measures vary considerably depending upon whether one uses data:

1. for individuals or for families (households),
2. for income before or after taxes and transfers, and
3. for complete versus partial sets of transfers, including, for example, subsidized schooling, subsidized health services (as in the U.S.S.R.), and so on.

Moreover, as shown by Simon Kuznets,[2] the distributions and various summary measures are often quite sensitive to family size, the age distribution of the population, and other demographic characteristics. By most measures, lifetime income distributions are substantially more equal than moment-in-time distributions.[3] Anyone familiar with human capital theory and the (transitorily) low incomes of students, apprentices, etc., relative to their lifetime income could have anticipated that finding.

As a consequence of such measurement problems, it is often not clear which of the various measures is the appropriate one (or ones) for comparison and analysis. For example, although a particular summary statistic (e.g., a Gini coefficient) may change over time in a given nation or economy, income inequality for individuals may be increasing while measured inequality for families may be decreasing. Family formation and the division of energies between market and household are obviously factors that can interfere with assessing the changing degree of inequality.

Similar problems exist and similar caveats apply to comparisons among nations and economies. Thus, various moment-of-time comparisons across nations may reflect different lifetime patterns of human capital acquisition as those patterns are conditioned by all the opportunities and constraints discussed in Chapters 4 and 8, while simultaneously reflecting the existing distributions of human (and physical) capital in each nation. It is equally clear that the summary measures reflect the division of the various economies into market and household sectors, a matter of no small consequence when comparing developed to developing countries. Recall that the various size distribution measures contain only market income (plus, in limited instances, some imputations for income in kind). They do not reflect "full income" in the Beckerian sense (see note 23 in Chapter 1). Inequality comparisons across time or countries are also risky since the inequality measures reflect cyclical patterns of employment[4] as well as private and socially determined responses to these dislocations (unemployment compensation, voluntary and involuntary unemployment, etc.). Comparisons at different stages in the business cycle and among countries at different stages can therefore give contradictory or misleading results. Finally, the measures reflect the property right systems, the patterns of physical asset distributions, and the sets of implied contracts across nations and time (e.g., land ownership, the extent of socialism). Distributions of income in kind may also be of importance (e.g., perquisites for tenant farmers), as may the distribution of returns to socially owned capital (e.g., the value of "free" health care, the value of special benefits—summer homes, transportation, etc.—provided to leading members of the ruling political party out of the "social dividend").[5]

These measurement and interpretation questions are complicated by analytical difficulties in the structure of the summary measures themselves. For example, as shown in Fig. 13–2, different Lorenz curves can yield the same Gini. Few analysts would argue, however, that the two distributions pictured here are equal in a meaningful sense. Indeed, the shape of a Lorenz curve can be infinitely varied while yielding the same Gini. The geometrically minded reader can develop his own example(s).

Figure 13–2 *Unequal Distributions on a Lorenz Curve*

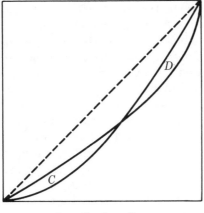

Area C = Area D

(Hint: try bimodal distributions.) More importantly, A. B. Atkinson showed that each of the summary measures of inequality which he studied reflects a particular value system, and that many of these imply social welfare functions that "are not likely to be accepted" or "are unlikely to satisfy any broad political consensus."[6]

In light of these considerations, it is not surprising that many economists and other scholars examining the size distribution of income reach sharply differing conclusions when they seek answers to questions concerning the changing degree of inequality, when they seek to rank countries (economies) by extent of inequality, and—most importantly—when they seek to test why measured changes or differences in inequality occur or exist. Nor is it surprising that the technical journals throughout the 1970s contained lively debates about the most useful measures of inequality.[7]

The Impact of Income Redistributions on Income Levels and/or Income Growth

Because the inequality measures used to assess the extent of redistributions are themselves suspect, those who seek to understand the impact of redistribution on income levels or income growth are indeed "playing on a very muddy field." Nevertheless, the question is a vital policy issue in both developed and developing nations.

Some attempts to wrestle with this question approach it from a macroeconomic perspective, concentrating on the impact of governmentally directed redistributions on national propensities to save and/or consume, and/or on the foreign trade balance or balance of payments effects of altered distributions.[8] "Macrogrowth model" studies of this type have been heavily influenced by W. Arthur Lewis's theoretical contention and by Simon Kuznets's empirical findings that growth and inequality are positively related in the course of development.[9] Note that the Lewis-Kuznets inquiry is broader than the one pursued here. Theirs looks not only to the effects of income redistribution efforts on growth (usually initiated through government policies), but also to the effects of endogenous growth developments on the income distribution—a full, simultaneous adjustment process. Thus, given the limits of our inquiry, detailed exposition and critical examination of the many fine macrogrowth model studies are left to others. We note only that by the late 1970s, research by Fei, Ranis, and Kuo, and by Chinn on Taiwanese development strongly suggested that there is nothing inevitable about the Lewis-Kuznets relationship.[10] Moreover, Felix Paukert's studies indicate that there is generally greater income equality *in developed nations* than in developing ones. His research, however, also suggests that economic growth may be accompanied first by a widening and then a narrowing of income inequality.[11]

Our more limited question fits into the macrogrowth-distribution controversy to the degree that income redistributions induced by governmental actions have positive or negative effects on the growth of the economy. Evidence on this narrower issue makes the multiple conclusions emerging from the macrogrowth literature seem reasonable. For example, three summaries of the income distribution literature suggest that improvements in levels of schooling could lead to either more or less inequality.[12] More pointedly, the analyses of Winegarden and of Marin and Psacharopoulos show that income redistribution for schooling can lead to more income equality if the redistribution widens the schooling franchise, so to speak, and less equality if it does not do so.[13] Thus, concentration of schooling subsidies among those individuals who are already well educated could yield a very low social rate of return, particularly in developing nations. It follows from the human capital theory developed in Chapters 4, 6, 7, and 8 that economic growth should increase with increases in the schooling or training franchise *if* internal social rates of return to these investments exceed alternative returns *and if* the "taxpayers" generally agree with the implicit social contract established for financing the schooling. The reallocation of resources into investments with greater "payoffs" necessarily increases economic growth, *ceteris paribus*. Lack of a broad sociopolitical consensus, of course, can lead to all the "tax avoidance" and even the "tax evasion" phenomena discussed in Chapters 1 and 2, thus inhibiting growth.

Applying such a human capital approach to Mexican development, Robert Looney concludes, for example, that:

a greater share of human resources at all levels will facilitate the redistribution of income by widening the distribution of human skills. This is in fact an invest-ment policy that would meet the objectives of economic growth and social progress in a positive manner.[14]

Looney also looked at marginal rates of return to schooling in Brazil, South Korea, and Iran, concluding that as in Mexico, there is no tradeoff between growth and redistribution for schooling in these nations. That conclusion follows, he notes, because in all these nations returns from human capital investments exceed those for physical capital, and because per capita differences in income are more readily traceable to differences in human capital stocks than to stocks of physical capital.

Income redistribution, however, need not be directed solely or largely toward investments in schooling or similar forms of human capi-tal. It may be directed toward income maintenance (e.g., for the poor or aged), toward improving the health status of the population, or toward a number of other goals. In each instance, the two elements discussed above are of crucial importance to the influence of the redistribution program on growth rates—that is, the social rate of return, if any, on these investments and the nature and degree of the social consensus underlying the respective redistribution(s). In addition, there may be "price effects" resulting from the changes in the prices of goods and leisure that are built into the structure of the redistribution programs themselves. Such price effects, of course, influence the allocation of efforts and goods, and therefore influence incomes and national output. The price effects of the proposed FAP (President Nixon's work incentive pro-gram, examined in Chapter 2) is an example, as is the effect of unemploy-ment insurance payments on the duration of unemployment (discussed in Chapter 12). Although the potential for such effects resides in most redistribution and social insurance programs, generalizations about those effects are difficult to formulate because their nature and extent depend directly upon the rules and regulations of each of the programs.

Finally, governmental efforts to reallocate incomes may involve redistributions of physical assets, as in the case of land reform. Such efforts may involve negative or positive effects on output depending upon changes in the nature of the inputs available for given production func-tions (e.g., the withdrawal of managerial capital), upon whether the ini-tial owners were cost minimizers (remember Chapter 5), and upon the presence of monopoly or monopsony influences in the market(s) prior to the redistribution of physical assets.

Our preliminary and not fully satisfying analysis suggests, therefore, that it is the *uses* of the income redistributions and the potential production or price effects that we must examine if we are to solve the redistribution-growth issue addressed at the beginning of this chapter. It is likely that no generally "correct" answer can be given. Social rates of return differ for the various levels and types of schooling, health, and other social investments. Moreover, these rates of return differ over time (remember Chapter 8). There is always a possibility that particular redistributions will elicit negative responses among the "taxpayers," who may then seek to opt out or reduce their commitment to the "commune." Finally, it is conceivable that the production or price effects will result in reallocations of efforts and inputs (and the demand for goods and services) that are not or were not anticipated by the framers of the programs.[15] Thus, at the end of Chapter 13, it would appear that we have come full circle—back to the communality issues raised in Chapters 1 and 2. Although we have not arrived at a definitive answer concerning the effects of communality in a complex economy, we have, it is hoped, widened our understanding of the implications—both positive and negative—of communal redistributions.

Notes to Chapter 13

1. William Cline, *Potential Effects of Income Redistribution on Economic Growth: Latin American Cases* (New York: Praeger Publishers, 1972), pp. 102–7.

2. Simon Kuznets, "Demographic Aspects of the Size Distribution of Income: An Exploratory Essay," *Economic Development and Cultural Change* 25, no. 1 (October 1976): 1–94.

3. Milton Moss, "Income Distribution Issues Viewed in a Lifetime Income Perspective," *Review of Income and Wealth* 24, no. 2 (June 1978): 119–36.

4. C. M. Beach, "Cyclical Sensitivity of Aggregate Income Inequality," *Review of Economics and Statistics* 59, nc. 1 (February 1977): 56–66.

5. For an interesting international comparison tracing the lower Ginis in socialist countries largely to differences in property right systems and labor market duality under capitalism, see J. Cromwell, "The Size Distribution of Income: An International Comparison," *Review of Income and Wealth* 23, no. 3 (September 1977): 291–308. Also see N. Rimashevskaya and S. Shatalin, "The Structure of Personal and Social Consumption in Socialist Countries," *Problems of Economics* 20, no. 4 (August 1977): 46–68, for a discussion of the valuation of socially provided income flows. For comparative data covering many nations, see Shail Jain, *Size Distribution of Income: A Compilation of Data* (Washington, D.C.: The World Bank, 1975) and Felix Paukert, "Income Distribution at Different Levels of Development: A Survey of Evidence," *International Labour Review* 108, nos. 2–3 (September 1973): 97–125.

6. A. B. Atkinson, "On Measures of Inequality," *Journal of Economic Theory* 2, no. 3 (September 1970): 244–63. Also see S. Yitzhaki, "Relative Deprivation

and the Gini Coefficient," *Quarterly Journal of Economics* 93, no. 2 (May 1979): 321–24.

7. See, for example, Morton Paglin, "The Measurement and Trend of Inequality: A Basic Revision," *American Economic Review* 65, no. 4 (September 1975): 598–609; B. Bressler, "The Measurement of Income Inequality Revisited," *Review of Social Economy* 36, no. 2 (October 1978): 212–16; S. K. Singh and G. S. Maddala, "A Function for the Size Distribution of Incomes," *Econometrica* 44, no. 5 (September 1976): 963–70; J. S. Cramer, "A Function for the Size Distribution of Incomes: Comment," *Econometrica* 46, no. 2 (March 1978): 459–60; E. K. Browning, "The Trend toward Equality in the Distribution of Net Income," *Southern Economic Journal* 43, no. 1 (July 1976): 912–23; T. M. Smeeding, "On the Distribution of Net Incomes: Reply," and E. K. Browning, "On the Distribution of Net Incomes: Reply," *Southern Economic Journal* 45, no. 3 (January 1979): 932–44 and 945–59, respectively. Also see G. S. Fields and J. C. H. Fei, "On Inequality Comparisons," *Econometrica* 46, no. 2 (March 1978): 303–16, and Henry Phelps Brown, *The Inequality of Pay* (Berkeley, Calif.: University of California Press, 1977), for some interesting insights into inequality measures.

8. For representative examples, see Cline, *Potential Effects of Income Redistribution,* and John R. Stewart, Jr., "Potential Effects of Income Redistribution on Economic Growth: An Expanded Estimating Procedure Applied to Mexico," *Economic Development and Cultural Change* 26, no. 3 (April 1978): 467–86.

9. W. Arthur Lewis, "Economic Development with Unlimited Supplies of Labour," *The Manchester School* 22, no. 2 (May 1954): 139–91; Simon Kuznets, "Economic Growth and Income Inequality," *American Economic Review* 45, no. 1 (March 1955): 1–28.

10. J. C. H. Fei, G. Ranis, and S. W. Y. Kuo, "Growth and the Family Distribution of Income by Factor Components," *Quarterly Journal of Economics* 92, no. 1 (February 1978): 17–53; Dennis L. Chinn, "Distributional Equality and Economic Growth: The Case of Taiwan," *Economic Development and Cultural Change* 26, no. 1 (October 1977): 65–80. For some opposing evidence from Costa Rica, see M. J. Carvajal and D. J. Geithman, "Income Distribution and Economic Development: Some Intra-country Evidence," *Southern Economic Journal* 44, no. 4 (April 1978): 922–28.

11. Paukert, "Income Distribution at Different Levels of Development."

12. Jacob Mincer, "The Distribution of Labor Incomes: A Survey with Special Reference to the Human Capital Approach," *Journal of Economic Literature* 8, no. 1 (March 1970): 1–26; L. A. Lillard, "Earnings and Human Wealth," *American Economic Review* 67, no. 2 (March 1977): 42–53; G. S. Sahota, "Theories of Personal Income Distribution: A Survey," *Journal of Economic Literature* 16, no. 1 (March 1978): 1–55.

13. C. R. Winegarden, "Schooling and Income Distribution: Evidence from International Data," *Economica* 46, no. 181 (February 1979): 83–87; Alan Marin and George Psacharopoulos, "Schooling and Income Distribution," *Review of Economics and Statistics* 58, no. 3 (August 1976): 332–38. Also see the special issue on education and income distribution, *Journal of Political Economy* 87, no. 5, pt. 2 (October 1979).

14. Robert E. Looney, *Income Distribution Policies and Economic Growth in Semi-industrialized Countries* (New York: Praeger Publishers, 1975), p. 30.

15. Communal redistribution and its necessary condition, a supportive so-

cial contract, has a relationship to the so-called Laffer curve. The Laffer curve argues that there is a rate of taxation that optimizes government revenue via the connection between national output and those revenues. Higher taxes may or may not result in sufficient negative output effects so as to reduce governmental revenues. Unfortunately, the precise nature of these macrorelationships is not developed fully in any works of which this author is aware. For a popular exposition of the Lafferian point of view, see Jude Wanniski, *The Way the World Works* (New York: Simon and Schuster, 1979), especially Chapter 6.

Index